# Financial Crime Investigation and Control

# Financial Crime Investigation and Control

## K.H. Spencer Pickett
## and
## Jennifer Pickett

JOHN WILEY & SONS, INC.

*This book provides a general introduction to fraud investigation and control. However, each individual fraud is unique in terms of its features and context and therefore, legal counsel should always be sought whenever investigating fraud and designing specific controls to address financial crime.*

ISBN: 0-471-20335-1

Printed in the United States of America.

10 9 8 7 6 5 4 3 2 1

*This book is dedicated to
Lloyd and Frederica Livermore*

# ACKNOWLEDGMENTS

W e would like to thank all those friends and colleagues who have contributed their stories and ideas. Special thanks to Professor Gerald Vinten, Professor Andrew Chambers, Neil Cowan, Richard Kusnierz, and Isabel Picornell for the personal comments they have supplied for the book. Thanks to Nigel Freeman and The Association of Certified Fraud Examiners for their continued support. And a very special thanks to our children, Dexter and Laurel-Jade. We hope, in a small way, to contribute to the drive to getting fraud prevention, detection, and investigation onto the agenda of managers, supervisors, and employees generally. In this way, everyone may be part of the solution to the growing threat from corporate white-collar crime.

SPENCER AND JENNIFER PICKETT

# CONTENTS

# Financial Crime Investigation and Control

# CHAPTER 1

---

# Why Financial Crime?

*There is no little enemy.*

## WHAT IS FINANCIAL CRIME?

There is no precise legal definition of financial or white-collar crime that we can turn to, to start this book. The term is much like the associated concept of fraud, which again has no fixed legal definition. There are, however, various general definitions of white-collar crime that have evolved over the years. *Black's Law Dictionary* defines *fraud* as:

> An intentional perversion of truth for the purpose of inducing another in reliance upon it to part with some valuable thing belonging to him or to surrender a legal right. Bad faith—the conscious doing of wrong.

*Webster's New World Dictionary* describes fraud as:

> Intentional deception to cause a person to give up property or some lawful right.

Another useful definition comes from the Federal Bureau of Justice Statistics (Dictionary of Criminal Justice Data Terminology), which defines white-collar crime as:

Nonviolent crime for financial gain committed by means of deception by persons whose occupational status is entrepreneurial, professional or semi-professional and utilizing their special occupational skills and opportunities; also nonviolent crime for financial gain utilizing deception and committed by anyone having special technical and professional knowledge of business and government, irrespective of the person's occupation.

In practice, there are numerous definitions of financial crime that can be used as a starting point. They tend to be similar and cover a number of key aspects of human behavior. It is the contrast between white-collar crime and other types of crime that is most interesting. Smash-and-grab robberies, rape, murder, muggings, and other such crimes are easier to describe and categorize. Violent crimes promote a clear response from citizens and law enforcement agencies in terms of various quick and effective countermeasures. In contrast, white-collar crime is, in the short term, perceived as being nontraumatic because it is generally nonviolent. It is in the longer term that deceitful behavior has a traumatic impact on business and communities. White-collar crime contains several clear components:

- **It is deceitful**. People involved in white-collar crime tend to cheat, lie, conceal, and manipulate the truth.
- **It is intentional.**   Fraud does not result from simple error or neglect but involves purposeful attempts to illegally gain an advantage. As such, it induces a course of action that is predetermined in advance by the perpetrator.
- **It breaches trust.**   Business is based primarily on trust. Individual relationships and commitments are geared toward the respective responsibilities of all parties involved. Mutual trust is the glue that binds these relationships together and it is this trust that is breached when someone tries to defraud another person or business.
- **It involves losses.**   Financial crime is based on attempting to secure an illegal gain or advantage and for this to happen there must be a victim. There must also be a degree of loss or disadvantage. These losses may be written off or insured against or simply accepted. White-collar crime nonetheless constitutes a drain on national resources.
- **It may be concealed.**   One feature of financial crime is that it may remain hidden indefinitely. Reality and appearance may not necessarily coincide. Therefore, every business transaction, contract, pay-

ment, or agreement may be altered or suppressed to give the appearance of regularity. Spreadsheets, statements, and sets of accounts cannot always be accepted at face value; this is how some frauds continue undetected for years.

- **There may be an appearance of outward respectability.** Fraud may be perpetrated by persons who appear to be respectable and professional members of society, and may even be employed by the victim.

For the purposes of this book, financial crime involves the use of deception for illegal gain, normally involving breach of trust, and some concealment of the true nature of the activities. We now have a working definition, but it covers a whole array of activities that fall under the general banner of financial crime. In this book, we will use the terms *financial crime, white-collar crime,* and *fraud* interchangeably.

A lot of illegal activity can occur in both the commercial and public sectors. In one sense, so long as there are weaknesses that can be exploited for gain, companies, organizations, and private individuals will always be taken advantage of. Some of these illegal activities include:

- **Consumer fraud**—attempts to coerce consumers into paying for goods not received or goods that are substandard, not as specified, or at inflated prices or fees. The growing use of attractive Internet Web sites, as an alternative to unsolicited phone calls or visits to potential customers, compounds this problem.
- **Credit card fraud**—use of stolen credit card details to secure goods or services in the name of the cardholder. Sometimes a brand new credit card is forged using known details. Cards can be stolen or details obtained from files that are not properly secured; credit card details may also be purchased from people who are able to access this information. This is another growth area.
- **Kickbacks**—generally involve an employee with influence over who gets a particular contract, who is able to obtain something for assisting the prospective contractor. Likewise, bribes may be paid to inspectors to turn a blind eye to substandard goods coming into a loading dock. If bribes do not work, the dedicated fraudster may well turn to blackmail and threats.
- **Bid rigging**—When a vendor is given an unfair advantage to defeat an open competition for a given contract. A vendor may be provided with extra information to bid low but then raise more income

through many variations to the set contract. This may be linked to the receipt of kickbacks. Election rigging is a similar but more sinister type of fraud.

- **Inflated invoices**—when a company inflates its bills without agreement from the bill payer, who may be a customer. Conversely, an employee may arrange to pay a vendor more than is due in return for an unauthorized payment or some other gain. An employee could also pay an amount to an entirely fictitious supplier, and divert the check to a personal bank account.

- **External fraud**—schemes by people who do not work for an organization but seek to defraud it. Advance-fee fraudsters attempt to secure a prepaid commission for an arrangement that is never actually fulfilled or work that is never done. Many international frauds committed via the Internet require advance payments for fictitious or substandard goods or services. Billions of dollars worth of health care fraud has resulted from several parties in the health industry conspiring with individuals to submit fraudulent medical bills for services not provided. Insurance companies suffer multitudes of fraudulent claims, often from sophisticated parties who conspire to commit a series of well-planned scams. In short, any organization or public body that provides something of value (for example, food stamps, cash grants, compensation payments, claims, refunds, loans, and equipment) may be subject to efforts by external parties to defraud it. In Europe, the European Commission has found that fraudsters can obtain millions of dollars from irregular claims if there are not adequate controls over the process, including physical verifications.

- **Inventory theft**—straightforward stealing of stock from an employer. It can also involve stealing scrap and goods that are returned by customers, as there may be less control over these items. A bigger problem is shoplifting: customers rather than staff steal billions of dollars worth of goods from retail outlets each year.

- **Theft of cash**—misappropriation arises when cash comes into a company and is diverted. *Skimming* occurs when cash is taken before it enters the books; for example, by a cashier. *Embezzlement* involves a direct breach of trust, when someone entrusted with the cash diverts it for personal use. *Lapping* is a technique whereby the theft of cash or checks is covered up by using later receipts so that the gap in funds is not noticed, sometimes for many years. Some argue that the reported figure for these types of frauds is only around 10 percent of the actual losses.

- **Basic company frauds**—when an employee fakes sickness to obtain paid sick leave, submits inflated overtime claims, or uses company equipment for an unauthorized purpose which may be to operate a private business. When this private business competes with the employer's business, the fraud may also involve theft of ideas and company information such as a client database. A more dangerous development is the sale of information and ideas that the employee has access to. Pilferage relates to small items taken home by staff. Fabricated time sheets can constitute a theft of time (and therefore pay) from businesses. What used to be a basic deception, but is now a major problem, is falsified information on résumés from persons seeking employment. In some cases, the person being employed is very different from the person on paper, who appeared to have the skills, competencies, and credentials needed. Some argue that more than half of the material that appears in a typical résumé is misleading. Someone who lies to a prospective employer from day one may be the type of person who will engage in deception as he or she settles down with the company. Many organizations have some staff who engage in basic company deceptions.
- **Travel and entertainment (subsistence) claims**—when claims are falsified, inflated, or there is basic abuse of the scheme. Small-scale abuse occurs when people simply overstate their claims. It gets more serious when the claimants put in fabricated sums and even forge the line manager's signature. Fraud by an accounts clerk who operates a payments scheme can be substantial, as the aggregate amount grows over time.
- **Check fraud**—when a company check is stolen, altered, or forged, it may be diverted to an unauthorized person who accesses the funds and then closes the account or simply disappears. Company secretaries and accounts personnel may also slip additional checks into a signing routine to effect significant levels of fraud against a company. An extension of check fraud is bank fraud, whereby individuals (and businesses) seek to defraud banks of funds, normally in the form of unsecured loans.
- **Identity fraud**—this is now a major issue in society. There are many reported cases where people have had to defend themselves against claims, because others have stolen their identity, using personal data

such social security number, address, date of birth, and so on. The costs of reestablishing a reputation that has been impaired through credit card fraud and other fraudulently incurred debt can be tremendous in terms of both money and time.

- **Ghost employees**—getting extra names onto a company payroll and diverting the funds to a bank account specially set up for this scam. If an employee can stay on the payroll after having left the company, again extra funds can be obtained for a while. Unauthorized changes to payroll times, rates, and claims can also result in money being diverted for illegal gain.

- **Misappropriation schemes**—come in many forms and guises; detection is made more difficult by efforts to conceal the nature of the funds lost to the company. Writing off income that was actually received is one concealment technique. Altering sales figures, obtaining blank purchase orders, amending documentation, diverting vendor discounts, and writing off balances that are thrown out from account reconciliations are all ways that an employee can misappropriate funds and balance the books at the same time.

- **Computer-related crimes**—computer hacking can be a stepping-stone to securing data, accessing rights, and providing a means to commit fraud. Therefore, fraudsters may be involved in sabotage, software piracy, stealing personal data, and amending or damaging records held on computer systems. Younger people brought up in a computerized environment can run rings around their senior managers, who may not appreciate the opportunities for unauthorized transactions that are inherent in automated information systems. In some organizations staff have more access rights than they need to have to do their jobs. Computers have great facilities to hide irregular transactions, but at the same time can capture lots of information on the trail of each transaction.

- **Financial statement fraud**—this can be very serious and can be used to encourage investment and loans through fabricated or falsified financial figures. Inaccurate earnings figures may also be used as a basis for performance bonuses. Popular frauds involve people buying stock and then "talking up" the price and selling before the market spots the distortion and falls back in line. Some credit card frauds link into share frauds, in that the stolen cards are used to buy stock in the name of the rightful card owner to help boost share prices.

Alternatively, a company may be entirely fabricated to attract funding; once the money is obtained, it and the bogus company disappear from the face of the earth.

- **Sundry frauds**—there are many types of fraud that have not yet been mentioned, such as illegal price-fixing cartels; pyramid investment schemes; environmental abuse, such as waste pollution; money laundering, where illicit money is turned into legitimate usable funds; mail fraud; counterfeiting; and racketeering, where someone operates an illegal business for personal profit.

A lot can and does go wrong for both organizations and private individuals when fraud is allowed to prosper. Note that, for the purposes of this book, we will be primarily concerned with employee fraud. The Association of Certified Fraud Examiners (ACFE) has tried to put this into context: in its *Report to the Nation on Occupational Fraud Abuse* (Case Study 2389), the ACFE argued that employee fraud is big business. Smaller businesses were found to be most vulnerable because they tended to have less sophisticated financial controls, and to place more trust in managers. According to the ACFE, employee fraud is costing the nation some $400 billion a year, which is around $9 per employee and 6 percent of turnover. Losses caused by fraud among executives and managers were found to be some six and four times greater, respectively, than losses caused by other employees. Typical frauds found were asset misappropriation (cash, supplies, information, and equipment), fraudulent statements, illegal gratuities, bribery, and corruption. Typical perpetrators were college-educated, white males; the frauds examined ranged from a $22 misappropriation through to a $2.5 billion investment swindle. The ACFE quite rightly feels that fraud is an important issue in society and that the rate of its occurrence is rising.

## MODELS OF FINANCIAL CRIME

Only some of the myriad of frauds that exist were discussed in the preceding section. In practice, there are hundreds of methods by which an employee may defraud an employer. Likewise, there are many ways that outsiders can deceive an organization into parting with something of value. Private individuals, particularly the elderly and more vulnerable members of society, can fall prey to con artists in a variety of ways. To help put these

|  | **Theft** | **Misreporting** |
|---|---|---|
| **Internal** | embezzlement<br>pilferage | fraudulent reporting<br>bonus schemes, loans |
| **External** | health care fraud<br>shoplifting | share-price scams<br>pump-and-sell schemes |

**Figure 1.1**   Types of Fraud

issues into focus, we need to develop some basic models of financial crime. The first one distinguishes between fraud by members of an organization and fraud by external third parties, as shown if Figure 1.1.

An organization may be attacked from all sides. Employees may engage in both minor and more serious fraud; outsiders may also seek to obtain something for nothing, if given the chance. The other side of the coin is misleading the public through distorted information on the business (i.e., financial misreporting). Pump-and-sell schemes occur when company shares are acquired, the price is artificially inflated (say, through false Internet reports), and then quickly sold. Figure 1.2 looks at the potential layers of fraud affecting larger organizations.

Here the type of fraud varies with the position of the potential fraudster, although there is scope at all levels throughout and outside an organization. The more senior the employee, the greater the opportunity for committing more material fraudulent activity. Fraud can entail small amounts of regular

| **Criminal<br>Gangs** | **The<br>CEO** | **Unethical<br>Individuals** |
|---|---|---|
| check fraud<br>fabricated invoices | financial accounts<br>misreporting | Medicare fraud<br>shoplifting<br>government claims fraud<br>food stamp fraud |
|  | **Directors**<br>share-price scams<br>conflict of interests<br>concealed debts |  |

**Management**
bribes, kickbacks, travel and expense misreporting

**Employees**
petty cash, misappropriation, pilferage
false overtime, use of company equipment

**Figure 1.2**   Layers of Fraud

items that are misapplied or misappropriated, or it can involve huge sums in a scheme to artificially inflate profits. Scams can be custom and practice, when everyone adds a few hours to their overtime claims as a matter of course. Other frauds can be one-time hits, where funds are transferred to an overseas bank account and then quickly disappear from the system—along with the perpetrator. It could consist of a security guard who fails to turn up with thousands of dollars that he was conveying for the company. Fraud happens in thousands of health care claims that are regularly overstated by fairly small amounts. An entire company could embark on a scheme to rip off investors with promises of huge returns that fail to materialize. The point is that there is a risk of up to $400 billion of fraud in the U.S. economy from all aspects of business, and if there are no real safeguards against white-collar crime, the consequences could be devastating. Professor Andrew Chambers sets out the real impact of financial crime on society:

> With breathtaking cynicism we build the cost of fraud into the price of our products and are often prepared to require our customers to pay 5 or 10% more to subsidize the defrauder. Of course, this area of debate is shot through with moral tones. In particular, there is the immorality of the defrauder, notwithstanding that many defrauders find it hard to see that any individuals are hurt as a consequence of their frauds. But there is also the issue as to whether it is moral to launch new products and services which are prone to fraud. Do not enterprises have a moral obligation to minimize the temptation of fraud? Might this not also be in their enlightened self interest? We suggest that the situation has now become so acute that it calls for urgent action at senior levels of government, by regulators and in the boardrooms of companies and other entities.

## REAL-LIFE EXAMPLES

The press is full of stories of fraud and some cases go into extreme levels of detail. This book does not seek to reproduce the various stories, or embarrass named organizations and individuals, but it is appropriate to briefly mention some past cases that can help us understand and appreciate the problem:

- *An insurance claims settler stole $1 million, to support a gambling habit, by sending 417 checks to his friends in payment of bogus claims. He was jailed for eight years.*

The key factor was an addiction to gambling and the huge losses that this entailed. The solution for our friend, the claims settler, was to conspire with his friends to defraud his employer. A jail term concluded this story of greed and abuse.

- *A Post Office worker falsified travel expenses by $4,500 to improve family finances. He forged claims and his manager's signature and was convicted of false accounting. Instead of helping the family, he is now in jail.*

In this case, the fraudster felt that crime would be the solution to financial problems. There was a worthwhile motive—to provide for his family—but the net result of these endeavors had the opposite effect.

- *A company director gave a friend a corporate credit card. The friend racked up $17 million over 2.5 years, which was discovered when the director went on leave and a box of receipts was found in his desk.*

The director was someone in a powerful position, such that his actions were not questioned at all. In fact, the fraud was uncovered by accident; the extent of the losses is astounding.

- *An attorney who was mild, unassuming, and of good character stole from his clients' accounts. He went to Monte Carlo to bet on roulette in an attempt to pay it back. He was subsequently convicted of theft.*

Many fraudsters excuse their actions by maintaining their intention to repair any damage done. Their need is great and once they settle their problems, they will pay back the sums taken. In most cases this intention is simply an attempt to soothe a guilty conscience.

- *A promising young law student was attacked during a road-rage incident. She had to take sick leave and fell behind in her studies, although she still attempted to take her exams. She subsequently broke into the university at night and altered her exam results, but was found out. She could not face the shame of a court hearing and committed suicide at a nearby beach.*

People of high social standing face the prospect of irreparable damage to that standing if they get caught committing fraud. This sad case shows the emotional extremes that drive a person to commit an act of deceit and the impact of this dishonesty being uncovered.

- *A security guard stole £1.5 million in gems and cash from Versace in London.*

  A person who is given a position of trust is able to do much more damage than someone who is kept away from valuable resources. When breach of trust occurs, it can be disastrous. What's more, if the same person is fairly junior and is presented with an opportunity to divert a large sum, there will always be some temptation.

## UNDERLYING COMPONENTS

There are many and varied types of fraud that threaten all organizations. These attacks can come from a variety of sources, and can be directed toward government, public bodies, and commercial enterprises. At this stage, we need to extract the essential components of financial crime to complete the initial analysis of this problem. There has been a great deal of detailed research on why people commit fraud and what circumstances are required for fraud to arise. One of the founding fathers of fraud theory is Edwin H. Sutherland, who felt that opportunity, means, and motive together provide the impetus for white-collar crime. Donald R. Cressey, in *Other Peoples' Money* (Patterson Smith 1973), developed three key factors in fraud, shown in Figure 1.3.

Opportunity exists where there are poor controls over organizational resources. Severe pressure in the form of financial problems can occur in any family at any time. When the problem is not shared at all, feasible solutions like asking family members for temporary assistance may not be considered. Likewise, help may not be obtained for problems such as

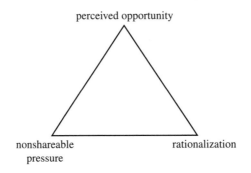

**Figure 1.3** Fraud Triangle

alcoholism or an addiction to gambling. Rationalization is a really interesting concept, because perpetrators are able to justify their actions, at least to themselves. Excuses may be simple—say, that most staff engage in similar or worse behavior—so pilferage or taking kickbacks is seen as the norm. Other excuses may be less obvious, such as when an employee feels that the company "owes" him for many hours of unpaid overtime, so he recoups it through regular kickbacks. Society values both business success and personal integrity. When these two concepts conflict, the individual has a clear decision to make. Which is more important?

- To obtain a high standing in society?
- To alleviate a financial crisis, such as college fees, medical bills, or a divorce settlement?
- To acquire a better car, vacation, property, school education?
- To assist a friend or family member with a major financial commitment?
- To fuel an addictive lifestyle that involves vices such as gambling or drugs?
- To observe, above all, the highest standards of personal integrity?

There may be great pressure to lower one's standards of personal integrity and choose between loyalty to one's employer or solving a major financial problem. Rationalization may allow someone to forgo integrity because of the compelling weight of the financial problem. Moreover, perpetrators may argue that they:

Will pay it all back later on.
Take what's only their fair share.
Just do like all the rest of them.
Don't worry because no one really cares about this anyway.
Must bow to a greater and more pressing need.
Are getting their own back on a corrupt employer.
Take what won't be noticed from a wealthy company.

The point is that professional, respected, and trusted members of an organization may commit fraud against the organization for a variety of reasons that make sense to them. They are not members of violent criminal gangs and they do not walk around armed with guns and wearing heavy scowls on their faces. They may appear and act like honest, law-abiding citizens, even while breaching their fiduciary duty to their employer.

Trusting your co-workers and bosses and staff is part of organizational life. It is difficult to know how to work together without this mutual trust and understanding. The new world of staff empowerment makes this reliance on trust even more of an issue. Researchers have found that there are many reasons people may turn to fraud and in many cases both the fraud and the precipitating factors for it come as a shock to their colleagues. The position is not simple. The world does not consist of criminals and honest people—it is more complicated than this. The world is full of people acting under tremendous, and in many cases conflicting, pressures which can lead to behavior that, although wrong, can be explained and even excused. Often a fraudster, if discovered, risks only his or her reputation. It depends on the value the person places on reputation and whether this is a risk worth taking. One thing that most organizations now accept is that people are, if anything, unpredictable.

The chances of getting caught also come into the equation: fraudsters will want to secure the desired gain, but also retain their freedom and perceived status in society as honest and upright. Where controls are poor, ethical standards are nonexistent, and real oversight in the organization is lacking, substantial employee fraud and concealment become much more likely. This lethal combination of forces—components of what some now call economic crime—make this a major growth area in business, public services, and society generally. Professor Gerald Vinten has described the real dangers of white-collar crime in today's society:

> White collar crime seems like the nice end of criminal activity, since it does not usually involve violence, and the perpetrators are just like the people next door. However, its economic consequences can be devastating, and in the wider scheme of things it can be even more lethal than crimes of physical violence. White collar and other types of crime tend to operate hand-in-glove and even be symbiotic. Money laundering is another illegal activity that makes the cross-walk between the 'nasty' end of crime and the 'nice' end. What is clear is that 'white' collar crime is not the preserve of the angels although policing agencies tend to treat it as a low priority compared with other types of crime. It is a difficult balancing act between civil liberty and minimizing crime, but a system which plays into the hands of the organized white collar criminals has a mushrooming impact on crimes generally. It is already expensive economically, and is a price that the law abiding are forced to pay, a redistributive tax which has all to do with human rapacity and nothing to do with the public good. It has to be time to confiscate the ill gotten gains of such activity, and to place the burden of proof for once back on the suspected perpetrators. The huge excitement

and promise which greeted the onset of the 21st century is in danger of being undermined if the white collar crime threat is allowed to perpetuate itself unchecked.

# REASONS FOR NOT BOTHERING

So far, we have outlined the great potential for financial crime to undermine our economy. The statistics are shocking, but fraudulent activity is both wide in scope and difficult to detect. The growth in fraud depends in part on the financial pressures placed on normal working people and the value placed on ethical behavior. There are always tensions resulting from these two factors; the third factor that completes the cycle of damage is the way organizations respond to the perceived risk of fraud. When fraud is not seen as a priority business risk, there is little incentive to tackle it head on. When directors and managers are not bothered about fraud as a corporate issue, their response contributes to the forces that are driving fraud further and deeper into all organizations. In this section we address some of the reasons why people, companies, directors, nonexecutives, and others do not always hold fraud as a key concern.

## General Lack of Awareness

Many managers and staff members do not have a particular interest in white-collar crime. It is generally seen as an unfortunate occurrence that occasionally happens to other organizations and when it arises, specialist investigators are brought in to deal with it. There is no real appreciation of the power of greed, nor the pressures that lead individuals to become deceitful. The typical manager may fail to think through why a staff member who has a small workload is always very busy. Managers do not follow through the implications of the accountants asking for more deductions in certain areas to get profits down. Some feel that men and women in suits rushing around the office indicates that all is well, as people in suits are by definition perceived as respectable.

## Not Seen as a Personal Threat

Fraud tends to be nonviolent and therefore does not have an immediate physical impact on the victim. Not bothering about fraud at times simply reflects society's priorities; people respond first to issues that threaten their physical safety and comfort. White-collar crime is not "in your face," as are other crimes. It is not something that will necessarily be on the tip of the tongue of police officers and security staff. As such, it may be seen as unfortunate or bothersome rather than criminal.

## No Real Victims—Write It off

Industries such as retail and distribution recognize that a degree of fraud is inherent in the nature of operations that possess, display, or move around valuable and portable goods. Some see crimes against such organizations as victimless because the losses are built into profit margins. The aim is not so much about removing fraud as it is about ensuring that the company does not exceed industry norms. Losses are written off, insured against, and lived with. This high-level policy sets the tone for the entire organization.

## Business before Security and Not Vice Versa

Linked to the preceding point is the view that securing company resources, if taken to the extreme, will mean little or no business gets done. A phone inquirer may hang up if asked dozens of questions to verify identity. Likewise, a grocery store owner may spend an hour making goods readily accessible to street thieves, just to get them to the eyes of potential customers. New information systems tend to be installed with the security and audit trail facilities set to zero, to be activated in a manner that suits the client. The point is that the more secure the system, the more resources it uses and the slower it becomes. Entrepreneurs have a keen eye on the business but less thought about the potential for abuse. This is also true in the sales arena: businesses love to supply large quantities of goods even when most of it is on credit. Turning customers away because of poor credit ratings has caused pain to many a dynamic salesperson.

## Not Understanding the Link between Fraud and Controls

*Controls* are mechanisms that guard against unacceptable risk. Most people accept that fire alarms are in place to detect and warn against fire. Plans are prepared and put into action to help counter the risk of not meeting strategic objectives. Performance appraisal systems may likewise counter the risk of failing to set and meet personal and group targets. Fraud is an invisible risk, in that it is potentially everpresent but may actually never materialize. Many people see fraud as something that happens if the company is unlucky and has taken on the occasional "bad apple." Not everyone links control standards to safeguards against fraud. When you spot your boss signing dozens of blank check request forms and handing them over to an assistant manager, just before he takes his vacation, you are witnessing this concept in action. When the reception staff allow visitors into the building without checking ID cards, the failure to link controls with fraud is obvious. If a purchasing manager asks for some checks to be handed to him rather than sent straight off to the suppliers, because he wants to insert a note with each check, then once again a fundamental breach of control is in action.

## Not Seen as a High-Risk Area

Risk management is happening in most dynamic organizations. Operational risk identification, risk assessment, and formulation of risk management solutions are basic to ensuring business success. The problem is that many risk assessment processes ignore fraud as an operational issue. Everything is discussed, examined, and addressed except what happens if someone in the team decides to defraud the business. In team-building mode, the risk workshops work well to get people together in a positive environment to tackle threats and exploit opportunities. Stunned silence is the usual response when deceit, corruption, and criminality are thrown into the debate. It's a little like hosting a dinner party and asking the guests how to prevent one of them from stealing the silverware.

## Not Built into Information Systems and Performance Indicators

Most people respond to challenges at work with one eye on their performance targets. An organization may devise dozens of value statements to guide employees' behavior and safeguard its resources. But if there is nothing in the performance framework that suggests preventing, detecting, and being able to respond to fraud is important, then there is little impetus to act. In fact, the absence of fraud issues in performance indicators, arguably helps reinforce the stance of "not bothering" about fraud, as it is usually perceived as being outside the ambit of most staff.

## Security Seen as a Doorkeeper Issue

Much fraud prevention is based around security systems. When security is seen as the responsibility of a lowly paid contractor in a shiny black uniform, it is deprioritized. Again, corporate policy implies that fraud prevention is not an issue when high-profile physical methods of fraud prevention are relegated to uniformed personnel.

## No Employer Loyalty

A commitment to fraud alertness and responsiveness enables people to see behind the veneer and glimpse the reality of an apparently innocent activity. These glimpses many times do not register at first. Being alert to fraud requires action above and beyond the call of duty, which is more likely when staff is loyal to the employer. Loyalty means that people feel a sense of belonging and responsibility for ensuring that things are done properly and corporate resources and interests are protected. What's more, the feeling of loyalty extends to pride in the reputation of the organization. Some argue that employer loyalty is under great pressure because of social and demographic trends. They suggest that a large proportion of the workforce will be temporary staff in the near future, along with contract people and self-employed business associates. The ties between employer and employee retain an economic dimension but no social or mutual bonding of trust and honor. This transforms the "why bother" attitude into one of "I'm not paid to bother."

## Pressure of Work

If we were to ask a typical middle manager what she is responsible for at work, we would probably get a detailed account of the many problems, issues, and stressful activities that constitute her daily workload. The manager may hint at peripheral issues such as health and safety, staff motivation, customer care practices, and other less obvious matters. The manager would certainly not try to take on other, more distant responsibilities that are less obvious. Fraud tends to be one of these "don't grab at" matters that cannot be squeezed onto the current To-Do list. Many managers and operational staff might get involved in fraud awareness, prevention, and detection if only they had more time.

## Less Experienced Managers with Less Understanding of Human Behavior

Fraud occurs because people behave unpredictably. People may be dishonest and in many cases manipulative, at least in terms of hiding their actions and forging records. More experienced managers have a better understanding of human nature than less experienced and sometimes younger managers. A newly qualified MBA graduate has studied business management, but may not have experienced the impact of dishonesty from staff. As we look to enthusiastic youngsters to drive the business of tomorrow, we must be careful about discarding old values of supervision, checking, and questioning and what can be referred to as healthy professional skepticism. Conversely, older managers may not realize that younger staff have a detailed knowledge of information technology (IT) systems and audit trails, and may know how to erase specific transactions. Any parent who has tried to block inappropriate Internet access will soon realize that most school kids have advanced Internet skills.

## Face-Value Assumptions

We have already referred to the fact that many frauds depend on an outward appearance of regularity. When people trust in initial appearances, it is hard to detect irregular transactions and activity. Some shop workers seem to gain weight at closing time, as they depart through the exits, only to slim down the following morning when they return to work. If managers always suspect fraud, they will overreact and want to search the employees each day. However, if everything is accepted at face value, the company is open to abuse on a daily basis. One way to test your susceptibility is to ask whether you are one of the people who have never challenged the accuracy of a spreadsheet that is placed in front of you.

## Less Time for Formal Procedures

As a general rule, controls cost money and take time. Frauds occur because of poor controls, whereas business flourishes when people are given lots of freedom to act. Workers are given responsibility and have to get a signature or an approval only when absolutely necessary. Getting bogged down with formal procedures is, for many, a thing of the past. Business has less time for written rules. The downside is that fraud is facilitated by an environment of unclear roles and procedures. When a rule violation is neither clear nor provable, it makes it more difficult to bring forward a case. Say there are no clear procedures or policies about storing equipment at home: it would be difficult to bring charges against a worker who has been taking equipment home and has a ready explanation for this apparent irregularity.

## Overreliance on Insurance Coverage

Insurance is a risk management technique for transferring or spreading risk and is normally associated with risks that are high impact but unlikely to materialize. If employee fraud is likely to happen, it will be hard to get insurance at an affordable price. However, if an organization is insured against employee fraud and has fidelity bonding, there may be little emphasis on effective controls to guard against fraud.

## Perks Are Just Perks, Not Real Criminal Intent

A real driver for the lack of interest in employee fraud is the view that every company has perks for its people. There must be some kind of nontaxable perk in place to keep everyone happy. This stance translates white-collar crime into harmless scams and cons. No victims; no real losses; no threats; no distress; so no one is bothered. The cycle of neglect is the basis for real crime that can escalate to great heights in this type of culture. An organization that does not view company perks as an issue undermines its ethical values. When a staff member resigns or asks for a transfer for no discernible reason, this type of situation could well be the cause of their discomfort.

## Undetected Fraud Is Not a Crime

Some argue that reported fraud is around 10 percent of the real picture. One reason why people don't bother about fraud is the feeling that it does not affect their industry. So why worry about something that occurs in another neighborhood?

We point to the story of an operative of a railway company who was convicted of stealing trains and selling them to individual collectors, as an example of fraud in an area that was not at all obvious.

## Only Happens to Chaotic Organizations

Many frauds rely on poor records, confused staff, and slack authorization and reporting lines. Some are so complicated that only charges of false accounting can be brought, because the underlying trail of transactions crosses through, around, and over so many different accounts and records. In contrast, some frauds flourish where there is an abundance of rules and regulations, where everyone is double-checking everyone else. The problem here is that people assume that someone else will pick up any concerns; responsibility is diluted if not completely dispersed. Rigid organizations can be abused by people who know the systems well, and depend on this rigidity to get around the controls.

An organization may issue an ID (employee initials) and a public password (say "password") to all new employees for access to the network. The new employee is then asked to alter the password as soon as possible. This system can be abused by someone who knows the initials of a new employee who has not yet begun work.

People in these types of organizations may assume that fraud is a non-issue when rigid checks exist everywhere, but again, this is not always the case.

## We Need to Trust Our People

It is hard to get around this one. People do not want to hear about fraud at work because this stops them relating to colleagues and having social engagements and ultimately life fulfillment from their employment. In some cases they react vigorously and quite unfavorably to suggestions that a system that depends primarily on trusting your staff is not always a good control against fraud. By taking fraud off the agenda, this debate can be avoided. Fraud is seen as unfortunate, negative, and disruptive to business life. Talking about fraud and guarding against its eventuality is seen as much the same. Ignorance is used as a shield and the issue is brushed aside as irrelevant.

## Board Agenda Crammed

Perhaps the most important factor in fraud dereliction is the state of most directors' agendas. The agenda is crammed full of issues that require boardroom buy-in. If all organizational issues were put onto the agenda, the board would have to meet 24 hours a day, 7 days a week, for many months. What is on the boardroom agenda is first and foremost business success and stakeholder opinion. If fraud is not seen to relate to these issues, then it won't make it onto the table. The force that usually drives fraud awareness is the growing interest in long-term corporate reputation as an adjunct to short-term business profits. It is here that fraud fits into the debate, in terms not only of cost but also of impact on standing in the business community. A "don't bother" attitude is much harder to defend in this scenario.

So where do we stand now? Management change theories sometimes revolve around action models that have driving and resisting forces. For the fraud debate, the potential resistance is great, and there are many reasons why people who are not bothered about fraud in their organization can nonetheless rest easy at bedtime. On a sliding scale of concerned—not concerned, we have so far argued that many organizations are closer to the latter end of the scale. If the explanations for not bothering about fraud are not countered, there is very little opportunity to argue that fraud is a substantial corporate risk and should be managed with this in mind.

# SO WHY BOTHER?

External auditors, financial controllers, certified internal auditors, investigators, certified fraud examiners, and other like-minded professionals talk about the problems associated with white-collar crime with relish. In many cases they form an inner circle to debate and decide on the best way to defend the organization against attack. Everyone else is outside this debate, because it apparently does not concern them. This is unfortunate. Here we list the reasons why people in all aspects of organizational functions should be concerned about the threat of fraud.

### Financial Costs

The costs and time of investigating fraud can be high, and investigation could involve law enforcement and state prosecutors. It requires time in court appearing as a witness in the case and time for internal disciplinary action when the case involves a member of staff. A fraud requires a press release and work to manage any press inquiries that may arise. Repairing damage to the corporate reputation can be costly and again, has to be managed carefully to ensure that the share price and customer loyalty do not suffer. The cost of hiring replacement people to cover for the employees implicated in the fraud can likewise be high. Lost time while staff is assisting in the investigation should be added to time lost while the suspect is suspended or unable to perform.

### Product Cost

The standard response to the cost of fraud is to finance the losses through higher prices. So the consumer pays in the end—the consumer being everyone. Employee fraud can be funded, as an alternative option, in lower wages, if product price increases are not feasible. With this option the fraudster's colleagues pay for the misdemeanors.

## Business Costs

Building on the preceding, the impact of a material fraud can be loss of business or a lost business.

> In one case, a small bakery business employed five local people to work and prosper in their small community. Several workers decided to defraud the business and sold large quantities of bread on the side by diverting stocks from the main legitimate business. These workers were assisted by the fact that they started baking at four in the morning but the owner did not arrive until many hours later. Eventually, the business crashed, owing debts. The local community lost its bakery, the workers lost their jobs, and the owner swore he would never invest in a local business again.

This is not an unusual story, unfortunately; businesses in many local communities have taken similar blows.

## Resource Issues

Areas where there are high levels of external fraud—the food stamp system, insurance, government contracts, and health care, for example—are staffed with large fraud teams. This puts a strain on government resources because public officials are diverted to fraud work. It can be argued that high levels of fraud tie up law enforcement resources and prosecutors, as well as valuable court time.

## Culpability

Companies that have no concern about whether their employees are committing fraud may be held partly responsible for their employee's deceitful behavior. Federal sentencing guidelines allow companies to pay lower fines if they have good compliance mechanisms in place to counter the risk of fraud. Much depends on the culture and perception of fraud throughout the organization.

## Company Accountability

Company shareholders employ directors to oversee the company. The directors in turn employ managers to run the show. Managers employ people to make things happen, and so on. If the directors give no guidance on fighting fraud, the share price may decline, reflecting the losses that will probably be suffered, and the shareholders may not reinstate the directors as a result. New directors may be brought in to redress this position, and set the much-needed guidance and oversight in place. The cycle of accountability should ensure that in the long run the shareholder's concerns are addressed and resolved. But the cycle is costly and time-consuming and can lead to lost markets and lost business.

## Encouraging Dishonesty

Organizations that are not bothered about fraud have virtually painted a sign on their front doors saying, "we are open for business and anything else." It is a dangerous position that may encourage dishonest people to act on opportunities. Not acknowledging corporate fraud as an issue means not acknowledging the importance of controls that guard against abuse. This is particularly so for criminal gangs interested in, say, check fraud and internally, the level of basic company swindles. In both instances a lack of concern creates a greater potential for fraud. Not being aware of past frauds is simply no excuse for not caring about the subject. In extreme cases, the known figures are low because the real extent is not being detected at all.

## New Business Context

Perhaps the single most important driver for coming to grips with fraud is the trend toward online business. Figure 1.4 illustrates this point.

Future businesses will have to be online because of the lower costs, greater accessibility, and basic market expectations. The biggest threat is consumer reluctance to risk their money through, for example, credit card transactions over the Internet. The sensible business response is to achieve a reputation for reliability and trustworthiness and perhaps seek official recognition and even some form of certification. Failing to recognize the

**Figure 1.4**   New Business Contexts

risk of corporate fraud will eventually affect the business negatively. Accepting internal and external abuse and breach of systems security again will mar the organization's public reputation. Thus, the only way online commerce will succeed is for all sectors of the economy to engage fully in the fight against fraud. Neil Cowan, the Director General of the Confederation of European Institutes of Internal Auditors, has been able to bring home the importance of fraud prevention:

> Fraud can occur in any organization in every sector of economic activity. The perpetrators may be found at all levels of the organizational structure. Fraud is no respecter of national or cultural boundaries. Sometimes, fraud can be committed in the name of the organization in a misguided attempt to keep it going or to be able to sell it on. Always, however, fraud is committed for gain and always at somebody else's expense. Fraud is a business risk in the widest sense and may be perpetrated at the highest levels of an organization, the lowest levels and everywhere in between. All that's needed is opportunity, gain and a reasonable chance of getting away with it. Take away one of the sides of that triangle and you begin to mitigate the risk.
>
> Prevention of fraud provides a far better pay-off than detection. Prevention and deterrence costs money—cultural changes, control changes, risk assessment changes—but detection costs potentially far more. The cash or assets have gone, the organization [is] unable or unwilling to prosecute the perpetrator. And, anyway, what chance of a reasonable recovery? So, assess the risks of fraud, make prevention cost effective and take away the moral dilemma of the organization and the individual when a temptation arises. No opportunity, no temptation, no fraud.

# CONCLUSION

We can now list 10 key points relating to the importance of addressing financial crime:

1. Fraud is a billion-dollar business.
2. There are many different types of fraud.
3. Fraud is on the rise.
4. Trusted employees can become fraud perpetrators who will rationalize their behavior.

5. There are many reasons why organizations do not see fraud as an important corporate issue.
6. There are also many reasons why there must be a powerful and positive response to combat fraud.
7. Organizations can be victims or protected; much depends on the adopted approach and culture.
8. Fraud must be seen as a business risk and then tackled along with other known risks.
9. The actual scale of fraud risk may be unknown in an organization.
10. Many organizations are being defrauded either with or without their knowledge. A lack of reported fraud is not a good guide to whether an organization will be targeted in future.

Financial or white-collar crime has a depth and breadth that is all-consuming. It has a global dimension in all societies and all economies, to a greater or lesser extent. Developed countries, the third world, and emerging democracies are all subject to illegal business practices and fraud undermines the efforts of funding agencies across the world. Public perception of fraud and corruption also affects the level of charitable donations and grants for countries struggling with natural disasters. If the funds cannot get to the right places, there is less impetus to give generously. It is with this in mind that we examine the structures that should be in place to address the issue of fraud, in Chapter 2.

# CHAPTER 2

---

# An Action Model

*Opportunity makes a thief.*

## WHY ACTION?

This chapter introduces the "stop light" model (Figure. 2.1) as a way of illustrating the philosophy behind the entire book.

Many risk models break the organization down into zones that are marked red, yellow, or green: Red is high-risk areas that have to be urgently tackled; green denotes safe areas that can be accepted, or exploited for greater gain; yellow reflects parts of the organization that should be kept under review. We turn the standard risk model on its head and suggest that fraud risk management is about sending the right message to would-be perpetrators. We want potential fraudsters to read red as dangerous to them so they avoid attacking our systems. Fraud is intentional and involves the use of deceit to gain an illegal advantage. Thus, our model must have a more proactive dimension to counter this potential risk. The colors in this model are used as follows:

**Red:** These are parts of the organization that are geared up to combat fraud. People at red include specialist fraud investigators, auditors, compliance teams, financial controllers, and others who have a clear mandate to address the risk of fraud as part of their work role.

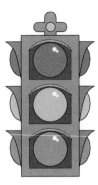

**Figure 2.1**   The Stop Light Model

**Green:**   These are people who wish to breach organizational systems for gain. They are career criminals who have access to corporate resources (for instance, hackers), shoplifters, credit card fraudsters, and also people who work for an organization but would commit fraud if given the chance. These people want to see a green light to fraud where little or no safeguards are in place.

**Yellow:**   Everyone else who works for an organization is essentially at yellow. That is, the vast majority of employees are not concerned about the risk of fraud. They have no involvement in thinking through the potential for fraud and how this may be assessed to ensure that any opportunities for criminality are minimized.

The stop light model is useful in that we can get people to position themselves at red or yellow and then find ways of encouraging the "at yellows" to move toward red. The strength of the model lies in the pictorial representation, which provides a simple yet effective way of getting people to assess their current position, set clear targets, and devise strategies for making the target. If people in an organization can be moved up to red, we have a good start on combating fraud and protecting resources and reputation. If this happens, there is a better chance of escaping corporate culpability if an employee acts in an unlawful manner. If there are good antifraud procedures, ethics training, good controls, and a history of compliance, then there will be some protection under the federal sentencing guidelines. Moreover, if staffers are alert and understand that minimizing the risk of fraud is part of their overall responsibilities, the employer has a head start over its competitors. The message that needs to reach all employees is that preventing fraud starts with each and every individual in the organization.

# WHO'S AT THE STOP LIGHT?

### Green

Fraud involves people behaving in a deceitful manner. There is no fraud without deceit. If employers do not accept that they may have employed people who, given the right circumstances, would resort to criminal acts, then there is no incentive to install safeguards. There are many fraudsters and potential fraudsters who work for organizations or have access to corporate resources. Career criminals make a living out of crime. In employee fraud, these criminals earn their salary plus "extras" and it is these extras that are secured through deception. When the extras are more substantial than the basic salary, the employee may be more interested in illegal rather than legal gains.

### Yellow

Directors, managers, associates, and employees all fall at yellow. They have set targets and workloads that reflect their day-to-day activities. Managers have a pivotal role in all organizations, in that they take responsibility for planning, organizing, allocating resources, directing activities, and monitoring performance. Most would argue that these managers are also responsible for ensuring that controls are firmly in place, that actual performance is compared to targets, and that any variances are explored. In addition, known risks are assessed and, when appropriate, controls put in place to ensure that the effects of these risks are minimized. One way of assessing risk is to get the team together to work through the operational risks that must be managed. At yellow, team members do not focus on fraud risk to any extent, as it is seen as being outside their scope of responsibility. A review of management development training programs and their contents will reveal that the vast majority do not address fraud prevention, detection, or investigation. Management competencies, again, do not normally include items relating to employment fraud issues. The only exception is front-line staff, such as cashiers and delivery personnel, who may be asked to watch out for con artists and false documents.

### Red

At this level, fraud awareness is normally quite good. Specialist fraud teams will by definition have a good handle on employee fraud and irregularity. Security staff and people handling important items such as large sums of cash will also regard watching for criminal activity as part of their role at work. There are other high-risk areas involving, for example, credit cards or unsecured loans, where there are obvious opportunities for things to go wrong. Auditors, both external and internal, have an eye on indicators of fraud and are trained to respond appropriately if they come across inconsistencies or unusual transactions. People at red will get some training, depending on the type of work they do, though it may be as little as handling ultraviolet pens to check the validity of bank notes received. At the other extreme, some public-sector staff may get detailed forensic training in isolating forged personal documentation, such as drivers' licenses or passports. The training will be specific to the job and will involve some depth only if staff has a specialist role in investigating fraud. In short, only a small amount of the workforce will tend to be positioned at red. Unfortunately, even when an organization employs a team of in-house fraud investigators, these teams do not normally have an educational role in spreading best practice across the organization. They tend to carry out detective work and then launch into action when a particular fraud is spotted.

## MOVING FROM GREEN TO YELLOW

We have already suggested that if everyone was at red and felt they should combat fraud, there would be no fraud. In an ideal world, everyone would behave honestly and there would be no need to consider the possibility of fraud. In the real world, however, there will be a core of individuals who are dishonest. Some argue that achieving rewards and advantages through deceitful behavior is learned very early in life and that, once set, this pattern cannot readily be altered. This is a cynical view that fails to recognize the blurred lines between right and wrong that individuals are faced with on a daily basis. People, in the workplace, behave lawfully because:

- They believe it is the right and proper thing to do.
- There is trust between employer and employee.
- It mirrors the behavior of other respected persons in the organization.

- The risk of getting caught outweighs the benefits that could be secured through the fraudulent act.
- There is no other alternative.

We can take each of these issues in turn to assess the potential for moving people away from temptation to criminality.

### It Is the Right and Proper Thing to Do

An organization needs to make clear what is right and proper and what, in contrast, is not. Going back to our point about learned behavior, it is hard to alter values set at an early age. All an employer can do is to make clear its expectations. Tell your people what is right in terms of general aspirations and then ask them to follow this line. The rest is up to them.

### There Is Trust between Employer and Employee

There is much interest in the "trusting" organization, where the staff and employer have a relationship based on mutual trust and acceptance. Trusting employees does not mean turning a blind eye to misdemeanors or forcing a position on staff by threats and inducements; rather, it has more to do with making clear what is expected from people and helping them achieve it. The work relationship is a series of mutual promises whereby the employer promises fair treatment, support, feedback, and listens to staff. The employee promises to meet targets, work hard, and behave in accordance with set standards. Each side is asked to keep these promises and build them into the decisions that are made at work. When the promises are broken and trust breaks down, the relationship is terminated. Managers and workers who are considering fraud as an option will have to calculate that this trust is not worth retaining and that defrauding the organization is fair. One further point concerning the trusting organization: There is still a need to install effective controls against fraud, on the basis of trusting the systems to make sense and not trusting someone such that they can commit fraud and conceal it.

### It Mirrors the Behavior of Other Respected Persons in the Organization

More than 90 percent of communication is nonverbal, through actions and responses rather than what is actually said. Likewise, an organization communicates its standards through the behavior of its senior people, not through formal policy documents and colorful logos. When top managers send inconsistent messages, such as giving themselves huge pay raises or expensive "exploratory visits" or "networking opportunities" to exotic locations abroad, the tone is set for others to follow. The difference is that the managers' corrupt behavior is legitimate (i.e., authorized); the fraudster's behavior is similarly wrong and differs only in that it is unauthorized. Simply put, this means the potential fraudster will view high-profile individuals at work as either an encouragement or discouragement to unethical behavior. The obvious solution is to ensure that standards and behavior are ethical—which gets more difficult when we try to relate this concept to, say, huge annual increases in directors' fees, bonuses, and share options paid by some companies for no apparent reason.

### The Risk of Getting Caught Outweighs the Benefits that Could Be Secured through the Fraudulent Act

For people firmly located at green, the single biggest deterrent is the risk of getting caught and punished. People commit fraud simply because of an anticipated gain. The need to secure funds arises from many and varied sources, including a wish to help others who are less fortunate. If there is little chance of being discovered, or if there is a lax policy on repaying losses and punishing offenders, then the door is open for crooked employees to rest easy at green. There must be good controls that guard against fraud and managers who are proactive in acting against perpetrators. Make it hard to commit fraud; make it easy to investigate, recover losses, and dismiss and prosecute the offenders to move some people out of the green and up to the yellow zone.

### There Is No Other Alternative

When an individual is confronted about inappropriate behavior, the standard response is one of guilt. Counseling, advice, staff welfare, emergency funds, and financial management advice on loan rescheduling and financing options can all be made available through work. If employers take the initiative to enable staff to feel financially secure, then these become real options. In addition, if organizations make sure their new appointments are financially sound, they will not hire people who are desperate for extra funds, particularly in high-risk areas. By giving people alternatives, some of the green employees may look at other options before resorting to extremes. Any help line should be set up with this sensitivity in mind.

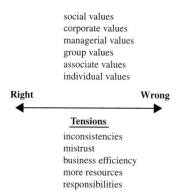

**Figure 2.2**  Values System

To tackle "green" people, employers need to consider the preceding strategies and ensure that as much as possible is being done to keep people on the straight and narrow. A system of cascading values may appear as in Figure 2.2.

The value system starts with social values that are learned first at home and then at school, and later on via peer groups and friends. Television and other mass media can also have an influence.

> Above the cheers and screams of fans, a commentator at a major wrestling match stated: "Now's not the time to play fair. Now's the time to win. Do whatever it takes to win."

Within the confines of the organization, there has to be a solid set of corporate values that give employees a clear sense of direction. Whatever the official values, individual managers will have a big impact on the way values are translated to and observed in the workplace. In general, staff will act in a way that is acceptable to their manager. Real-life, day-to-day decisions happen quickly, and there is always a balance between what has to be done and what is allowed. The manager should point to the right direction in these circumstances. Tremendous pressures are exerted by the work group, too, and affect the way each group member behaves. If it's a norm to skim, to idle, or to turn a blind eye, then all members of the group may adopt the norm in order to be accepted. When the manager's values differ from the group's view, the individual group member will side with whichever source is most influential. The strongest force will reign supreme, for better or worse. It is within this cascading system of values that the individual's own values are located. Strong-minded individuals will go their own way, come what may; others may be swayed by the corporate value system. If there is a strong link between corporate values, managers' values, and group values, we have a chance to influence the individual's decision to do what's right. There is not much an organization can do about social values, although an employer can try to discover a person's personal value system as part of the recruitment and selection process.

# MOVING FROM YELLOW TO RED

The most important aspect of the stop light model is that it supports the process of moving employees from yellow to red. This is the challenge. If organizations can get their people to view corporate fraud as "The Invisible Enemy," they will be positioned to succeed. If teams start to incorporate fraud issues in their risk assessment training and workshops, then fraud prevention can be addressed through suitable controls. Strategies to increase employee awareness and understanding across the organization mean that appropriate risk assessment will naturally follow. This section deals with fraud awareness workshops. The best way to get an important issue across to staff is to give the initiative the proper resources, and get teams together to work through the subject and assimilate key learning points. There are three main approaches to fraud awareness training.

### Focus on Ethical Values

This first approach deals with getting people to understand ethical concepts and find out where they and others stand. One way of convincing people that fraud happens only if it is allowed to, used by many fraud specialists, is a model that suggests people in most organizations fall into one of the categories shown in Figure 2.3.

We would go through the following process:

1. Do all the usual preparation for launching the fraud awareness workshops and getting support from the board and top management.
2. Get the operational teams together and introduce the topic and workshop objectives.
3. Go through the background to the antifraud policy in brief.

**Figure 2.3**   Dimensions of Honesty

4. Prepare forms that list the three categories of staff, but do not include the 25, 25, 50 percentages. Ask the group members to discuss the issue in pairs, and then individually put in what they feel the percentages are for people who work for their organization. Each person will come up with his or her own percentage breakdown between the three types of employee.

5. Seek feedback and ask the group members to reveal their personal scores (percentages); the workshop leader can write them on a large chart or display board.

6. Stimulate a discussion on the assigned scores and discuss the variances. Get the group to engage in the debate across the room. People who score extremes—for example, 100 percent honest or 100 percent dishonest—may engage in a minor debate about the discrepancies.

7. Work through the idea of honesty and the fact that if everyone were completely honest, there would be no fraud at all.

8. Work through the idea that although some people are honest, organizations cannot design controls over valuable resources and interests around an assumption of complete honesty.

9. Tackle the all-important concept of the middle percentage (50%), where people who are ordinarily honest and trustworthy could suffer severe financial or emotional pressures and succumb to temptation. When opportunities to defraud are provided by lax controls, those opportunities, together with the temptation factor, will lead to problems.

10. Give team members time to think through the implications of the workshop and how powerful forces can erode people's ethics. Use the exercise to get across the importance of good controls at work.

Underscore this with the point that responsibility to combat fraud lies with each individual group member. Refer to the antifraud policy and the material (which should be present) on staff responsibilities.

11. Work on an action plan to address the potential for fraud. This is best linked to general risk assessment exercises that the team should be carrying out, but the fraud angle should be prioritized in future exercises.

12. Debrief the group and ensure that participants do not feel they should spend their time spying on each other as a result of the workshop.

### Focus on the Set Policy

This approach is completely different. The ethical approach just described can become evangelical if not managed well. Thumping the table and preaching about right and wrong can be unsettling for some people. The second approach simply relays the corporate antifraud policy to team members, through the following process:

1. Do all the usual preparation for launching the fraud awareness workshops and getting support from the board and top management.

2. Get the operational teams together and introduce the topic and workshop objectives.

3. Briefly discuss the importance of the antifraud policy.

   At this stage, the workshop approach can be further broken down into two alternative options:

   a. The first option is to present the antifraud policy to the group by going through each aspect and taking questions as they arise. After each section, there should be time to discuss and reflect and possibly give brief examples to illustrate.

   b. The second option is to divide the group into smaller groups and give each subgroup part of the corporate antifraud policy to work on. The trainer will ask each small group to present that part of the policy back to the main group and make clear its importance, relevance, and content, along with an example or two of its impact at work. Each subgroup makes a presentation, with time for debate and discussion following each presentation. Taken together, the presentations will deliver the entire policy to the main group, with involvement from all. The challenge is to get groups to concentrate on aspects of the policy that were not covered in their individual subgroup.

4. Work on an action plan to address the potential for fraud in conjunction with the antifraud policy. The action plan is best linked to general risk assessment exercises that the team should be carrying out, but with the fraud angle prioritized in future exercises.

5. Debrief the group and ensure that everyone has a good understanding of the corporate antifraud policy and how it affects their day-to-day work.

### Focus on Practical Implementation

The final option is to get people into pragmatic mode. Here the trainer will focus on practical exercises and the learning that occurs if done well, through the following process:

1. Do all the usual preparation for launching the fraud awareness workshops and getting support from the board and top management.

2. Get the operational teams together and introduce the topic and workshop objectives.

3. Briefly go through the background of the antifraud policy.

4. Construct an exercise that takes the group through key aspects of fraud, such as integration of fraud policies into operational practices, fraud detection, responses to a particular fraud, fraud prevention, and staff discipline in cases of suspected employee fraud. The exercise can be based on one short case study that asks each subgroup to deal with a particular aspect of fraud, as in the exercise described in the preceding section. The exercise should have at least passing relevance to the work of the teams in the workshop. The best exercise to use can be chosen from a suite of different case studies after doing some pre-workshop research.

5. Monitor groups as they prepare their presentations on the aspect of fraud that has been assigned to them.

6. Make sure each subgroup listens and questions the other subgroup members as a way of getting into the material.

7. Give the team members time to think through the implications of the workshop and how they need to learn about fraud prevention,

detection, and response. Investigation is perhaps too strong a word for nonspecialists, as any forensic work should be done by experts. Make clear the importance of prevention as the basic philosophy behind proactive antifraud measures. Refer to the antifraud policy and the material on staff responsibilities that should be present.

8. Work on an action plan to address the potential for fraud. This is best linked to general risk assessment exercises that the team should be carrying out, but with the fraud angle prioritized in future exercises.

9. Debrief the group and that ensure participants feel they are equipped to deal with aspects of fraud that have been covered in the workshop.

10. Make sure people know when to call in the fraud experts.

Each approach has its own merits and disadvantages. The first approach could become almost evangelical, and consist mainly of a series of general aspirations, which some people will find frustrating. The second approach can be dry and boring if the company policy is presented in a classroom format. Interaction is helpful but again may be frustrating when group members have no influence on the policy document. The last approach may involve exercises that are too far removed from the workplace environment, and so encourage some group members to switch off.

If core competencies include the ability to manage the risk of fraud, then a matrix can be developed and used to assess the three basic approaches. Competencies are made up of skills, knowledge, and attitudes; the impact of the approaches can be plotted as shown in Figure 2.4.

Training is about promoting positive and dynamic change, and ideally should concentrate on the skills, knowledge, and *attitudes* of the workforce. The first approach, which focuses on ethical values, is designed to change

|  | 1. Ethics | 2. Set Policy | 3. Practical Exercise |
|---|---|---|---|
| Skills |  |  | X |
| Knowledge |  | X |  |
| Attitudes | X |  |  |

**Figure 2.4**   Developing Competencies

*attitudes* and get people thinking about the chances for deceit in the workplace and how they can guard against it. The end result is that attitudes can be altered so that controls and alertness will be seen as essential. The second approach, where trainers simply work through the antifraud policy, provides a *knowledge* of the policy so that people understand it and are able to incorporate the requirements into their everyday work. The exercises in the final approach are linked to acquiring *new skills* for tackling employee fraud. If employees are able to develop positive and dynamic skills, knowledge, and attitudes in managing fraud, they will move closer to protecting the organization against the threat of fraud. A combination of the three training approaches would greatly aid staff development. One integrated approach, using all three options, is as follows:

1.  Do all the usual preparation for launching the fraud awareness workshops and getting support from the board and top management.
2.  Get the operational teams together and introduce the topic and workshop objectives.
3.  Briefly go through the background to the antifraud policy.
4.  Present the importance of ethical positioning to the group.
5.  Go through the 25/25/50 percent ethical exercise and establish the importance of dealing with fraud in the organization.
6.  Present the antifraud policy and fraud response plan in an interactive manner. This can be done either with the group analyzing the policy or by subgroups presenting the material along with discussion points.
7.  Put the policy into action by working through set practical exercises covering fraud prevention, detection, and response, along with internal staff discipline.
8.  Give the team members time to think through the implications of the workshop and their need to learn about fraud prevention, detection, and response. Investigation is perhaps too strong a word for nonspecialists, as any forensic work should be done by experts. Make clear the importance of prevention as the basic philosophy behind proactive antifraud measures. Refer to the antifraud policy and the material on staff responsibilities that should be present.
9.  Work on an action plan to address the potential for fraud. This is best linked to general risk assessment exercises that the team should

be carrying out. However, the fraud angle should be prioritized in future exercises.

10. Debrief the group and ensure that they feel equipped to deal with the aspects of fraud that have been covered in the workshop.
11. Make sure people know when to call in the fraud experts.

This type of workshop is really intensive and would probably take a whole day to complete. The morning would cover items 1–7; the afternoon would involve breaking the group into subgroups and giving them time to work on their exercise, and then present back to the main group. There could well be several spinoff benefits from such a workshop, including enhanced communications, team performance, problem solving, and presentation skills.

## MEASURING PROGRESS

One criticism of training and development programs is that although they create an intention to effect change, the planned changes do not always arise. Managers and staff members attend the workshops, get involved and at the time excited, only to drift back to the old ways of working soon after the workshops are over. The way around this is to establish a measure and assess how staff is progressing against this measure. For fraud awareness, the measures can be derived from a series of questionnaires that seek to find out how much people know about antifraud strategies and to what extent they are managing the risk of fraud in their operational areas. The questionnaire may be sent out annually or every six months and in this way score the level of awareness and responsiveness from staff and monitor progress. Each organization will have to decide on the key questions that it will ask, and this will vary with policy. Questionnaires could ask the following:

1. How does the organization define fraud?
2. Do you have a copy of the antifraud policy?
3. Are you aware of its contents?
4. Do you have a copy of the fraud response plan?
5. Are you aware of its contents?
6. Who would you report suspicions of fraud to?
7. How do you build fraud prevention into your operations?
8. How do you ensure that you are able to detect fraud if it is happening in your area of responsibility?

9. How is your staff managing the risk of fraud (if appropriate)?
10. Have you experienced any frauds or irregular activities at work?

Each return could be assessed and marked on a scale ranging from "highly aware and responsive" through to "very poor awareness." The returns can be used to gauge the success of fraud awareness workshops. In addition, it is advisable to ask group members who attend the workshops to score the events as to which of the set objectives have been met and whether working practices now include the need to respond to the risk of fraud. The two sources of information will provide a good indication of whether the workforce is moving toward the red light.

## ZERO TOLERANCE

The stop light model suggests that if employees are at red, there will be no problems with internal fraud. Obviously, this is wholly unrealistic. What is more realistic is to set some form of standard and try to stick to it. One approach is to use zero tolerance as the baseline, where the highest ethical standards are expected by the organization. Many "yellow" issues arise when lines are blurred and the rules are not clear, so zero tolerance is about:

- Having a clear and direct message on employee fraud.
- Having a position that is, in the main, uncompromising.
- Setting demanding targets about what is accepted at work and what is not condoned.
- Trying to keep things one-dimensional (if something appears wrong, unacceptable, or questionable, then do not do it).
- Establishing responsibility for the behavior of staff. The responsibility lies with the individual employees and their managers.
- Matching words with action. Sanctions should be applied to everyone who engages in fraudulent activities, even a company director.
- Asking senior people to set a good example and show leadership.
- Monitoring activity and ensuring that irregularities are picked up.
- Keeping the staff discipline procedures vibrant and clearly linked into the corporate fraud policy.

If zero tolerance is adopted, the organization should follow through on it. Organizations cannot give everyone a red badge, say they have been through the fraud awareness training, and then check the appropriate box. Fraud prevention is not about assigning a color and then walking away. Prevention has more to do with ensuring that people are responding positively to internal policies and are able to internalize the requirements and make sense of them. Detached consensus is not enough. A grudging acceptance that everyone should be doing more about fraud is a start, but real commitment is needed from all employees. Fraud risk should be an agenda item and it should stay on the agenda and stimulate decisions on making systems more dependable and robust. Zero tolerance is about accepting nothing less than that.

There are forces that make fraud a real issue in society. There are organizations that will never achieve zero tolerance because there are too many flaws in the systems and thinking across the organization. Fraud thrives where:

- People who work for the organization are assumed to be honest at all times.
- There is little or no supervision of staff and their activities.
- Systems are not developed with a view to protecting company resources as well as conducting the organization's business.
- Contracts are arranged informally, without proper tendering or open competition.
- The important control inherent in segregating duties, where one person checks the work of another as a natural part of a process, is absent. When this key concept is ignored, it is easier to commit fraud.
- Authority levels are not clear and sensible. If almost anyone can spend against a particular budget, things can go wrong. By the same token, there should be several people involved in monitoring budgets to ensure that discrepancies are isolated and addressed.

A zero-tolerance environment is based on tackling these potential weaknesses. Strong systems, alert staff, clear rules, and quick and effective follow-through on problems underpin the zero-tolerance concept. It is not simply a stated intention, but effective procedures and responsive attitudes throughout the organization.

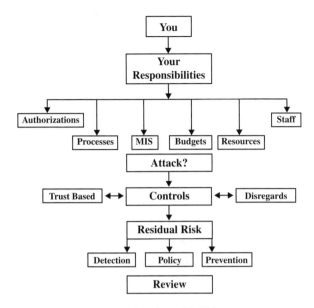

**Figure 2.5**  Critical Fraud Self-Assessment

# TURNING TRAINING INTO ACTION

In the training workshops mentioned in the preceding sections, we stressed the need for action planning as a conclusion to the training event. Action planning is fairly straightforward and typically involves going though the steps that must be taken to get the various training concepts to the workplace. In terms of fraud, there is an assessment technique that can be used. It goes under different names, but we can call it Critical Fraud Self-Assessment or CFSA. This technique is derived from Figure 2.5.

The CFSA model provides a context within which operational teams and individual managers and staff can assess the extent to which they are at risk from fraud and ways they may ensure that controls are put in place to guard against this risk.

**You:**  This starts the model by ensuring that people understand that antifraud action is the responsibility of everyone in the organization. It's simply reinforcing the "at red" state of the stop lights. The model is directed personally at the individual, regardless of where they stand in an organization, from the boardroom to the mailroom. We impose personal responsibility for fraud management and ask each employee to look inward at his or her own position in the workplace.

**Your responsibilities:**   The next stage is to determine one's exact responsibilities at work. This sounds simple at first, but in practice it can become complicated when other factors (such as projects, temporary staff, shared programs, group targets, associates, and temporary promotions) are taken into account. Some frauds slip through the system because of a lack of clarity as to who is responsible for what. An example is a staff travel-and-expenses procedure that falls between personnel, accounts, and the authorizing manager, with resulting uncertainty over who should be checking what to ensure that claims are valid.

**Authorizations:**   We come now to the vexing question of authorization. Documents, screens, forms, or systems access that are authorized should be carefully listed and examined. The act of authorization constitutes a key control over fraud and abuse and it is with this in mind that each employee needs to assess how he or she applies this task. An example of authorization failure is a payments system whereby the supervisor authorizes a batch of live transactions by glancing at dozens of payments on a screen and pressing the send button. Where there is no healthy skepticism, there is no real authorization. Unfortunately, the act is still seen as a control and the transactions are deemed to have passed some form of test. Others considering the same items may well feel that further checks are not warranted.

**Processes:**   An important next step is to consider carefully the organizational processes that are used and how activity is verified or checked at all. A payroll clerk may interact with the payroll system, personnel system, claims, deductions, check issuing or bank transfers, time sheets, overtime claims, and many other internal processes. External systems, such as tax and government returns, may also affect many of the people in an organization. A purchasing manager may get involved in tenders, contracts, payments, returns, and so on. Again, the idea is to assess the processes that affect each person at work from the point of view of the potential for fraud. Interaction with organizational processes creates a responsibility to ensure that all actions are proper and that the employee is alert to any inconsistencies or weaknesses that are apparent.

**MIS:**   Some argue that the future of fraud is located in information systems. Tomorrow's fraudster will be able to commit a crime and then convince everyone that the figures are right by manipulating the database and resulting reports. This stage of the model involves employees checking their access rights across the organization and considering whether these are excessive. The question to ask is this: If you were a dedicated criminal, what damage or manipulation could you create using your current access privileges? The secondary concern is what harm others could do if they so desired?

**Budgets:**   The budgetary control system is a great control in its own right because it locates authority to spend with budget holders, and income and spending patterns can be monitored. The first point to make is that people must protect their budgets, ensure that only official and correct items use their budget codes, and investigate any unusual ones. Also, the budget reports should be used to isolate strange trends that cannot readily be explained. Again, some investigation is required. One word of warning:

> One fraud involved the misappropriation of cash that should have come into the head office on a weekly basis. The first reaction of the finance manager was that all the cash that should be appearing in his income statements was coming in, according to the weekly statistical returns. The income returns had been understated by around 30 percent for years, because the fraud had been going on—undetected—for such a long time.

**Resources:**   The basic misappropriation fraud targets what can be called attractive, portable items, that is, items that can be taken, stolen, lost, or misplaced. The opportunist fraudster will misplace an expensive item at work and see whether it is missed at all. After a while, the items will disappear completely. An employee who is responsible for company assets such as laptop computers, mobile phones, cameras, televisions, video recorders, finished goods, expensive chairs, and so on, must consider the risk of theft. Other resources are less obvious; perhaps someone has control over a customer database or the pricing arrangements for specific jobs. Sometimes it is about having the means to get into company resources; for instance, when one person is responsible for awarding contracts or personal loans or discounts, unsupervised. These situations all have great potential for fraud and corruption, so it is a good idea to list the precise areas in question.

**Staff:**   Corporate fraud prevention is primarily about the way people behave at work. In this context, the single most important control is the lead that managers give to their staff. The next step is to work out which teams the employer is responsible for and assess the way these teams are positioned to recognize and respond to the threat of fraud.

One must always bear in mind the potential for staff committing fraud. Some have described fraud as the enemy within. Fraudulent gain can be uppermost on the mind of a member of staff, unbeknownst to the manager and the rest of the team. When a manager has staff that work in an at-risk area, this possibility should be kept in mind. To repeat our position, the best guard against a deceitful employee is a team of colleagues who are close to this person and who are alert.

**Attack:**    This is a most interesting part of the model. It consists of asking a number of searching questions along the lines of:

1. How could my staff perpetrate a fraud against the organization?
2. What is at risk?
3. What would be the impact of a fraud in my work area?
4. What types of fraud have we had in the past and why?
5. What problems have occurred in other similar operations/ companies?
6. What parts of the operation are weak and possible to abuse?
7. What are my auditors telling me about weak controls?
8. What is my staff telling me about potential problems and concerns?
9. What have I read in the press or journals about new frauds that could affect my area of work?
10. Is there anything that is worrying in terms of inconsistent and unusual activities?
11. Are there parts of the operation where procedures are being breached?
12. How could our systems be breached by people outside the organization?
13. Is there any way that I could commit a fraud against the company and get away with it?
14. Are we taking the threat of fraud seriously?
15. Is there anything else we should be doing at work?

These questions can be addressed in "brainstorming" mode either alone, with a team of specially selected people, or with the work groups. The important thing is to address the potential for fraud at the workplace in a systematic and dynamic fashion. If the manager, the staff, or an outsider can get into a system or abuse trust, there is no reason this may not already be happening now or some time in the future. What's more, it would be wrong to be aware of a system's weakness and not take quick and effective action.

**Controls:** Having established the risk of fraud in the operations, the next stage is to have a look at the types of controls currently in place, to try to prevent and detect any abuse. A careful examination of controls that focus on protecting company resources, in conjunction with an assessment of fraud risk, is a great way of working toward improvements. Employers need to go through each control and ask a series of questions:

1. How important is this control?
2. When was it last reviewed?
3. Is the control clearly defined and properly set out?
4. Does staff understand the control and its importance?
5. Does this control work in practice?
6. Is the control being breached at all? If so, why?
7. Does the control address all the known fraud risks that it is meant to deal with?
8. Can I double-check a few transactions to ensure that the control is doing what it is supposed to do?
9. What is my overall assessment? Do we need to make any improvements?
10. Can I issue formal assurances to my manager on the adequacy of the control?

After going through this procedure, each employee will have a good idea of the state of existing controls, and in particular fraud risks that do not appear to be managed at all (that is, areas where no suitable controls are in place to guard against an unacceptable risk of abuse). The next two items in the model also affect control assessment.

**Trust based:** If the fraud risk self-assessment follows from the training workshops discussed earlier, the issue of employee honesty will have been considered. The reality of nice people becoming crooked, because of a whole variety of reasons, will have been discussed. This stage of the fraud assessment model develops the idea of honesty further. The important point to drive home is that controls that depend entirely on the honesty of a pivotal member of staff are by definition unreliable. If, for example, one senior director has the final say in awarding large contracts and even overturning the recommendations of the tender board, an organization cannot simply argue that its directors are trusted and so end its responsibility for fraud prevention. There must be more than this. When a less senior person reports unbelievably good income figures and everyone gets a bonus for exceeding targets, this does not mean income figures are not checked for accuracy and reliability. Unfortunately, many control systems rely on this single-person trust, and when it breaks down the effects can be disastrous.

**Disregard:**   There are several types of controls that do not really stand up to scrutiny; before relying on them, employers should assess their value. Password protection on sensitive systems is not always reliable—systems can be breached by a hacker or someone who has access to the password. Signatures can be forged quite easily. Segregation of duties is a powerful control on paper, but when two parties work closely together there is always the chance that collusion will defeat this control. Also, the two individuals may become so familiar that they disregard the routine and rely on each other for checks, perhaps naively rather than deceitfully. For example, the formal procedure may be that the line manager prepares and signs an order form before placing an order, and this form is checked by the payments clerk before the invoice is paid. In practice, the payments clerk may ask the manager, who has been a colleague for some time, to make up an order retrospectively every time an invoice is received with no associated order on file. This brings us to the linked point that official procedures may not be a good guide to what really happens at work. People may bypass the procedures to save time. Some organizations have a policy of not selling on personal computers to staff unless data on the hard disk drive is permanently erased. A friendly IT manager may bypass this procedure and simply delete (not erase) data before selling the PC. Managers need to bear in mind weaknesses that are inherent in what are normally good controls, and carry out their assessments with this in mind.

**Residual risk:**   After suitable controls have been designed and put into place, risks may then be managed. Unlike other risks, fraud usually cannot be accepted. The option to leave things alone is a valid part of risk management strategies when the risk is either insubstantial or too costly to mitigate. This is unlikely to apply to illegal abuse. Some fraud risk may be transferred by getting a contractor or associate to take responsibility for the particular service. It's simply about assigning responsibility elsewhere and perhaps seeking compensation if appropriate. The most common form of risk transfer—or perhaps risk sharing is the better term—is fidelity bonding, whereby staff is insured against committing fraud and causing subsequent losses. In the main, antifraud strategies will consist of controls that seek to prevent fraud, discover any fraud that may have occurred, and then contain it as far as possible. The risk that remains after controls have been put in place is known as *residual risk*. Decisions must be made on whether the residual risk is acceptable and, if something untoward happens, whether all actions can be justified and the employer can avoid culpability. Not an easy task.

**Fraud policy:** The context of the CFSA model is the corporate antifraud policy. All action taken in assessing fraud, and analyzing where it could happen and how it may be dealt with, should conform to the antifraud policy. It is essential that the red-light approach not result in people throughout the organization setting up their own fraud exercises and surveillance operations or accusing their staff out of hand. It is also essential that people are not asked to tackle fraud with no help or advice from specialist fraud professionals. The antifraud policy pulls everything together. The policy should set the direction, assign staff responsibilities, and indicate where advice may be obtained. It is important that the policy be adhered to, or the organization may be vulnerable to civil suits.

**Detection:** The fraud workshops are meant to raise awareness and get people thinking about fraud as a real threat to business success. One question that should spring to mind, either directly or more subconsciously, is whether any abuse is happening in parts of the organization that is not obvious. Fraud detection is an important part of the control system and acts as a deterrent in that it increases the chance of the would-be fraudster getting caught. Fraud risk self-assessment may result in a great action plan to tackle fraud. But this becomes embarrassing if there is already a fraud going on that has remained hidden for some time. In fact, the perpetrator may be taking part in the self-assessment workshops and be aware of all the steps that have been proposed to deal with the type of abuse the perpetrator is actually involved in. Detection can be the result of signs that all is not well, such as a supplier that only wants to deal with one person. Moreover, discovery can be the result of a planned exercise; for example, checking all supplier invoices for phone numbers that coincide with phone numbers belonging to employees. The point is that initiatives should be in place to ensure that fraud, if it exists, can be isolated and dealt with.

**Prevention:** The focus of fraud awareness is really on prevention. This is against the background of the controls that were assessed earlier in the model. Prevention is simply the implementation of a system of internal control that recognizes that fraud is a priority and that controls need to work well, in harmony, to promote success.

**Review:** The final part of the self-assessment model relates to the review process. Reviews should occur regularly, either as a regular event or when there are gaps in the current arrangements. Taking stock is also important when a new process is being designed and implemented or when a material new project is set in motion. Business is constantly changing and the risks change as new opportunities for fraud are presented (for example, through greater empowerment for all staff). Likewise, there must be a consideration of how to guard against these risks. This cycle of assessment, action, and review should be dynamic and not a one-time event. The main drawback of training events is that they can become stuck in time, lead to short-term changes, then flounder. The only way to get around this problem is to stress the review aspect of agreed action plans.

# CONCLUSION

The stop light model is designed to give people a target to aim at: a level of awareness, understanding, and subsequent action that places everyone in the front line of the fight against fraud and abuse. People should move from yellow to red as they realize the fact of fraud and its impact on their organization. There should be a degree of loyalty in place if the model is to work, and a sense of belonging as well. Accepting this, the model should lead into a self-assessment routine that embeds the culture of proactive risk management—particularly for fraud, a risk that at face value may seem invisible.

# CHAPTER 3

---

# Ethics at Work

*A door must be either shut or open.*

## WHY ETHICS?

Ethics underpins the fight against corporate fraud. It is essentially about doing the right thing and assessing the benefits and harm caused by an individual's action. An organization may secure a reputation for being highly ethical and seek to attract investors who see this as an important part of their assessment criteria. The Foreign Corrupt Practices Act of 1977 (FCPA) came about because of the many hundreds of companies making illegal payments to foreign officials. Directors, shareholders, agents, and employees are covered by the act and fines, imprisonment, and suspension from the stock exchange can result if the FCPA requirements are breached. Enforcement of the legislation is through the stock exchange for civil action; the Department of Justice deals with the criminal implications. In practice, compliance programs are fundamental to ensuring that the FCPA is adhered to and, in the event of a suit against a company, that any accusations can be defended. The need to apply moral standards comes to the fore when antifraud policies are being developed. In a volatile business environment, where people have to make quick decisions, the pressure is on business expediency. It is here that short-term gains may be considered over and above the longer-term reputation of the company. If the mission statement contains no mention of integrity, there will be no platform upon which to

51

base the corporate ethical position. Fraud teams, fraud detection routines, the all-important preventive controls, and general staff alertness become weapons without ammunition if there are no real ethical standards. Some argue that ethics is about acting with good common sense, but this view ignores the labyrinth of conflicting issues and potentially mischievous influences that face executives and staff. Legitimacy and legality do not always coincide, and basic perks of the job can either remain routine behavior or mushroom into illegal behavior. This chapter deals with the place corporate ethics assumes in the fight against fraud. We consider the need to link ethics to the company's value system, and explore the idea of what is right and wrong. The reality of resistance from staff is also addressed. Blurred lines between right and wrong are discussed along with the need to ensure proper integration from concept to front-line action. The direction set at the top is what most people now call "tone at the top;" we also touch on the importance of having a strong beacon from an enlightened management. We close with an action model to help get the right structures in place.

Corporate ethics is a global concept. The Organization of Economic Cooperation and Development (OECD) has regulations similar to the requirements of the FCPA, and the OECD rules have been adopted by many countries. Ignorance and turning a blind eye to the behavior of sales and support people is no excuse for not adhering to the FCPA. A dynamic response is the only way to get hold of the ethical baton and run with the underlying ideas and ideals. Ethics policies cost money to design and install, but compensation claims against the company also cost money, as does repairing damage to the corporate brand name. The response is simple but at times difficult: that is, do the right thing and get something in place that works and makes sense to the workforce.

## ETHICS AND VALUES

When developing a value system, the ethical position must be internalized:

> In one case, six high-ranking staff members of a bank went out for a meal to celebrate a coup in the bond market and spent $62,000 at a restaurant at a time when the bank had been cutting staff and closing branches. When asked about this, which most people felt was at the least inconsiderate behavior, the bank insisted that it was a private matter that need not concern the public.

Unfortunately, corporate ethics tends to consist of a set of good intentions written into a formal code of ethics that, for the most part, is then filed away. Values have more to do with the way people are expected to behave toward others; values are broader in scope and linked to what each organization wants its customers and colleagues to get from the relationship. The problem is that the values tend to be prepared for the workplace and reflect what really happens at work, covering issues like communication, trusting people, keeping promises, and generally ensuring business success. The code of ethics, in contrast, may look more like a rule book, with a list of specific standards that must not be breached. The code only comes to the fore when there is a problem and the rules are used to discipline or sanction a member of staff.

Ethics should really be about corporate consciousness and involve a degree of guidance on how to put the ideals of integrity, openness, and accountability into action. That is how to get ethics into values into action. Many value systems are prepared without regard to the organization's ethical standards. This is a lost opportunity, as all the hard work in consulting staff and getting buzz groups together to discuss and debate proposed values would double the benefits if ethics were incorporated into the issues. The corporate mission statement should stress the need to deliver and be successful, but should also incorporate a guide on tempering success with a sense of moral direction. So, we may corporately promise to: *Deliver world-class services and meet all key targets.* If there is nothing further, employees might simply massage the sales figures and distort the performance data to meet this goal. If, however, the words *with integrity* were included in the mission statement, this would give much-needed direction. Intentional (or with careless disregard) over- or underreporting of performance means the goals have not been achieved as intended. This is a moot point, because when sales figures are climbing, everyone prospers. Performing with virtue creates a new tension, as senior executives have to question performance reports and challenge unusual trends, even if they mean bonuses for everyone. If items such as *Be honest and responsible, and always communicate the truth* were included in our value system, these would link directly into ethical standards and add to the overall direction of the company.

## DOING THE RIGHT THING

We have argued that ethics is about doing the right thing. Each organization will have its own interpretation and standards that it publishes to managers and staff. These standards will vary and include less or more detail, depending on how people work and whether there are high-risk areas in the organization where ethics is an issue. It is against this background that we produce a list of items that could be considered for inclusion in a code of ethics. The list is comprehensive, in that it covers much ground, but it does not go into excessive detail on any individual item.

*VALUES*

1. Be honest.
2. Treat all people with whom you deal with respect.
3. Be trustworthy.
4. Act with integrity.
5. Be loyal to the company.
6. Respect others at work.
7. Act with dignity.
8. Be tolerant of diversity among people.
9. Never engage in illegal, unethical, or questionable acts.
10. Keep all promises and contractual obligations, but act in the best interests of the company.
11. Make sure all inquiries are conducted with due process.
12. Take responsibility for your actions.
13. Provide leadership in promoting the code of ethics; above all, set a good example and demand the same from others.

*BASIC STANDARDS*

1. Make sure all transactions that require approval are properly approved at the earliest opportunity.
2. When approving items, make sure you are satisfied with their underlying integrity.
3. If there is any conflict of interest that affects (or appears to affect) any decisions being made, disclose it to your line manager.
4. Record the reasons for important decisions.
5. Do not make a promise that you cannot keep. If you become aware of anything that means you cannot meet targets, make sure this is brought to the attention of your manager.
6. Do not disclose company information to unauthorized persons. If in doubt, seek advice from your line manager. This includes making statements or comments about the company to outsiders.
7. Do not use the company's name for personal gain or advantage.
8. Do not accept gifts or inappropriate hospitality, and report all offers to your line manager.

9. Do not use nonprescription drugs or alcohol at work. Alcohol can be consumed only at official company functions.
10. Do not use company, or customers', facilities in an unauthorized manner or for personal gain.
11. Ensure that access to all company resources is secure and report all violations to the security officer.
12. Do not engage in private employment without advising your line manager and ensuring that the private work does not conflict with your role in the company.
13. Ensure that political activities do not conflict with your duties at work.
14. Ensure that you display your identification at all times, and challenge anyone who does not display appropriate ID.
15. Ensure that your standard of dress complies with the code used by your section.
16. Do not make or take excessive private phone calls.
17. Do not use company vehicles or other resources for private purposes unless authorized in writing by your line manager.
18. Do not engage in postemployment work that abuses the confidential information gained as an employee.
19. Keep your workstation in good order and ensure that it is tidy and clear, particularly at the end of the working day.

*RESPONSIBILITIES*

1. Ensure that you are accountable for areas under your responsibility and that this accountability is demonstrated at all times.
2. Ensure that you are able to demonstrate the basis for decisions you make and justify your actions.
3. Ensure that you adhere to all relevant legislation and regulations, unless a variance is justified and approved by your manager.
4. Ensure that you are aware of all the procedures, laws, and regulations that affect your area of work.

*DEVELOPMENT ISSUES*

1. Arrange sound procedures for your areas of responsibility and ensure that they are properly implemented.
2. Whenever possible, try to find and adopt better and more efficient ways of working.
3. Maintain good quality in everything you do at work.

*NONCOMPLIANCE*

1. Always follow procedures, if any variation is required, seek approval.
2. Report improper conduct to your line manager. Familiarize yourself with the reporting arrangements and use these arrangements as appropriate.
3. Report any instances or suspicions of fraud, corruption, irregularity, major error, breach of procedure, or any other questionable behavior.

*GENERAL*

1. The code of ethics will be reviewed and republished at least annually. Ensure that you familiarize yourself with its values and individual requirements.
2. The code applies to employees, agents, suppliers, and associates, who should ensure that they have knowledge of the code and are able to meet the requirements.
3. Uphold these principles at all times.
4. Breach of the code may result in disciplinary action for the offender, including dismissal.

# RESISTANCE

We have defined ethics and outlined the types of values and standards that fall under the ambit of ethical behavior. The result is a code of ethics that most companies will publish and send out to new and existing staff. This fairly simple model may lead to a dry and dusty document (the code of ethics) that remains in the top drawer and is ignored by most employees. It certainly will not alter behavior in any way. In fact, it may only come out of the drawer when there is a major disciplinary problem, when it is used as a weapon by management to punish offending staff. In this way the code could acquire many negative connotations. There are many reasons why ethical standards are not taken seriously in some organizations and many of these reasons have sound foundations. If an organization seeks to implement a newly revised code of ethics and ignores these reasons, the code may fail to have any real impact. Some of the factors that make it hard to get ethics on the agenda are as follows.

## Rationalization

This was discussed in Chapter 1. Employees may become involved in frauds against the company, but feel they are not necessarily unethical because they have rationalized their behavior.

## Meeting Targets

Performance targets create enormous pressure for most employees. This is the main driver for all their energies, which cascades upward into achieving team, section, department, and overall corporate objectives. The added complication of adhering to a vague set of stated intentions simply creates a further level of pressure that may detract from the main objective—that is, to achieve targets.

## Our Employees Are Okay

This view suggests that ethics is a negative concept to be used against people who are immoral. Teams and close groups of workers seek support from each other and build allegiances and dependencies that are based on mutual trust. The view here is that ethical standards are irrelevant because team members are good workers and trustworthy. The problem gets worse, and attempts to create an awareness of ethics may backfire, when the workforce falls into three main groups:

**Group one:** These people are generally well behaved and feel that the training in ethics management is patronizing and presumes they cannot be trusted.

**Group two:** These people may be less well behaved and at times in breach of the standards (for instance, claiming excessive overtime). They will feel uncomfortable and even marginalized if the workshops are seen as a way of targeting them.

**Group three:** These people may have no interest in ethics and feel that it is not relevant to them at all. They may see ethics training as a divisive way of categorizing people as good or bad.

## Our Company Is Okay

The organization may be seen as basically sound; that is, there are no current problems regarding claims against the company or excessive complaints or employee frauds. In this scenario, ethics management is seen as an unnecessary and costly add-on. The basic code of ethics is published, but anything more than this is seen as belonging to contingency planning, important only in the event of irregularities that so far have not happened. This viewpoint at times translates ethics management into basic social responsibility and nothing more. If the organization is not hurting anyone and is employing local people and making profits, then this is more than enough.

## Ethics Is a Vague Religious Concept

Some see the drive toward corporate ethics as a type of religious mission to get people to see the light. Setting standards and developing in-house training is one way of driving home the basic idea of good over evil; implementing the code becomes a matter of philosophy and even spiritual enlightenment. Employees may view the entire experience as personally uncomfortable. Codes that suffer from this problem are those that concentrate on aspirations but ignore the process as an important and practical management tool.

## Ethics Is Not Part of Management

In this scenario ethical standards are seen as belonging to the personnel department, not operations management. Ethics is viewed as the new flavor of the month, and not integrated into daily working practices at all. This happens when the code is prepared in isolation and kept away from the workers themselves. The worst-case scenario is when the codes are so unrealistic that they are more or less ignored by most people. Alternatively, the values may be so general that they float above the workplace with very little real substance or applicability.

## We Are All as Bad as Each Other

Here the workforce and management are engaged in a form of stand-off. Each side is equally to blame for the absence of ethical standards, because of mutual distrust. An example is the workers' injury compensation scheme, under which some employees make false claims and pretend to be sick. Meanwhile the employer is seen as just as dishonest because it misclassifies workers as low-risk and pays the wrong rates. So public opinion swings between fraud by employees and fraud by the employer. A university that gives scholarships to budding sports stars may get college staff to write their assignments, to ensure the stars don't flunk out. In this climate, it is hard to establish a set of ethical standards that will be taken seriously.

From the preceding, it should be clear that there are many reasons why ethics may not be taken seriously in an organization. There is also the view that rule books create dependent employees who cannot think for themselves. They need guidance on doing the right things or presumably they will falter. If ethics were simply a matter of right and wrong, there would be no difficulty in managing behavior. The next section deals with these blurred lines.

## PRACTICAL ISSUES AND BLURRED LINES

If enough people trample over the line between right and wrong, it disappears. This is what makes the study of ethics so interesting. Employee-driven white-collar crime would not exist if people were ethical all the time. Any problems would be caused by error or simple ignorance if deceit could be ruled out at an early stage in the inquiries. Unfortunately, this is an impossible ideal to achieve. A lucid metaphor of blurred lines is given in *The Final Death* by Harlan Coben (Hodder & Stroughton, 1999, p. 334):

> The line between good and evil is not so different from the foul [line] on the baseball field. It's often made of stuff as flimsy as lime. It tends to fade over time. It needs to be constantly redrawn. And if enough players trample on it, the line becomes smeared and blurred to the point where fair is foul and foul is fair, where good and evil become indistinguishable from each other.

Standards should be there to enable people to make informed choices about their behavior and the repercussions of breaking rules:

> In one city, eight bicycles were left unattended and then observed. The first was stolen in 12 minutes; the longest took 9 hours and 30 minutes to disappear.

What is "right" and "wrong" must be seen in the context of what is right for the individual, his or her family, or the employer. Moreover, an act may be wrong because it is frowned on, causes loss, or causes a sense of guilt. The competing forces are affected by the circumstances and balance between different perceptions of what is right and what is wrong. This is where blurred lines come into play: on the one hand, people act so as to benefit defined parties, but on the other hand they are constrained by factors that inhibit or restrict some activities. In part, it comes down to managing diverse values at work. Ethical standards will have to address several key factors.

### The Need to Fit into Stakeholders' Values

Shareholders and other interested parties have targets and aims. These have to be achieved, but there also must be a transparency in the way the organization reports its activities back to the stakeholders. There are conflicts. Some shareholders want quick profits, whereas others want long-term sustainability (for example, over three to five years). The key issue regarding stakeholders is transparency. Whenever possible, decisions made by powerful groups in the organization should be published as long as this does not hurt the business.

### Make Sense and Involve All-Round Fairness

Values have no effect unless they fit into the performance scheme used by the organization. Decisions are made in conjunction with the way the organization wants its people to behave and the way they are rewarded for their efforts. Therefore, the code should provide a clear sense of purpose and direction.

### Based on Individual Responsibility

The code of ethics must focus on the responsibilities of all employees and adherence to a set of basic minimum standards. A clear vision, driven from the top and located in the heart of the organization, is a fundamental component of a successful model of ethics.

### Address Dilemmas

Blurred lines relate to dilemmas that cannot be readily solved. There are competing forces that drive people in different directions. There must be a framework in place that allows some degree of objective arbitration on such matters. A feedback loop should be in place to ensure that once an ethical dilemma (say, a general problem of sales personnel overstating the benefits of a product to the extent that it becomes misleading) has been addressed, similar dilemmas do not arise in future.

## Sell the Benefits

This upside of bothering about ethics management as an important managerial tool involves specifying its benefits, including that it:

- Is good for the reputation of the company.
- Provides an environment within which employees can develop.
- Helps give direction when there are dilemmas and inconsistencies.
- Helps us stay within the confines of the law.
- Underpins positive group norms.
- Reflects the growing recognition of ethical and environmentally friendly companies.

# INTEGRATION

Getting ethics across to the employees is not an easy task. The document may well sit in the staff handbook, even though memos may be sent out to staff reminding them to look at the requirements every six months. This is not enough. The code has to become part of the reality of working for the organization. The model shown in Figure 3.1 can be useful.

The "gap" exists when the corporate code of ethics does not reach the workforce. Corporate functions such as legal and personnel may have a better appreciation of the codes. Organizations need to translate policies into procedures into practices as a seamless and dynamic process. Several steps are necessary to close this gap.

| Line Operations | Corporate Functions | Staff Functions |
|---|---|---|
| policies procedures operational standards plans | ethical standards | policies procedures |
| | *"The Gap"* | |
| | **Actual Working Practices** | |

**Figure 3.1**   Standard and Practice

## Establish an Ethical Standards Committee

A powerful forum at the highest level, reporting directly to the main board, is one way of getting ethics onto the corporate agenda. An ethical standards committee (ESC) may consist of nonexecutive directors who will oversee the way ethical standards are being developed and managed in the organization. Members of the ESC should have some experience in ethics management or undergo a short orientation process with guidance from an expert in the field. The terms of reference will be set to suit the organization but may consist of, for example:

- Ethical standards are carefully developed and are firmly in place.
- The ethics officer and other key players have well-defined roles and are discharging their responsibilities properly.
- Employees are behaving in an ethical manner as defined by the organization.
- The organization is complying with all laws, regulations, and rules that affect it.
- There is a system in place for resolving ethical dilemmas.
- There is an effective and robust system of compliance checks in place and all significant problems are reported to the ESC.

What is more, the ESC should encourage development and improvement of the way ethics are managed as an ongoing task. There may be some scope for promoting ethical standards for the board and taking a view on whether this is happening to an acceptable degree.

## Appoint a Corporate Ethics Officer

Organizations should identify a resource to support the drive to good corporate ethics, and this may well come in the form of an ethics officer. If there is concern over the ethics officer taking too much responsibility for an issue that should be shouldered by all employees, the resource may be called the ethics advisor to help clarify this point. The important thing is to ensure that there is someone with suitable expertise to support the ethics program. The ethics officer's role may be to:

- Support the ethical standards committee.
- Ensure that ethics is understood and managed across the organization.

- Provide support and guidance on matters that affect application of the ethical standards in the organization.
- Ensure that the code of ethics reflects best practice and the defined intentions of the organization.
- Oversee a compliance program and recommend disciplinary action as appropriate.
- Ensure that people in the organization understand their respective roles and responsibilities.
- Promote the integration of ethical standards into working practices.

The ethics officer should play an essential advisory role, providing support and advice across the organization. Orientation training for new staff will be an important feature of this role, whether the training is provided by the ethics officer or outside specialist trainers.

## Identify Key Players

There are people throughout the organization who should have a say in how ethical issues are being managed and who should be taken on board to support the ethics program. Some of these players include the personnel department, company trainers, legal staff, the director of internal audit, and the chair of the audit committee. Someone senior from the CEO's office should sponsor the program and help with the design, implementation, and review stages. In fact, the entire program should be endorsed (if not driven) by the CEO. Select people may come together to present special forums, say, to review the code of ethics, to hear special cases of ethical dilemmas, or to consider cases against employees for breach of the code. The ethics officer should be able to call upon these individuals to assist and support the company efforts as and when required. It would be helpful if these people were identified beforehand, in the ethics policy.

## Design a Proper Code of Ethics

Some argue that a code of ethics is merely window dressing. This view holds that the code is a document that has no power or impact on its own and so should not be prioritized. This is a questionable position: having a code is fine, but the code must be supported by an effective program of training, review, and integration. If the code itself is impoverished, the "window dressing" will be uninviting. The code should be carefully constructed so as to make sense. It should reflect best practice. One way of making it work is to call on focus groups of people in the organization for their input into the design, review, and preparation. In fact, a code that comes up from front-line services will avoid the problem of being removed from real work, which constricts many codes designed by top management. Again, it is not the code itself that is important, it is the process that engages people around the issues of ethics and gets them to reflect on and recognize the complexities of blurred lines. One way of achieving this focus is to pare the code down to, say, the top eight to twelve main values, to avoid too much dilution.

## Allow Some Form of Arbitration

To instill a sense of justice into the ethics program, it is a good idea to pro-mote a form of appeal. When decisions are made on what staff can do and how management should handle a specific problem, there should be a forum to review these matters and ensure consistency and reasonableness across the organization. For specific circumstances, employees should be able to call for review of decisions, by a person who takes on the role of inde-pendent ombudsman, as and when required. One main task of the ombuds-man is interpreting policies when there is a lack of clarity on what should be applied where. It may be that different parts of the organization have dif-ferent standards in place, depending on the type of risks that exist at a local level. When there is disagreement over whether something is acceptable, it is a good idea to have in place a set procedure for assessing specific cases:

- Does a conflict of interest exist? What are the implications?
- What different courses of action are available in the circumstances?
- What parameters should be considered in weighing the options?
- What is the impact of each of the options? Who is affected and how?
- Do we need to secure more information? How difficult is this task?
- What is reasonable, given the information available?
- What is in the best interests of the organization?
- How should we publicize the decision, and does it change any com-pany policies?

## Implement an Ethics Program

The final task is to get a suitable ethics program up and running. This involves all the work covered in preceding sections, but features a series of events to ensure that people understand the program and how it affects them. This is similar to the fraud awareness training in Chapter 2, and a three-point model can be used to design the program, as shown in Figure 3.2.

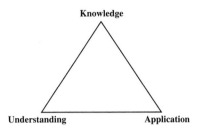

**Figure 3.2** Applying Ethics

**1. Knowledge.** Staff should know about the code of ethics and its underpinning structures, as well as the roles and responsibilities of key players. This is mainly about getting the code and policies to staff and making them read and sign for it. It may also involve presenting the material in an awareness seminar that is attended by select teams on a rolling basis. The main objective is to make sure that people have access to the code and that all reasonable steps have been taken to get the key message across to them.

**2. Understanding.** People relate to the code through a series of proactive exercises that forces them to work through the contents of the code and present their views. The code is used as background. Participants can be asked to express their understanding through a multiple-choice exercise, whether on paper or online. Understanding is about having a good appreciation of the code and what it means to the individual employee.

**3. Application.** The final stage of the model moves into practical translation of the code to workplace practices. This task involves two things. First, employees work through practical exercises in which they are asked to decide on the most suitable course of action given a set of difficult circumstances. The circumstances should be as near to the work role as possible, and so a portfolio of different exercises must be made up for this purpose. The second part is to get an action plan made up by the individual or team to help integrate the learning points into the operational plans and targets. The participants should be encouraged to develop their own action plans, with support from the group.

It is better to use workshops and exercises as a way of getting the message across to staff rather than to try to force the standards upon them through threats and manipulation. The organization itself may be seen as unethical if it takes the latter course.

### Keep the Entire Thing under Review

It is nice to be able to say, at a board meeting, "Ethics policy and program looked at, revised, and sorted out. Next item on the agenda!" In truth, this is what happens in many organizations suffering from agenda overload. A better response is to say:

> We have considered the issue of ethics management and have established a suitable strategic response that will be reviewed in six months' time. Meanwhile, we look forward to receiving the first report from the Ethical Standards Committee next month.

In other words, the thing is kept alive and dynamic. As long as the system in place works, the board can sit back and simply keep it under review.

The preceding steps constitute a process that forms the ethics code, policy, and program. Anything less than this will impair the essential linkage between the corporate ethics policy, acceptable standards of conduct, and the resulting working practices.

## ETHICS AND FINANCIAL CRIME

The Committee of Sponsoring Organizations of the Treadway Commission has developed a control model commonly known as COSO. Controls exist to guard against unacceptable levels of risk, including the risk of fraud. The key components of COSO are reproduced in Figure 3.3.

For our purpose, the foundation of COSO is the control environment, and in turn the key aspect of the control environment is the ethical stan-

**Figure 3.3** The COSO Model

dards that are applied from the top to the bottom of the organization. All activities in the organization attach to the corporate view of what is acceptable and what by default is not. An antifraud policy, a fraud response plan, fraud prevention tactics, or for that matter anything relating to employee behavior cannot be developed without an effective ethics policy in place. Corporate efforts to fight financial crime are foundationless without a clear set of baseline standards. The dynamic is simple: Fraud standards start with ethics standards.

Employee fraud breaches the mutual trust between employer and employee, and indicates a lack of loyalty to the welfare of the organization. This link between fraud and loyalty is interesting because it provides an additional insight into the forces that lead to dishonesty. The model shown in Figure 3.4 reinforces the links:

Points 1 through 4 are briefly explained as follows:

1. Where there is no real discussion on corporate ethics at work, but loyalty to the organization is otherwise strong. This may still result in a balanced set of employees, but with some blurred lines as to acceptable behavior.
2. Where all corners are covered, that is, a loyal team and clear sense of ethics, the majority of people should behave in an acceptable manner. All management development programs should contain elements of encouraging employee loyalty and ethical standards.
3. This is a worse-case scenario that exists where employees do not really care about the business and there is a complete vacuum regarding expected and proper behavior.

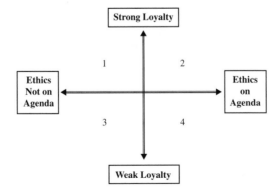

**Figure 3.4**  Loyalty and Ethics

4. Where high standards are set but the workforce is not very loyal, there will still be the potential problem of questionable behavior, even if the consequences have been made clear throughout the organization.

The question is, how can we get our people on our side? There are numerous books that deal with the task of promoting a balanced and committed workforce and all the recommended techniques should be used to this end. Impoverished management encourages unacceptable behavior and the code of ethics alone cannot counter the risk of irregular activities. The code has to be used in conjunction with good managerial practices to be of any use in tackling fraud.

## AN ACTION MODEL

The final section of this chapter introduces an action model that can be used to tip the scales and encourage fair and responsible behavior from employees. The basic action model is shown in Figure 3.5.

Let's deal with each aspect of the model in turn.

### Problems

We start in the middle of the model with an outline of what goes wrong when ethical standards are not set or met by employees of the organization. Some of the problems may be, for example:

- **Conflict of interests.**   Employees may make arrangements and decisions that create conflicts of interests that are not declared. Personal gain results from a mismatch between benefits for the organization and personal benefits to the individual employee.
- **Corruption.**   Bribes, kickbacks, and under-the-counter payments are problems for many organizations. When there are no clear rules covering unacceptable behavior, it is hard to stop regular, off-balance-sheet payments.
- **Shady deals.**   Fraudulent arrangements involving deceit or unauthorized transactions are another symptom of an ethically bankrupt organization.

| Resisting Forces | Problems | Driving Forces |
|---|---|---|
| **Self-Interest** | **Implication** | **Legitimacy** |
| greed | conflict of interest | compliance |
| no values | corruption | hiring policies |
| no redress | shady deals | values and codes |
| group norms | false claims | sanctions |
| resentment | fraud | group working |
| vacuum | | motivation |
| | | leadership |
| | | support |
| **Rationalization** | **Reputation** | **Ethical** |

**Figure 3.5**   Driving and Resisting Forces

- **False claims.**   Fabricated overtime, travel reports, compensation, insurance, and other claims are examples of problems that arise when fraud is not properly controlled.

If these problems are not dealt with, the reputation of the organization will be damaged.

## Resisting Forces

The left-hand side of the model deals with reasons the balance may tip over to the unethical side under the pressure of forces that resist the drive toward legitimacy. Here self-interest reigns supreme and is considered by many employees to be more important than legitimacy:

- **Greed.**   The pursuit of more and better consumer goods is really sheer greed. This greed is driven by a view that society values possessions more than any other qualities and judges a person on what he or she has managed to acquire. Drug traffickers tend to fit into this category.
- **No values.**   When the organization has no system of values, there is little hope of progress in moving people toward legitimacy.
- **No redress.**   One factor that helps get—or keep—people on the straight and narrow is the chance of being discovered and punished. When there are no clear, appropriate sanctions, the pendulum again tips toward the wrong side of the line between right and wrong.

- **Group norms**.   Another force that is often ignored is the power groups hold over their members. When it is common practice to engage in questionable activities that benefit the group but not the organization, problems may arise.
- **Resentment**.   "Getting your own back" is a factor that further blurs the line between right and wrong. It is also linked to poor morale and demotivated personnel.
- **Vacuum**.   The final part of the resisting forces relates to the space that is left when top management does not have a view. The vacuum will be filled with whatever fits into it. Much will depend on the current balance between the conflicting aspects of self-interest and legitimacy.

Left alone, there are many resisting factors that lead to a corrupt and unethical workforce, one that is able to rationalize unethical behavior.

## Driving Forces

The final part of the model consists of solutions that support legitimacy and seek to tip the scales in the right direction:

- **Legitimacy**.   It may help if the organization makes a clear statement on legitimacy and sets boundaries.
- **Hiring policies**.   An ideal situation is when thoroughly honest people are employed and their personal details are carefully vetted. One technique is to allow applicants to fabricate as much personal information as they wish, and then check the details extensively. Misrepresentation, lies, misleading details, and exaggeration can each be used to rule the person out as unacceptable.
- **Values and codes**.   The cornerstone of the fight is the code of ethics and linked corporate values. Clear and concise statements on expected standards of conduct, which make sense to everyone, are a great driver for legitimacy.
- **Sanctions**.   Sanctions are a last resort. As with many models of justice, there has to be a bottom line for hard-core fraudsters who simply break the rules without a good excuse. Selling, encouraging, and motivating are all part of the strategy to keep people on the right track, but firm enforcement has to underlie the entire package.
- **Group working**.   The group can be used to reinforce proper behavior. Reward good role models and stress the importance of keeping

on the right side of the model. Encourage the group to set rules that fit with corporate standards and work with groups in recognizing the risk of unethical actions and how fraud may be spotted and managed.

- **Motivation.** A well-managed and highly motivated workforce makes it harder for individuals to slip into bad practices and justify their actions.

- **Leadership.** Ethics starts with the leaders of the organization and the tone they set for others. If the top people demonstrate high standards, it goes a long way to creating the right control environment. Leaders should know all about the ethics program and take responsibility for spreading the word. Promotion policies should consider this factor when deciding on the leaders of tomorrow. Remember that actions have more impact than words and leaders need to set a positive example.

- **Support.** The final part of the driving forces relates to support systems around the organization where advice can be obtained on ethical standards, dilemmas, and reporting of specific problems. The vacuum is tackled with suitable and well-trained resources such as an ethics officer and an ethical standards committee.

The hope is that the driving forces will tip the scales to what we can call an ethical organization, notwithstanding the resisting forces. The model itself is quite useful as a high-level training vehicle. For example, a group of senior managers might come together in a development workshop to identify the problems that result when ethical standards are lacking. The result will probably look similar to the items in the middle part of the model. The next stage is to isolate the resisting forces that encourage people to put their own self-interest above legitimacy, much as in the left side of the model. Then solutions for moving the workforce toward legitimacy will fall in line with the drivers on the right side of the model. The final stage is to develop a working strategy for dealing with the resisting forces while also designing and implementing the various solutions that have been identified. This approach has been used to achieve a dynamic response to managing ethics in many organizations.

This approach has been used in a wider context for developing countries that are trying to combat fraud and corruption. Transparency International (TI) constructs an annual index of countries, rating each one in terms of its perceived propensity to require bribes to conduct business with international companies. Having identified where the country sits on the latest TI scale, the task is to get the government in question to accept the implications and then work through the model—that is, highlighting known problems like extensive bribery, reasons why this happens (the resisting forces), and ways forward in terms of solutions (change drivers). Again, a dynamic and practical set of solutions can result from this exercise, to be incorporated into long-term government and business reform programs. Nevertheless, change will happen only if the final solutions are owned by the government in question. For countries with particularly poor TI ratings, much depends on a culture change. There can be no change overnight; the idea should be to set realistic targets at the outset and monitor progress over what could be many years. The preferred behavior, which meets the needs of stakeholders, is defined and then the program aims at the changes required. Some form of amnesty may have to be established as formerly acceptable behavior (e.g., extensive nepotism) is redefined as unacceptable.

## CONCLUSION

The Association of Certified Fraud Examiners' *Report to the Nation* cited an example of shrinkage (employee theft) in one company where more than half of the thefts were carried out by company supervisors. When people in managerial positions commit most of the fraud, then what hope is there for the remaining employees? When trusted employees breach their fiduciary duty by setting up their own competing businesses while still employed, then the employer has a problem. When the directors are engaged in insider dealing, concealing debt, or misreporting accident claims to their insurer carriers, it gets worse. When doctors exaggerate the severity of their patient's illness to ensure they get paid for their services, then the need for proper ethical standards comes once more to the fore. When an international company has a slush fund to pay for bribes to win large contracts and regularly classifies these payments as "fees to consultants," business becomes a series of shady deals. When senior government officials live way beyond their means through massive kickbacks and rip-offs as a matter of routine, funding agencies such as the World Bank, International Monetary Fund, European Union, and U.S.A.I.D. have no means of ensuring that their funds are going to the right places. When young people are taught that success is everything, no matter how this success is achieved, the foundation for the future looks shaky. These conditions provide a breeding ground for fraud. Tackling individual instances of financial crime creates short-term wins, but standing back and reflecting on the actual value base of the organization allows a wider, long-term solution. Much can be done to isolate problems, check underlying causes, and move toward a better framework for managing ethics. Safeguards against fraud will have little meaning without a robust and feasible ethical framework in place. The three cornerstones of corporate ethics—integrity, openness, and accountability—are difficult to achieve, but they form the real challenge to top management. If successful in this task, an organization may publicize its achievements in the published annual report to shareholders and claim the badge of being an ethically aware organization.

# CHAPTER 4

---

# Whistleblowing and Detection

*The squeaky wheel gets the grease.*

## IMPORTANCE OF DETECTION

The earlier chapters dealt with fraud as a concept and with the importance of establishing the right ethical environment. Everything possible should be done to reduce the risk of fraud to a reasonable level. The words *reasonable* and *risk* go hand in hand since, by definition, *risk* is something that may or may not happen and *reasonable* relates to the fact that no absolute guarantees can be given for most risks, including fraud. The reality is that employee fraud, can occur no matter how hard an employer works to prevent it. This is why all organizations should have in place a process that enables the detection of fraud, as well as a process for preventing this risk from materializing. We deal here with the responsibility for fraud detection, whistleblowing, how to spot something going wrong, and the importance of using suitable detection routines. If the chief executive officer (CEO) and management team believe there is no fraud in the organization, they must be able to answer the question, "Are you sure?" The only acceptable answer is to check whether there is anything that sheds light on irregularities (i.e., implement a program of ongoing detection). Frauds are detected through controls, by accident, by tip-offs, by auditors, and also through well-constructed programs of detection. Without good detection routines, most frauds will be discovered only by accident, which is not the best way to manage the risk of fraud.

# RESPECTIVE ROLES

The starting place is to isolate and describe the respective roles and responsibilities for detection within an organization. Risk ownership is an important part of the fraud risk management cycle and it is only after defining clear accountabilities that employers can start to discuss detection as a dynamic process. If, in contrast, no one has any responsibilities for fraud detection, there is no meaningful deterrent against the dedicated fraudster. The key players in the detection stakes are as follows.

## Shareholders

The company owners sit above the organization and on paper oversee the way it is run by the directors. Unfortunately, many shareholders have very little involvement in the way their investment is being handled. Larger shareholders, in particular the institutional investors, should really get involved and ask searching questions about the policies and standards of their company directors. This model of stewardship only works when shareholder meetings are vigorous and well thought through. The shareholders should ask about the level of employee fraud and whether efforts are being made to uncover any problems. They should inquire about the directors' policies on fraud detection and ask for material issues to be reported to them.

## Main Board

The board of directors has a responsibility to the shareholders to administer the company through its best efforts and endeavor to meet all profit targets and underlying objectives. Fraud either directly affects the bottom line, or affects the reputation of the enterprise, which in turn will affect the bottom line. Employee fraud also opens the organization to claims under the federal sentencing guidelines. The main board should provide a statement on internal control in the annual report; it is from this statement that users of the financial accounts will gain comfort. An antifraud policy, a response plan, and suitable preventive controls exist to help keep fraud under control. There should also be in place an active process for ensuring that fraud is not happening and, in the event it does occur, that it is quickly detected and addressed. In this way, the task of detecting fraud is firmly placed on the shoulders of the board of directors. A sense of direction, for actively rooting out fraud wherever it exists, should come straight from the boardroom. Anything less highlights a failure of the board's oversight role.

## Chief Executive Officer

The chief executive officer should take the fraud policy and drive it down through the organization: down, across, and around the sections, units, teams, and people who make up the business. The CEO is the most powerful person around and the person we look to to set in motion the task of ensuring that a fraud policy is in place. It is very hard to ask managers to place an item that may not exist on their agenda. It's like asking a plumber to check out your house when there is no evidence of a water leakage. The CEO is the person who should really galvanize the troops into this ongoing search for wrongdoing.

## Senior Executives

Top management members need to implement a form of risk assessment in work teams around the organization. In terms of fraud detection, the directors say it should be done, while management decides how to do it. The executive management team needs to:

1. Coordinate the strategies for isolating fraud in the organization.
2. Ensure that suitable resources for special exercises are identified.
3. Make sure suspicions of fraud can be relayed to the appropriate officer.
4. Insist that the operation's people are actively alert to the possibility of fraud.

Management's task is to turn the stated intentions of the board into action by putting the right structures in place to underpin the required action, and then monitoring the results. This task is what most would call providing the enabling framework, concentrating on resources, procedures, and results.

## Audit Committee

The audit committee is the final solution to good corporate governance. At least this is what those who draft stock exchange and public sector regulations on audit and accountability assume. In practice, much could go wrong when the audit committee is really not very independent from the main board, or when the members do not possess the right competencies to exercise an effective oversight role. Accepting this, we would ask the audit committee to be concerned about the level of reported fraud: if it is high, ask why; if it is low, ask whether the organization is doing as much as possible about uncovering hidden irregularities. If the audit committee has no real interest in concealed impropriety, an important part of the detection machinery is missing.

## Ethical Standards Committee

We have already mentioned the need for independent oversight of corporate ethics and suggested that a suitable committee should be in place to address this gap. Although the ethical standards committee (ESC) may not have direct input into the fraud detection routines, there is still a link between ethics and fraud. Employee fraud necessarily involves a breach of standards of ethics. The ESC should be concerned that all violations are uncovered and dealt with by management.

## External Audit

The organization's external auditors are required to form an opinion on the final accounts and determine whether they are reliable and show a true and fair view of the enterprise's finances. This opinion is reported in the published annual report along with the directors' report, the accounts, notes to the accounts, and other pertinent information. The external auditors' report is used to defend the validity of the accounts, which means that shareholders and other users of the accounts can rely on the figures, trends, and bottom-line profits. Users may also assume that the accounts are free from fraud and manipulation. This sounds simple in theory, but in practice the external auditors' responsibilities are fraught with many difficulties. The most pressing problem is the potential legal liability facing the auditor, when employee fraud causes investors who relied on the published accounts to lose money. External audit cannot be held responsible for discovering all frauds against an organization, although it does have a role in the fraud detection process. The auditor is expected to conduct the various tests with a reasonable expectation of uncovering significant frauds that would lead to a material misstatement of the financial accounts. Moreover, auditors should be alert to the red flags of fraud and also comply with professional auditing standards, using reasonable skill and care. If the auditors found that documents were missing or the explanations from directors and others did not tie up with the examination, or if reconciliations contained unexplained differences or large items appeared in suspense accounts for many months, then they are put on alert. Once alerted to these red flags, the auditor would expand the tests carried out and explore problem areas. There are several further points regarding the external audit role that can be summarized as follows:

- Management holds primary responsibility for the detection of fraud in an organization.
- External auditors have a secondary responsibility to be alert to the possibility of fraud as it affects the financial accounts.
- Most lay people feel that the audit role revolves around proactive fraud detection; hence, some argue that there is an "expectation gap," because the public believes the auditor's main role is to look for fraud perpetrated by the directors and management.
- Ironically, certified public accountants (CPAs) have the kind of skills and professionalism that make for good fraud detection and investigation.
- CPAs are also independent from the organization and so can undertake a thorough job without too much interference from people within the organization. However, excessive consulting fees can undermine independence.
- Some CPAs feel that the idea of becoming sleuths is quite exciting and good for career development.
- Meanwhile, there is always great pressure to get the annual audit done efficiently, but also quickly.

This scenario creates a series of conflicting, and at times confusing, priorities. There is no way the external audit process can be relied on to uncover all frauds against the organization and there are some frauds that are very hard to detect anyway. A supplier may write off an account from a company, but a determined accounts clerk may get a payment released in settlement of this account that is no longer due and payable and divert the check to a personal bank account. An investigator would have to follow the check through the banking system and get the vendor to confirm nonre-ceipt of the funds to bring the fraud out in the open. But if a company expects to pay the account and the vendor does not expect the money, there would be no reason to suspect an irregularity. Also, the payment in question may fall outside the sample selected by the external auditors for closer examination. External auditors place some reliance on representa-tions from directors and may not necessarily search for red flags, because of the great pressure to complete the testing and verification routines. A few auditors have been sued for recklessly failing to conduct audits in compli-ance with generally accepted auditing standards, missing red flags, and not having an appropriate degree of professional skepticism. An organization may commission a review of fraud from its CPA and ask for a risk assessment of vulnerable areas and some penetration testing to explore the possibility of fraud in target areas. The CPA in this instance would contact the com-pany lawyers and professional investigators and look carefully at the rules of questioning, the use of original documents, rules of evidence, and other sensitivities. Most employee frauds involve financial losses and will affect the financial systems that the CPA knows quite well. The external auditor is part of the window between the organization and society, as the audit process enables an independent commentary on the published accounts. When there is a cover-up by the board or top management, the auditor may report any concerns to the audit committee and, if pushed, withdraw from the audit and inform the new incoming auditor of any particular disquiet. The external auditor may also inform third parties when there is a legal obliga-tion to do so, the Securities and Exchange Commission (in some cases), the successor auditors, in response to a subpoena, and also government agen-cies (if public funds have been provided). This is a powerful mechanism to ensure that any frauds found are properly brought to light and addressed.

## Internal Audit

Internal auditors work for management and carry out a plan of work agreed on with the audit committee. The work of the internal auditor is now driven by risk and an assessment of priority areas where controls need to be in place to ensure success. Several control objectives set the scope of internal audit coverage, including the need to ensure that:

- Objectives are accomplished.
- Operations are efficient.

- Information is reliable.
- Resources are protected.
- Compliance with standards, legislation, and regulation is achieved.

Implicit within these objectives is the prevention and detection of fraud. Internal auditors ask whether resources are protected, information is sound, and procedures are adhered to by employees. The internal auditor will be concerned about the risk of fraud, noncompliance, waste, abuse, manipulated or erroneous information, basic failures, and that risks are being managed through good controls. When controls are missing or break down, risks could materialize and the internal auditor will not only consider weak control but will also probe the implications of any weaknesses, including the possibility of fraud. Having said this, the internal auditor still holds no primary responsibility for detecting fraud, which is a role properly located with the management of the organization. Moreover, the internal audit staff will tend to possess the skills and knowledge needed to penetrate concealed fraud and carefully explore the implications. Internal auditors will also have a good knowledge of the main financial systems and the indicators of fraud and irregularities. Like external auditors, the internal auditors are seen by some as a main safeguard against fraud. The correct situation is that the real safeguard against fraud is the system of managerial and financial controls that should be in place in response to an assessment of the risk of fraud. The internal auditors may uncover frauds through the audit process, although the various tests will not be designed primarily to detect fraud. There is still the need to conduct the audit with a reasonable expectation of uncovering irregular transactions, particularly when the systems are found to be unreliable in some areas. Tests are based on samples, which by definition involve only some, not all, of the underlying transactions. Also, a well-designed fraud may on paper look innocent and may pass several audit tests, if the documentation and explanations appear satisfactory. In terms of fraud detection, the internal auditors may be seen as an important resource to undertake an exercise that scans at-risk parts of the organization to probe the possibility of fraud. The computer auditor is particularly useful in this respect, because interrogation software can be used to search for inconsistent, duplicated, or suspect items that could be related to employee or external fraud. Much depends on the terms of reference of the audit outfit and whether there is an in-house team set up to do this type of work. The bottom line is that simply relying on the internal auditors, working through a program of high-risk planned audits, to uncover fraud is unrealistic.

## Security and Compliance Teams

Fraud necessarily involves noncompliance with procedure and breach of the organization's security. Compliance teams can be asked to direct their efforts to fraud detection routines and engage in an ongoing search for internal problems. Many such teams have a clear focus on probing parts of the organization where things could go wrong. Security personnel tend to have a protective role that concentrates on restricting access to company resources. IT security people will extend this role to logical as well as physical access, so that computer systems and databases are kept safe from unauthorized access and the resulting manipulation or destruction of data. The building security personnel also have a major role in both preventing and detecting abuse of company resources, although for the most part this is not always appreciated. Security cameras and video can also uncover many frauds involving unauthorized access to restricted parts of the building. The problem is that the security personnel are often the most lowly paid members of the organization; often they are not even employees, just "uniforms" supplied by a contractor. The entire profile of security and the crucial role it may play in protecting company resources can be sadly understated and underappreciated, and so impair the fight against fraud. If compliance teams and security staff are part of the detection process, they should be told that this is part of their job, and should be trained and properly resourced to carry out this task.

## Legal Representatives

Generally, due process and the rights of a person suspected of criminal activity mean the case must be properly investigated, prosecuted, and proved in court, if the person does not plead guilty. The seasoned criminal will have a reputation for hard-line offending and a spell in jail may enhance his or her status in the criminal world. Financial crime is similar in some respects, but different in that the suspect will probably cherish his or her reputation and depend on it for continued employment and ongoing career prospects. Because white-collar crime tends to be concealed, the investigation involves identifying company frauds and tracing any problems to the ultimate suspect. In setting up detection routines and probing into large numbers of transactions, companies may tread on toes and delve into data relating to their employees, supplier, customers, and others. Mistakes made during any part of the inquiry can mess up the project; an investigation could breach federal and state laws on privacy and the admissibility of evidence, and mean that any findings are ruled out of bounds. This is where the lawyers come into play. No detection routine should be set up without first checking the details with the company attorney. The plans, the probes, the decisions made during the exercise, the follow-through on suspicious items, and the location of suspects should all be cleared with the legal people.

## Top Management

Although the board of directors sets the policy on fraud detection, senior management puts in place the mechanisms necessary to enact the policy. Thus, the company's management should be the people to establish the detection project and determine the terms of reference and resources. They should also implement a whistleblowing process to ensure that colleagues or members of the public may pass on any specific concerns to the right place to act on the information. Top management should also ensure that the internal audit and compliance teams are working to the terms of reference set by the audit committee with respect to uncovering internal fraud. Senior managers should be able to sign a statement for the board that they are not aware of any fraudulent activity and have taken all reasonable steps to ensure that fraud is both prevented and detected. This and similar control statements on high-risk areas will help the board get a view of the state of the company's internal controls. One way to promote fraud detection is to get senior management to convene a series of appropriately resourced fraud detection projects, each sponsored by a senior board member. Locating responsibility with senior management for the overall program is important for ensuring that fraud detection is taken seriously and that someone is able to drill down into high-level reports and corporate statistics, searching for problems.

## Operations Managers

We come now to the people at the front line. Line managers hold operational responsibility for controlling and protecting the resources under their care and making sure that these resources are not abused or depleted. The way around this is to take the internal auditors' control objectives (mentioned earlier) and relocate them with management. Managers should ensure that:

- Objectives are accomplished.
- Operations are efficient.

- Information is reliable.
- Resources are protected.
- Compliance with standards, legislation, and regulation is achieved.

In this way, management do not wait for the auditors to review whether these goals are being met, but ask each and every line manager to assess their operations and assure themselves that they are achieving these goals. The self-assessment concept is derived from the empowerment concept, from which we argue that management is not only about achieving targets but also about addressing issues of integrity, openness, and accountability— not as add-ons but as central themes that are nonnegotiable.

## Employees

While management is in the front line, the employees are down in the trenches in the battle to win business, deliver services, and maintain quality. Employees operating controls are closer than anyone else to the basic company frauds that were described in Chapter 1. They should be aware of the red flags of fraud and be alert to any irregular behavior, which should be reported. People will not be equipped for this role unless they have received some kind of training and development in fraud awareness and proactive detection. An employer cannot give additional responsibility to staff without giving support, encouragement, and practical advice as well.

## Personnel

The other part of the equation relates to the personnel (human resources) staff. Fraud checks relate to the way people at work behave and whether this behavior is suspect, illegal, or questionable. Whenever an organization embarks on an exercise that affects staff and people it deals with, it must think through the implications for morale, employee rights, and the overall well-being of the workforce. If, for example, fraud detection is built into performance frameworks for line managers and teams, this will change the nature of the staff appraisal scheme. If work teams do a fraud risk self-assessment and take time out for this task, it may create a different culture and working regime for many such teams. Personnel can advise on staffing issues. For example, an exercise carried out on "milking the clock" could result in dozens of dismissals. It is best practice to call in the personnel representatives at an early stage to think through all the repercussions of this exercise. If all bonus payments are being checked and dubious payments struck out, the personnel staff will need to provide some advice on the way this is handled. Whatever the fraud detection plans, they have to be designed and enacted properly and all players with relevant expertise should be consulted. Good fraud detection does not work when shortcuts are taken.

## Employee Representatives

It is a good idea to advise any staff unions about the policy on fraud detection and the fact that the organization may embark on special exercises from time to time. The unions can comment on the general policies, but should not be involved in specific exercises that must be kept confidential at the early stages. Unions may be involved in attempts to review questionable working practices that have to be clarified. An example is claiming hotel expense allowances even if the person on location stays free of charge with a relative. Here the intention may not be to discipline and prosecute but to eradicate the practice and get things back on an even footing.

One fraud detection and control cycle that highlights the importance of clear roles and responsibilities is illustrated in Figure 4.1.

**Recognition:** The importance of detecting fraud should be appreciated throughout the organization. The fact that some frauds can be well hidden makes it crucial that people in the organization actively look for problems. Frauds do not always comply with set rules and most fraudsters do not recognize set boundaries; anything that provides value to them, that can be got at, is seen as fair game.

**Responsibility:** This is the crucial component. People will play no role in policy implementation if they feel the matter falls outside their area of responsibility. Respective responsibilities for making sure that

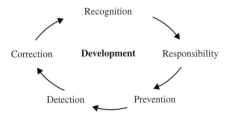

**Figure 4.1**  Fraud Detection Cycle

no double-dealing is going on should be made clear. Again, a way of enforcing this point is to get managers, teams, and individuals to sign off on an annual antifraud declaration.

**Prevention:**   Most managerial effort should go toward fraud prevention as the best way of managing the risk of fraud. Moreover, a sound system of internal control that guards against all unacceptable risks in an organization should be in place.

**Detection:**   Experienced fraudsters seek to conceal their fraudulent activity and collusion will defeat many controls based on segregation of duties. Detection is the next line of defense. Managers, teams, and review agencies need to keep looking for problems and respond to any unusual transactions. Prevention alone is not enough; searching for problems should be part of organizational culture.

**Correction:**   The cycle closes with organizational mechanisms to ensure that problems, once found, are addressed. Clear lines of responsibility for carrying out formal investigations of suspicious dealings must be established beforehand.

**Development:**   In the middle of the model is the reality of organizational life that staff need to get involved in fraud detection and understand the control cycle. This is no easy task and may involve full-blown team development workshops. Fighting fraud revolves around a learning process whereby people come to understand the nature of abuse and how it may best be tackled. Without this central development component, the cycle will not work. There will be no staff competence on which to base the newly defined responsibilities.

## WHISTLEBLOWING

The easiest way to find out about a problem is to ask people close to its source. Alternatively, make sure that these people have the opportunity to disclose any problems and are encouraged to do so. Fraud is an emotional issue, because it not only creates a problem for the organization, but also depends on dishonest behavior from persons within or outside the organization. Reporting fraud incorporates a view of the honesty of the person suspected of allegedly dishonest behavior. Whistleblowing means the informant may have to make a judgment about the honesty of someone who is known or who has come into contact with the informant, which necessarily involves emotion. A whistleblower is someone who informs with a view to putting a stop to something that is wrong. We have already touched on the negative aspects of blowing the whistle. There are other factors that make this task even more difficult.

## Loss of Employment

When someone commits an internal fraud against the organization, the mutual trust between employer and employee is broken. When someone informs on a colleague, he or she may be going against the culture of the workplace and be seen as impairing the trust between the informant and other employees. In this instance, many potential informants will think twice before pointing a finger at someone else. The fear that whistleblowing will backfire and eventually mean resignation (or worse) is a constant worry for someone who may wish to reveal a problem but does not feel able to.

## Physical Safety

We need to comment on personal safety issues when dealing with whistle-blowing. Telling senior figures or special advisors about what's going wrong at work is commendable. However, informing may carry a risk to the informant of physical threats, psychological pressure, and warnings (veiled or overt) of recrimination or intimidation. The real world is full of real people, and when an informant poses a threat, the suspect may wish to get rid of this threat. Commendable action may wilt in the face of intimidation, and the informant can feel completely isolated.

## Managerial Cover-up

The final reason people may not come forward relates to the perception that the problem will be covered up. Whistleblowers assess the likelihood of problems exposed being addressed and put right. When the likelihood is low, there is no real incentive to "go public." Even if there is a formal mechanism in place to relay concerns anonymously within the organization, there will be little activity if it is generally understood that nothing much comes out of the reports.

There is some protection for an employee with a nagging concern about fraud at work. The Civil Service Reform Act prevents retaliation against federal whistleblowers who are civil servants. Furthermore, each state has a similar law addressing the topic of harassment of whistleblowers generally. Organizations such as Employee Theft Anonymous encourage people to report vendor theft, gifts, collusion, milking the clock, swindling, embezzlement, and skimming. The informant will not be traced back and the employer will be notified straight away. If informants wish to use the False Claims Act and claim a reward (through a *qui tam* suit for frauds against the government), they must identify themselves using an appropriate form. The Office of Inspector General has a fraud hotline in place for social security frauds, and all allegations are analyzed.

Anonymous tip-offs and confidential information received are important ways of detecting fraud within an organization. Without this source of information, there is much scope for frauds to go on undetected for some time. When employees feel great pressure to tell someone about dishonesty in an organization, they may eventually go to an outsider if no one inside the organization is prepared to listen to them. The best response by an organization is to establish a formal whistleblower policy, and think through some of the reasons why people might keep information to themselves, when designing the policy and procedures. There are several key components to such a policy.

## Make Clear the Purpose

Make it clear that whistleblowing is part of the drive against fraud, to allow employees and external third parties to provide information in confidence. The board should support all avenues that help it detect fraud and irregularity. Make clear that the procedure is not for staff grievances or matters that should be reported straight away to line management. It should be only for issues concerning fraudulent activity of employees or associates that have not been properly addressed by the line manager. If the policy is to cover misadministration or reckless negligence by managers who fail to deal with allegations of fraud, then again, make this entirely clear.

## Define Employees' Responsibilities

Set out the role that employees play in bringing matters of dishonesty and regularity to the attention of the appropriate party. All staff should be alert to the possibility of fraud and have a duty to report anything that indicates fraud is happening; they should *not* confront the suspect or repeat the allegation after having reported it. In addition, informants should not launch their own investigation into the matter. Employees should not engage in unfounded accusations based on malicious gossip or vindictiveness, and should always act in good faith. Moreover, the organization has a responsibility to investigate all legitimate allegations that come to its attention.

## Keep Things Confidential

Encourage people to come forward by giving assurances of confidentiality. Information may be provided anonymously, or the informant's details may be provided. When personal details are provided, this information may be released to federal or state authorities when necessary or required by law, but otherwise it should remain confidential. Again, the reporting person should ensure that the information is kept confidential and that, whenever possible, the informant is prepared to assist in any further inquiries.

## Ensure Clear Reporting Lines

The reporting arrangements may involve an auditor, fraud officer, security officer, external agent, or some other nominated contact point, depending on the policy in question and the arrangements in place. Some schemes provide general feedback to the reporting employee; others take the matter up and do not contact the informant again. In feedback schemes, the informant will have to provide personal contact details.

## Link to Value System

There is a moral obligation to tackle fraud on all fronts, and this applies to everyone. Link the whistleblowing policy to other values of the organization, such as cooperation, standards, protecting the organization, corporate reputational issues, personal integrity, and so on.

## Monitor and Review

Ensure that reports are available on the activities of the whistleblower's hotline and the results of each case. The ethical standards committee will be interested in this type of information. Also review the efficiency of the arrangements and find out whether employees have confidence in the system.

The fight against fraud depends on good intelligence on what's at risk and what people out there are doing to access company resources. The hot line is a great way of getting inside information on wrongdoing, so long as people have confidence in the system and it is well organized. People may need to be acclimatized to the reporting process through various awareness events and practical examples. If staff feel a moral obligation to inform on fraudulent practices, detection will be so much easier. The worst-case scenario is to have a set procedure in place that no one knows about, understands, or has confidence in.

# INDICATORS OF FINANCIAL CRIME

"I guess there was something odd about it all . . . " This comment is what slips out after many a case of employee fraud has come to light. It is easy to be wise in hindsight. The feeling that things do not add up derives from inconsistencies presented to an observer, who may dismiss them or use such inconsistencies as the basis of an investigation to probe and discover the truth. Here we list the indicators that could suggest fraudulent activity.

## Behavioral Issues

These indicators relate to the way people at work behave. There are many and various legitimate reasons why someone may have excessive wealth and also be defensive about his or her work files, but nonetheless there could be other, less acceptable reasons, such as:

- **Regular absences.**   This could indicate a personal problem.
- **Low funds and lots of debt**.   A motive for some fraudsters is solving a severe financial problem. A person with mounting debts could have a strong motivation to commit fraud at work.
- **Protective behavior.**   When a person does not take holidays, works long hours, is hardly ever sick, and keeps his or her working papers very close at hand, there is little chance of anyone intruding into the person's work. Sometimes files are being doctored: for example, the person may be diverting refunds on loan interest on the final loan payment from clients, and paying these refunds into a private bank account. This scam could go on for quite a while, as long as no one checks the refund files. One indicator is an employee who becomes very defensive and aggressive, so as to ward off any unwanted inquiries.
- **Addictive behavior.**   Someone who drinks or smokes excessively, takes illegal drugs, or gambles will have to support an addictive and

possibly expensive habit. These activities may also be deemed anti-social. A loner is less able to share personal problems, and some argue that fraud results from having a financial problem that cannot be shared—hence, the person resorts to illegality.

- **Strange behavior.** When a person is involved in a fight between right and wrong and is not comfortable with this struggle, it may affect his or her personality. For example, by becoming really upset when someone tries to deal with a large supplier who is normally dealt with only by the employee in question. The individual may also become agitated when asked to explain an odd transaction.

- **Inappropriate wealth.** This indicator is pretty obvious. If an employee's income less expenditures results in a lifestyle and assets that do not add up, there is the possibility of unexplained income from illegal sources—although this is only one explanation.

## Poor Controls

Individuals will not be able to commit fraud without a lapse in the systems of internal control. The control environment is an important part of the basic control model and relates to the underlying ethos throughout the organization that promotes good control. When there are specific gaps in this control environment, there is a climate that does not help contain fraud. The following are specific problems that are symptoms of poor controls:

- **Lack of segregation of duties.** This is what we call a key control, where more than one person is involved in a transaction from start to finish, including recording and review. The idea is that two crooks would have to be employed and conspire to abuse the systems—not impossible, but less likely. When there are also other controls, such as review and supervision, the process should be pretty watertight. Where these principles are not in place, there is less control. The Association of Certified Fraud Examiners (ACFE) reports that smaller companies are more at risk of fraud because fewer people are involved in their business systems. Unfortunately, there are many smaller companies whose payments system consists of just one member of staff, who prepares payments, files paperwork, writes checks, reconciles bank accounts, files returned checks, follows up payment in suspense accounts, and prepares accounts for writeoff. This is a recipe for disaster.

- **Systems override**. Many controls are designed to ensure propriety and regularity. They are good and work well in incorporating sufficient checks over high-risk transactions, programs, and operations. These controls are tried and trusted and have passed reviews by external and internal auditors. The problem is that the official system is not always used, and it is the senior people—those who can do the most damage in terms of abuse—who can simply override the controls.

- **Poor state of controls awareness**. When parts of the organization appear to be in a constant state of chaos, there is much scope for fraud that cannot be readily uncovered. In this environment, reporting lines are unclear, as are levels of authority and supervisory arrangements. Desks may be clogged up with files and access levels to computer applications may not have been properly thought through. On the physical security front, people may wander around the section with no ID badges, and generally, there is a lax attitude to security. The hidden purpose of this set-up is to make life impossible for the audit people, who cannot find most of the documentation and end up simply asking team members for the required information.

- **Poor audit, accountability, and board oversight**. There is little more to say about this problem, which arises when the board does not accept that it has a role in overseeing the actions of management. The problem is compounded when the need for a robust audit process has not been properly recognized. If we add to this a lack of effective supervision from line and middle management and no real audit process, the total sum of this equation means either more employee fraud or an amount that cannot really be determined.

- **No controls over human resource processes**. When references of new employees are not properly checked and there is an inadequate performance appraisal scheme and no employee fidelity insurance, thing start to break down. When there are staffing problems generally and low morale, it is harder to get people to buy into corporate ethics. In this situation employees may view their managers as unfair in implementing staffing policies. Also, low morale and incentive among staff contributes to people's ability to excuse dishonest acts against the company. Also, it is hard to stress ethics and integrity in an environment where staff are highly competitive and adopt a win–lose stance in the way they relate to colleagues and management.

- **Large amounts of staff overtime.** The potential to place personal interests over and above legitimacy is higher in a climate where the workforce engineers the work situation to ensure extra benefits. When staff have gotten used to extra money as the norm, this can create problems when removed. Furthermore, some frauds create a stalemate situation, where managers are involved in scams but keep the workforce silent by giving them large amounts of overtime.
- **High staff turnover.** Large amounts of staff movement can result in a workplace where many team members have little experience of the systems, how they work, and how they should be checked. Also, many people join a company, section, or team and find they do not hold with the deceitful practices that are carried out there. Their answer is to resign or seek a transfer out of the section. Exit interviews in a confidential setting can elicit information on common scams. In some countries with high levels of corruption, excessive staff movement could indicate people leaving posts because there is insufficient opportunity to skim and take bribes.
- **Conflicts of interest.** When many different deals are being negotiated, there can be problems. Split loyalties create difficulty in maintaining the type of trust that abounds in a well-run organization. Knowing that dismissal from one job simply means more private work, or going self-employed full time (rather than part time), there is no real reason to want to achieve a career with the main employer. In addition, many frauds such as theft of ideas and customer (or design) data come to the fore when there is a conflict of interest for the employee.
- **Poor or risky organizational structures.** Some organizational structures create inherently high levels of fraud risk. An example is a decentralized set-up where many autonomous sites collect cash, make payments, and deal with the movement of stock. Retail outlets have a history of good controls in this type of environment and are pretty experienced at managing this type of business. Nonretail businesses may be less fortunate, as they design their systems to fit their own unique contexts. When there are many sources of income and junior people running remote locations with little involvement from a head office, the risk of fraud increases.
- **Poor accounting controls.** Symptoms include large amounts of outstanding debt, poor accounting documentation and missing records,

backlogs of work so that there are no up-to-date accounts, and many adjustments to the accounts. If the company also makes regular, large payments to individuals, the main ingredients of fraud are all in place. The final point that indicates problems is the constant use of post office addresses for delivery of checks and goods issued by the company. The question that should be posed is who benefits from the poor records and lack of controls.

## Straight Information

At times, information comes directly to light that on careful consideration should indicate something is wrong. Examples are:

- **Complaints from suppliers, partners, and customers.**   A great deal of information that comes from these sources is often ignored as an indicator of fraud. A supplier who complains that a check has not been received may be subject to a major fraud involving the misappropriation of checks. The problem is compounded if the replacement check is prepared by the same person who diverted the original check. Contractors may complain that the tender process is being abused, while customers may complain that goods have been incorrectly addressed and have gone astray. Altering the customer address so that the products go to the fraudster's address, or are returned to the company and then misappropriated, is a popular method of committing fraud. Many companies have good controls over products dispatched but poor controls over returned goods. A customer may open a shop credit account and pay cash for the goods, only to find that the account has been charged for goods already paid for. Many people do not check their credit card statements and will not follow up discrepancies, particularly when there is a joint account with a partner. A company that receives a customer's payment twice has a "dangling credit" that can be used to conceal an internal fraud.
- **I owe yous (IOUs).**   If IOUs are found in the cash till it is likely that a fraud is happening. Staff write these IOUs so that if they are found out, they can claim they were going to pay back the sum taken. The problem is that they simply replace the IOUs every day. The excuse may make the difference between dismissal and just receiving a warning. It is good practice to include clear rules in the accounting

handbook, such as "All cash *must* be banked intact and as soon as possible."

- **Information from whistleblowers**.  This has been dealt with earlier.

## Inconsistencies

Unlike straight information, other indicators of fraud are circumstantial in nature. Most are due to simple error, but others result from the intentional manipulation of records:

- **Trends inconsistent with business activity.**  Here profits may fall for no obvious reason, or there may be an excessive amount of inventory shrinkage. Payroll figures may have increased out of proportion to changes in the workforce, and there may be an excessive number of void checks. Scrap levels may have increased even while the income from scrap is declining. Large numbers of writeoffs could become the norm. Also, contracts may be placed for amounts just below the level where formal tendering procedures have to be applied. Growing amounts of unidentified credits and debits on the suspense account could easily mask an ongoing fraud. Staff expenses that suddenly jump just before the Christmas holiday season, without an increase in business, may be due to fraudulent claims by staff, to boost their finances at an expensive time of the year.

- **Reconciliation differences.**  When the bank reconciliation is off, the books do not entirely agree with the bank's records. Even when the bank reconciliation agrees, it may include old items that have not been identified. When the general ledger is off, it can indicate that funds have been fraudulently removed from the accounts. Internal figures may be in balance but when compared to industry norms may suggest a problem. Inventory figures are a good example of what is expected in terms of turnover ratios and losses. If stock ratios are higher than competitors', it could indicate error, waste, or fraud. If one or more managers are approving many more loans than other managers, it could be a case of bribery or fictitious accounts. If some of these accounts are subsequently written off, there may be an attempt at committing the perfect fraud.

- **Strange contract figures.**  When the lowest bidders do not win, this can mean bribes are being paid to staff. When the lowest bid is chosen (perhaps with unrealistic prices) but variations in contract prices occur regularly, this could mean insider knowledge is being provided to vendors and partners. Unauthorized changes to the contract again call for further inquiries. Contracts that have little supporting records or rely on photocopies could also suggest a problem.

- **Lost assets.** When the inventory is incomplete, wrong, ignored, out of date, or generally inefficient, theft of goods, equipment, and products, once carried out, may be easy to conceal.

- **Fictitious items.** Ghost employees, payments to unknown persons, and vendor accounts for people who cannot be verified are all signs of company fraud. A fraudster may establish accounts for people who do not exist or for people associated with the perpetrator. Another way of getting funds out is to make duplicate payments and then misappropriate the refunds while at the same time writing off the extra payment.

### Abuse of Information Technology Security

Some argue that the future of business is information and maintaining good customer and pricing data. Company records are mainly held in computerized information systems, and false accounting in practice mainly involves abuse of the IT security arrangements. Poor IT security is an indicator (or facilitator) of fraud and relates to:

- **Poor segregation of duties.** This was mentioned earlier. If a person can access a computer system, change data, and use this new data to send out goods, effect a payment, or commission a transaction, then the system is open to abuse.

- **Poor program control.** This includes poor controls over the way programs are written, stored, and amended.

- **No reconciliations.** A lack of reconciliation between related accounts may indicate problems.

- **Poor exception reports.** Problems in computerized systems are generally reported by the system. When these exception reports are not well designed, or when they are not examined and acted on, overall control of the system declines.

- **Poor virus detection.** Viruses pose a major threat to corporate data. Not only does the virus itself cause problems, and so constitute a criminal offense, but the resulting loss of data may mask a fraud and make the investigation more difficult.

- **PC activities not traceable.** A lack of audit trail makes it hard to relate specific transactions to specific people. Once the evidentiary trail is broken, fraud is harder to investigate and prove. All good systems should include extensive management trails and follow-up of suspicious items.
- **Password unchanged and uncontrolled.** Password control is still the single biggest safeguard against systems abuse and unauthorized access. Where password controls are slack, there are greater opportunities for fraud and abuse. Access controls should be properly focused. There should be good physical access and call-back controls for remote access to the corporate network to restrict fraudulent activity.
- **Output not verified.** Many users of computer systems assume that all output is correct. When no verification of output or checks is made, to ensure that the output makes sense and is consistent with other information available, false accounting and data manipulation are much easier to get away with.
- **Lack of proper sanctions.** When IT security is abused and severe sanctions are not imposed, the wrong message is sent to staff and external parties. An environment in which people swap passwords and leave workstations and laptops unattended, or generally are not aware of security provisions, helps the fraudster conduct business.

### Financial Misstatement

The final category of fraud and related indicators concerns fraudulent financial statements. When executives or the board are able to fabricate figures and invent performance reports and profits as and when required, the entire business community is affected. Unfortunately, many an investor has lost out because of this type of fraud. The environment in which financial misstatement flourishes has several features:

- **Performance pay.** Fees and compensation for directors and top management linked entirely to the financial performance of the company.
- **Share price.** Tremendous pressure to maintain a high share price and disastrous impact of a fall in the price. When a director's entire fortune is tied to the value of shares held in the company, there is a strong motive to "fix" things. This would be compounded when the

market is in a state of rapid development and high-risk venture funding is readily available.

- **Tax bills.**    Pressing need to keep tax payments low. Financial misreporting relates not only to keeping profits up, but also to keeping taxes down by massaging the accounts.
- **Board oversight.**    When no real board oversight is in place, and corporate ethics is seen as a dirty word, a small group can call the shots with no real control over their activities. In this situation, the audit process is unlikely to have a big impact and the staff may be in fear of losing their jobs, particularly the finance people. There will probably be a high level of staff turnover as people are fired and replaced overnight. There may also be a big gap between staff and managers and no real communication between the board and employees. The only part of the company that works will be the sales team, who will fight to meet demanding targets. When the chief executive and the chief finance officer decide to collude and commit fraud, they can create tremendous problems of misappropriation and concealment.
- **Financial problems.**    Improper accounting procedures can be associated with poor financial planning and a general lack of cash flow. Financial misreporting is a way of covering up fraud by directors or top management. A series of complex intercompany transfers and adjustments may be designed to confuse outsiders. This type of company may well lurch from crisis to crisis and have offshore funds (in tax havens) and many special accounts to ensure a swift exit for the key players in the event of a collapse.

There are many signals that fraud is happening. Taken out of context, each individual sign is not in itself significant, but the pattern and combinations that do not add up should lead to an "at-alert" status. If employers could train their staff to be aware of the indicators of fraud, there would be a better chance of detecting problems and resolving them quickly. It is the front-line staff who are closest to the signals of dishonesty and cover-up, and it is here that an entire army can be mobilized in the fight against corporate fraud.

## RISK AND DETECTION

Risk assessment is a useful tool to assist fraud detection routines. The idea is to focus detection strategies on parts of the organization that are at risk of fraud and abuse. The areas at risk were in one sense the items discussed in the previous section on indicators of fraud. The potential for the risk to materialize is affected by the motive of potential offenders and the opportunity available, that is, the type of person who may succumb to fraud and the state of controls. There is obviously no definitive personality type that typifies dishonest people. There are, however, circumstances that can alert management to the possibility of an employee's being involved in fraud. Drawing on the ACFE's *Report to the Nation* and other research, the typical employee perpetrator (if there is any such thing) is likely to be:

- Male, white, and college educated.
- A bit of a risk taker.
- Egotistical.
- Inquisitive (for example, spends time asking about corporate systems and the various interfaces).
- Eager to ignore or override the rules and take shortcuts whenever possible.
- Working long hours and even weekends, and as such may be seen as a hard worker.
- Under some stress and somewhat of a loner, although at the same time may have close working relations with select suppliers.
- Motivated by greed and material rewards; may spend a great deal of cash on a regular basis. This type of person is highly driven by money. One theory paints the fraudster as a opportunist who, given the chance, would get involved in as many scams as possible.
- In some financial difficulty (perhaps large credit card debts).
- Unhappy with the workplace and complaining about unfair treatment or the corrupt people at the top. Some people may be under pressure to meet difficult performance targets in an environment where most income is earned through bonuses and commissions.
- Have an attitude that the auditor, inspectors, and supervisors are the enemy.

This is a profile of the person who is most likely to commit fraud. But what exactly is at risk from this person? We can list some of these at-risk items in a typical organization:

- Cash.
- Checks.

- Income.
- Payments.
- Contracts.
- Equipment.
- Knowledge.
- Goods.
- Privileges.
- Staff travel and expense claims.
- Bonuses.
- Company claims.
- Loan rights.
- Compensation.
- Insurance.
- Valuable and portable items.
- Sexual favors.
- Promotions.
- Overtime.
- Payroll.
- Annual accounts.
- Investments and investment income.
- Consultants' fees.
- Research and development.
- Ideas.
- Pricing policies.
- Petty cash.
- Sales.
- Returns.
- Writeoffs.
- Mortgages.
- Government grants.
- Private work done by a company contractor.
- Credit cards.
- Personal data.
- Interest paid and received.
- Computer networks.
- Insider information that affects share price.
- The reputation of the company.
- Compliance with federal and state laws.
- Absolutely anything of value.

We have listed the attributes of fraudsters and the things that they might target in an organization. This is a good place from which to launch a proactive program of fraud detection.

## MAPPING SUSPICIONS

We have established corporate responsibilities and outlined what to look at in terms of high-risk areas, and can now turn to detection proper. The adopted detection strategy may include various options, as shown in Figure 4.2.

1. **Informant.** This strategy is based around reacting to direct information that alleges a wrongdoing. Great reliance is placed on the hot line and access to a special facility that is well resourced to receive confidential tip-offs. Exit interviews can be conducted with people leaving the company to gather information when the respondent has nothing to lose. The organization is on the lookout for fraud but really responds to information received.

2. **Red flags.** The second level is where people in the organization are on the lookout for indicators of fraud—so-called red flags. Staff are trained in general awareness and understand the significance of indicators that appear at the same time. Alert, active, and responsive people will watch for manifestations of dishonesty. For example, if inventory reorder levels are overridden, an excessive amount of returns that should go back into stores may disappear. Staff should be able to spot these irregularities.

3. **Regular searches.** The final, and most extreme, level consists of proactive resources that embark on regular searches of at-risk aspects of the business. These exercises are generally carried out by specialists such as external auditors, internal auditors, compliance teams, financial monitoring people, or fraud examiners.

**Figure 4.2**   Reactive and Proactive Detection

Each organization must decide on the most appropriate position on the spectrum. The choice must suit the context and type of business in question. The main point is, having decided on the best strategy, to tell everyone who works for or deals with the organization, and make sure they understand the implications. Levels one and two are important but pretty straightforward. Level three is more interesting and involves some careful thought about the following:

- **Random probes.** Make sure random probes can be carried out throughout the organization and that constitutional rights are not being infringed. Techniques such as security video, bugging phones, recording computer system interfaces, monitoring PC keyboard strokes, recording meetings, tracing PC audit trails, and discreet observation of employees all need to be cleared with the legal people. The key question is whether employees have a reasonable expectation of privacy in areas that are under observation.

- **Resources.** Ensure that the right resources are in the right place. Specialist staff do specialist work, and an employee-based exercise may lead to serious action against anyone found to be involved in dishonest and irregularity activities. The team may consist of external auditors, internal auditors, compliance teams, or certified fraud examiners. The exercise may result in criminal charges and/or disciplinary procedures against any alleged perpetrator discovered by the examination. The work should really be driven by a senior official who can call on extra support from computer experts, personnel staff, and legal advisors as and when required. This person may also need to make policy decisions as the work progresses.

- **Techniques.** Use all available fraud detection techniques. Data mining can be used to isolate potential problems by linking computerized data through a set assessment criteria. Patterns, trends, and unusual associations can be used to produce a set of data that should be examined further. In this way, huge amounts of information may be sorted and checked out very quickly using the right techniques. Appendix B provides more information on data mining.

> In one large government agency, a team of business advisors worked with local businesses to encourage them to apply for start-up grants from the government. The advisors would assess the business, explain the grant scheme, and ask the applicant to prepare a business plan and cash flow statement as a basis for applying for funding.

Acting on a tip-off, a data mining exercise was undertaken looking for links between the advisor, the client, the accountant, and the legal advisor selected by the client, and it came up with some interesting results. Several clients (new local businesses) had the same business advisor, accountant, and lawyer, and submitted applications just below the level that would have been subject to rigorous verification. As a result, a full investigation uncovered a conspiracy whereby the advisor and other parties fabricated the illusion of new businesses, fraudulently obtained grants, and then split the proceeds.

Clear associations between several parties, when there is no good reason why these parties should be linked so frequently, call for further inquiries. When some monetary gain is involved, this can indicate suspicious circumstances. Insurance companies use this approach to isolate claims that fall into a set pattern of parties involved in fraudulent claims. A theory about potential frauds should be developed and built into a database of information. The next stage is to apply suitable techniques to this data. Most computerized databases contain a wealth of information that will suggest there is something wrong, if only the right questions are asked and the data interrogated accordingly. If the need to explore and examine data is appreciated, and a basic interrogation tool is available to detect strange associations, many frauds can be quickly detected, investigated, and resolved. Further progress can be made by comparing internal and external databases. The hardest stage is developing a useful theory about how frauds could happen and what should be looked for.

In one data-matching exercise using internal and external databases, several retired ex-employees who were receiving company pensions were found actually to be dead. In a typical case, someone close to the deceased had assumed the former employee's identity and continued collecting the pension.

Another technique, called Benford's law, suggests that fabricated figures (an indicator of fraud) possess a pattern different from random (or valid) figures and that an analysis of figures used on (for example) invoices, orders, contracts, claims, and so on can uncover potential frauds.

- **Database of past frauds**.   What's past is gone, but what's happened before can provide a clue to what may happen in future. This is true of frauds against the organization. Many frauds over the years are similar in concept but differ in the way they are executed. There are dozens of ways company checks can be diverted to a fraudster's bank account, but each method essentially consists of getting hold of the check and paying it into the account. Many an organization has been embarrassed by the simple question, "Can you tell me the extent of employee fraud in your company over the years?" A frauds database not only gives this information, but also allows reflective insight into what has happened, why, and how to tackle it. Detection routines should take past problems into account and maybe even extrapolate trends into the future. An extension of this is to keep in touch with developments in the industry in question, on the theory that if it is happening elsewhere, it may well happen in our own back yard. Ensuring that there is an ongoing assessment of fraud trends can help an organization create a series of alarm systems. As one alarm goes off, the detection routine swings into action. There must be good information on fraud and how it affects businesses now and in the future.

- **Risk assessment for potential frauds.** Building on the preceding point, there should be an ongoing assessment of risk throughout the organization, based on the potential for fraud and significant breach of procedure. Parts of the organization or certain key operations may come up as high risk and so attract our attention. In these areas, consider actively looking for fraud through detection procedures. As the assessment of risk changes through new information, changing business patterns, and the analysis of key risk factors, detection routines should likewise change. Frauds can be profiled to an extent, although the range of possible scams is great and each one will be slightly different from the others. New IT systems should be watched very carefully because, although most frauds are variations of old themes, the way they are perpetrated is affected by new technology and therefore new opportunities.

> In one fraud, a person purporting to be an employee paid in $150 on official company documents at a company cash office and therefore was not asked for ID by the cashier. She then withdrew $2,500, again using official company documents. She spent $150 to gain $2,500 fraudulently.

Many businesses have a five-year road map of projected new technology that they use to guide company efforts and direction. This road map can also be used to think through frauds that may hit now and over the five-year period. In this way, good anticipation assists good fraud protection.

- **Analytical review.** If two sets of figures are compared between periods or across functions, differences may be discovered that cannot be readily explained or are inconsistent with known facts. A simple example is shown in Figure 4.3.

The increase in travel costs for Department B should be cause for concern. It may be that an increased output will be achieved in a later period, but on face value there is something that should be explored further. Again, it could be due to error, investment (say, attending a big overseas sales conference), misadministration (not keeping the budget under control), or fraud. It is when all sensible explanations have been explored that we eventually come to the possibility of fraud. Data mining could then be used to identify the people, places, authorizers, expenditure codes, and amounts in the suspect department to isolate any strange patterns for further investigation. One word of warning: If the fraud has been going on for some time, the returns and figures may have been understated for so long that they will be seen as being correct.

> In one fraud investigation involving regular cash skimming, the fraud had been carried out for so long that the figures were seen as acceptable even though they were 20 percent understated. An even worse situation arose when the section managers knew there was

**Staff Travel Expenditure $**

|         | Last Period | This Period | % Diff | Output |
|---------|-------------|-------------|--------|--------|
| **Dept. A** | 100 | 120 | 20 | 100% |
| **Dept. B** | 210 | 300 | 90 | 100% |
| **Dept. C** | 150 | 160 | 10 | 110% |
| **Dept. D** | 110 | 110 | 0 | 100% |

**Figure 4.3**  Analytical Review

something wrong with the reported earnings but ignored the signals because they were meeting their targets and did not want to rock the boat.

- **Assortment of approaches.** Many organizations make the mistake of seeing fraud detection as a sophisticated automated technique. They rely on the interrogations, like checking supplier details against staff details, and then sit back in comfort. The key is to use an assortment of different techniques and approaches to reflect the fact that fraud comes in different forms and disguises. Use a range of approaches, from computer-based interrogations, to assessment of video coverage, to PC network logs, to industry fraud trend comparisons, along with anything else that comes to mind. Detection is a little like a competition: When the fraudster is creative and daring in designing the crime, the target organization needs to respond by being just as creative and daring in sniffing out these crimes. The new atmosphere of empowerment and trust-based enterprises means that many old-fashioned controls of specific supervision and authorizations have been discarded in favor of the new business ethos of general supervision and blanket authority to spend against budget. Something should be in place to balance things; if one approach does not work, learn from this and try new approaches. Meanwhile, and as a footnote, remember that it is not possible to detect 100 percent of possible frauds.

- **Concentration on the bigger fish.** An organization may spend a great deal of time investigating fraud and breach of procedure and regularly dismiss staff as a result. Managers may even get a reputation for being tough on fraud and reckless behavior. Unfortunately, it may all backfire if the strategy is to hit soft targets, such as slightly optimistic overtime claims while the real corruption happens at senior levels, where top managers are bribed to push business in certain directions. The workforce becomes resentful, the investigators are seen as pawns, and the ethical base starts to crumble in this type of organization, even if there is a full-time fraud team. The lesson to learn is to take on the real fraudsters (i.e., senior managers) and then think about getting the ethical tone right for the rest of the organization. An abundance of low-level fraud is normally the tip of the iceberg, sitting comfortably on a bedrock of management corruption and neglect.

- **Forensic accounting**. *Forensic* means material relating to the criminal courts. When developing fraud detection plans, companies must think through the implications of the various routines and extraction of documentation. Many frauds have accounting implications: either records have been doctored to hide the fraud, or the records provide reliable evidence of the fraud in question. There is generally some kind of trail that leads back from the loss to the perpetrator. Accountants who understand the need for forensic evidence can contribute to the way evidence is gathered and preserved, as can forensic computer experts. It is good practice to get advice from expert fraud examiners before embarking on a detection strategy, particularly in terms of the admissibility of evidence. The motive for carrying out the exercise should be established up front, as this may be called into question as any resulting investigation progresses. The detection exercise may be the result of information received, or a response to an indication that there were suspicious circumstances, or simply a random search designed to sniff out scams. So long as the reasons fit with the fraud policy and people are aware that detection is accepted practice in the organization, management is well placed to defend against accusations of victimization or breach of workers' constitutional rights.

- **Documentation and information standards**. The way the organization compiles and stores documents and information may well have a bearing on the feasibility of fraud detection. In an environment where documents are regularly scanned and the originals destroyed right away, problems can arise because copies have to be relied on for evidence of fraud. The courts (or internal disciplinary hearing) have to be told how the documents were obtained and that they are reliable. In future, most evidence may be circumstantial in nature, which makes it even harder to prepare a case against an alleged perpetrator. At times, there is too much documentation; some frauds are based around securing confidential waste that has not been properly destroyed. A document, even if not original, by itself may tell half the story.

> In one scam, tenants were paying rent and then telling their banks not to pay the checks before they were banked by the housing company. The tenants would then produce the original rent receipt when sued for outstanding rent; the housing company was so disorganized

that it had a hard time proving that the rents had not been paid. Many cases of outstanding debt, for tenants who had since moved, were written off because of this problem.

Not all systems have good enough audit trails to trace transactions back to specific individuals in the company. Business is quickly moving toward total connectivity, with hardly any human interface at all. This is frightening, as most organizations are now entirely reliant on IT-based safeguards and controlling access to authorized persons performing authorized tasks only. Some feel that all corporate frauds will soon become Internet fraud, and because security costs money and slows things down, the fight against fraud becomes even more challenging.

- **Controls**.  Detection should lead to detailed inquiries into all suspect items, but do not forget the importance of controls. One way to focus on controls is to think about developing tools of detection— say, interrogation software that looks for related or duplicate transactions that are not at first glance obvious (such as suppliers with the same cell phone number)—and giving them to the front-line staff. With these controls, as an item is processed, the detection routine swings into action and the transaction may be rejected, or at least reported before it is paid or finalized. In this way, what was simply retrospective detection can be turned into the much more effective action of fraud prevention, so long as the controls are as dynamic as the frauds.

## CONCLUSION

The stop light model changes the responsibility dynamic by moving everyone in an organization to red. At red, employees, agents, associates, partners, and officers are all asked to engage in the ongoing task of preventing and checking for fraud. People who resign may be interviewed to ascertain whether anything untoward is going on in their workplace. Auditors may be asked to actively look for fraud when performing their audit routines; compliance teams should likewise look behind any breach of procedure they find in case there is any fraudulent intent. Meanwhile, the board should initiate regular searches for misappropriation and breach of security in what are deemed high-risk areas. Red flags come in a variety of forms, and if considered carefully may indicate a matter to be explored further. An accounts manager who owns a luxury condo on the east coast and lives well beyond the dictates of the salary paid by the company can be explained away quite easily. But if the same manager approves large refunds from suppliers and maintains sole responsibility for the process from start to finish, we should start to get concerned. Instead of this concern being just a nagging worry, the stop light model asks us to think through the implications and whether some detection should be undertaken. It does not mean people distrusting their coworkers and unilaterally launching grand surveillance operations. It simply means that people are aware of and think about the indicators of fraud and report any concerns to the right place in the organization so that steps may be taken to address these concerns. Under this model, all people should be actively alert to the possibility of fraud as it falls within their organizational responsibility, no matter where they sit in the organization:

- Procurement managers and staff need to think through the tendering or bidding process and how controls can be defeated by outsiders, collusion, or bribery. The bigger the bribe, the more influence provided to the bribe payer, although it is hard to bring organized bribery to light.
- Accounts staff need to think about transactions that go through their systems and large one-time payments or attempted requests for payment that are aborted until one finally gets through.
- Inventory managers need to think about the way returned goods disappear and why large amounts of stores are going to one site that is not currently doing much business.
- Personnel officers need to worry about people who claim qualifications that seem odd or list previous employment with companies that always to go out of business before the details can be verified.

   > One bookkeeper joined a company and misappropriated cash after having concealed convictions for doing the same thing to the previous employer.

- Managers need to work out why sales teams are claiming for expensive flights without deducting the large frequent-flyer discounts that are available.
- Security managers need to think about the people who have unlimited access to all parts of the organization to clean and empty trash bins.

- The legal people need to ask why an executive is spending $100,000 on a consultant with no formal contract in place for those services.
- IT people need to ask why some employees are logging unusual activity on systems that fall outside their areas of work.
- Shop and restaurant managers need to consider the way customer credit card details are handled by their staff, and whether the information is really kept confidential.
- The CEO should question why a personal assistant always asks for check signatures just before the CEO rushes off to an important meeting.
- The youngster manning the service desk needs to work out why customers are losing track of goods sent out to them and get reported lost, or why the quantities invoiced do not match up with what was shipped out.
- We all need to ask why a new and expensive contractor is located in the same street as the director of operations, when this particular director has had a new house extension at the same time as the contractor is building a similar extension at the head office.

The smugglers of old had a saying that townsfolk should "turn their faces to the wall," as illegal goods were taken off ships and escorted through the town at night; ignorance of the crime meant safety for all. The culture of turning one's face to the wall falls way outside the stop light model, and should be turned on its head. Everyone should push their heads through their windows and put a stop to the activities of the dishonest few. Detection is about getting everyone to do this as a reflex response to wrongdoing. Drawing on the knowledge of criminology, detection routines can be designed to feed into the fraud prevention cycle, because potential fraudsters fear being discovered and publicly exposed as dishonest. If the approach to detection is publicized in an aggressive manner, it may act as a deterrent for those who sit on the border between right and wrong behavior. In this way, rather than being a secret undercover operation, proactive detection may involve everyone cooperating with the searches, and sending a clear message to all who come into contact with the business. It may not put off the dedicated and intelligent criminal who seeks a challenge as one motive, but it may make others think twice about the pros and cons of stepping into the seedy world of deceit and concealment. Whenever an organization issues a representation along the lines of "We are pleased to report no incidences of fraud and abuse this year . . . " it needs to add "as far as we are aware" and then reflect on just what it is doing to make itself aware of matters that people work very hard to cover up. Certainly, if an organization is using the internet to stay in business, which is more than likely, ignoring the issue of fraud moves through a spectrum from lack of awareness, through basic ignorance, until it becomes more a question of reckless carelessness. If an organization adopts the stop light model of fraud protection, this trend can be reversed with a move toward a workforce that is alert, determined, and fully protects the organization from betrayal by criminal elements outside and from within.

# CHAPTER 5

---

# The Fraud
# Response Plan

*Diligence is the mother of good luck.*

## THE FRAUD POLICY

We have covered financial crime as a topic and its impact across all types of organizations. Ethics, detection, and the need for proactive action from front-line staff have also been described as key in the fight against fraud. We come now to the organization's need to embed relevant policies regarding the way fraud is handled and responded to if it does arise. It is essential that these things be considered in a calm climate when there are no obvious problems, rather than having people respond to fraud in an ad hoc, unco-ordinated way. An effective fraud policy is a major component in managing the risk of fraud. An ideal position is reached when no internal fraud is found despite all efforts to search for wrongdoing. This, however, is highly unlikely. Nevertheless, there is a second-best position where, having met with a problem, we can handle the situation properly and not make up the rules as we go along. A useful position is to be able to say:

1. We have a clear policy on managing the risk of fraud.
2. Our staff are aware of this policy and have been trained in the way it is applied in the organization.

3. All allegations of fraud are dealt with according to set procedures.
4. We undertake a standardized response to internal and external fraud in a standardized manner.
5. The adopted procedure ensures that we are able to perform a thorough and reliable investigation whenever this is required.
6. Any such investigation will meet all reasonable standards for gathering evidence in a way that protects the rights of all parties, including any suspects.
7. These measures have been formally adopted by our board of directors (or equivalent responsible body).

Anything less than the preceding seven points is not really acceptable. Not only must an antifraud policy and fraud response plan be designed, but they should also be firmly established within the organization. It is not a paper exercise that is done every five years; it is a process of integrating the required standards into the way people work and respond to day-to-day problems. As such, it is a boardroom issue that starts and ends with the direction set by the company directors. It is much better for each organization to design its antifraud policy in a way that suits the business and the way employees actually work. Decentralized organizations will have a different approach from those that have a head office focus; project-based businesses linked mainly by their PC networks will also need something that suits them. Thus, it is not possible to say what the fraud policy for all organizations will look like. An organization will make little real progress if it simply copies a fraud policy from another similar organization. There is nothing wrong with researching what others are doing about fraud, and to what extent standards may cross over between different organizations and business sectors, as long as the final product is designed and therefore owned by management and staff. The benefits from effective fraud management and the role of a suitable policy should be publicized as a further selling point. Reference to the bottom line (such as profits, good business, successful services, and a solid reputation in the marketplace) should anchor the policy in the hearts and minds of the workforce. The reduction of losses from fraud is another key factor that can be used to get the attention of busy managers. Budgets are diminished by dishonesty in such a way that an organization may not even realize that it is funding a fraudster's lifestyle. When describing the potential impact of fraud, it is best to use language that motivates rather than just frightens. Some of the standards that can be included in the fraud policy are outlined in the following.

## Define Fraud

The policy should start with a clear definition of fraud and irregularities. The definition should be simple and cover items such as misappropriation, false accounting, and bribery. Different types of fraud may be outlined, along with the fact that an employer cannot assume that people who work for or do business with the company are necessarily honest. There is probably no need to delve into criminology; it is enough simply to suggest that people can commit fraud while appearing to be solid, law-abiding citizens. Clear boundaries should be established so that it is clear whether the policy covers internal fraud, external fraud, employees' conduct in their private lives, and adherence to overall corporate standards of ethical behavior.

## Define Responsibilities

The chapter on fraud detection contained material on respective roles and responsibilities throughout the organization and its key stakeholders. Using this as a framework, the policy should establish various roles in the context of the overall fraud policy. One feature is the importance of informing third parties that are associated with the organization, such as business associates and partners, of the policies on acceptable behavior.

## Establish Overall Policy

There is little point in having a policy without setting out an overall mission. For fraud, this mission statement should be couched in terms that suit the organization and type of business provided. There may be a number of different aims, such as to:

- Ensure that the risk of fraud is properly understood, assessed, and managed by all employees.
- Ensure that all fraud, whenever possible, is eliminated through proactive detection.
- Aim at zero tolerance for all frauds, both internal and external.
- Ensure that all offenders are discovered, prosecuted, and that all losses are recovered in full.
- Ensure the prevention of fraud through dynamic and robust controls.
- Ensure that the organization is seen as well protected and not vulnerable to abuse.

- Create a stop light model to deal with fraud, through the combined efforts of everyone working for and associated with the organization.

Whatever the adopted format, the mission should be a focused message that gets to all employees and readily translates into everyday work practices. The message can be formal for organizations that want to be seen as serious and responsible, or it can be punchy for businesses in the creative industries. The bottom line is the ability to judge whether policy objectives are being achieved. At times, it depends how far we have gotten in the fight against fraud, in line with a range of strategies shown in Figure 5.1.

An examination of each dimension of this continuum will help clarify the model.

1. **General awareness.**  At this early stage, employees need a basic awareness of fraud, its impact, and how it can be contained. The policy here is focused mainly on the basic awareness stage; if staff become aware of a fraud or wrongdoing, they will simply bring in specialist advisors to handle the fallout and ensuing investigation. The idea is to increase overall awareness of the issues emanating from financial crime.

2. **Good understanding.**  Awareness of fraud has to be translated to a higher level to result in a proper understanding of what is at stake. Awareness is about sending out the documented guidance on fraud-related matters, such as control standards and security. Understanding is more about getting people together and working through these fraud matters. It is about driving home the guidance and giving staff time to work through the importance of being on guard for abuse, deceit, and cover-ups.

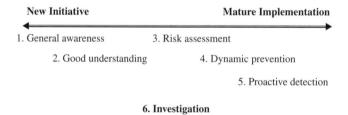

**Figure 5.1**   Implementing the Fraud Policy

3. **Risk assessment.** The next stage is to get people to build fraud into their ongoing assessment of business risks. Fraud guidance starts to get embedded into everyday operations when it enters into the action plans and operational strategies of front-line managers. Policies that aim at getting the message all the way to the shop floor are more ambitious and have considerably more guts than an approach that deals only with the corporate overview.

4. **Dynamic prevention.** Risk assessment is a strong tool for helping to identify obstacles to achieving our goals, whereas controls are really about overcoming these obstacles and promoting success. Controls come in different forms, but the best systems of control aim at prevention. Dynamic prevention is about controls that are risk-based and that flex with changes in the business context as a fluid and ongoing process. If the fraud policy aims at getting tight controls over fraud risks, there is a lot of ground to cover: all employees will be building controls that protect company resources as an inherent part of their work roles.

5. **Proactive detection.** An organization needs to understand fraud, the risks that fraud brings, and how these risks can be tackled. As a final add-on, it should get people to double-check and explore what appear to be good systems and look for inconsistencies. Again, if this attitude drives the fraud policy, the aims of the policy should reflect this somewhat demanding stance.

6. **Investigation.** As a backdrop to the entire policy, an investigation capability should be in place. This may take the form of an in-house team, external specialist, or an expert who can direct the project through whatever resources are secured. The fraud policy should be cross-referenced to the investigation standards and protocols.

## Corporate Interfaces

One reason that corporate policies fail is lack of integration with the rest of the organization. Many a policy floats above the organization without being attached to anything else that is seen as important to setting standards. The fraud policy should be cross-referenced to a number of other issues, including:

- **Operational risk assessment.** There is a need to get the topic of fraud into the risk workshops, which has already been mentioned.

- **Fraud response plan**.   This is dealt with later on. The fraud policy should cover the need to respond properly to allegations as they arise and then refer the reader to the response plan. It is probably wise to say that no employee should get involved in responding to an allegation or suspicion without first referring to the plan. In other words, take no immediate action that may jeopardize the investigation.
- **Investigation standards**.   Standards should be in place for carrying out special investigations, with a separate one for fraud and irregularities. The standards may be comprehensive, or may simply state that external specialists will be used and asked to follow their own professional standards for this type of work.
- **Ethics policy**.   Ethics provides a cornerstone for fighting fraud and breach of standards. In recognition of this, the fraud policy should refer the reader to the associated corporate ethical standards. Moreover, any fraud work should comply with these ethical standards and avoid shortcuts or quesitonable tactics in the conduct of an investigation.
- **Other policies**.   Other corporate policies, such as those addressing human resource issues, performance frameworks, customer service, dealing with associates, personal claims, and so on, should be interfaced with the fraud policy. The key is to examine the entire package of policies together and ensure that they are consistent and make sense. An example may be a conflict between the whistleblowing policy (which may be part of the fraud policy), a standard on confidentiality, and maybe a standard on company loyalty and following instructions from the line manager. All policies must tie into one another so that following one set of standards does not mean breaching another set.

It is necessary to think through the corporate interfaces and links between the fraud policy and other policies relating to staff behavior. There may be other matters, not previously mentioned in this book, that have been documented by the organization that must be taken into account. It really is about making the fraud policy make sense in the context of everything else going on in the organization.

## Prevention, Detection, and Investigation

The fraud policy should say something about prevention, detection, and investigation. Before these three matters can be addressed, a few examples of areas at risk in the organization can be included. Chapter 1 listed some of the typical at-risk aspects of the business, such as cash, payments, contracts, assets, and so on; some of these may be mentioned. There would be a section on detection and establishing the importance of looking for indicators of fraud. Likewise, there would be a section on controls as a means of preventing (and detecting) fraud. Lastly, as already noted, there may be a cross-reference to the standards on conducting special investigations. All these topics are covered in some depth in this book. Policy formulation is really about deciding on the level of detail of the policy document itself and what is best left to support training and awareness workshops. An excessive amount of detail in the policy will lead to an unworkable document that tries to do too much.

## Internal Discipline

One interesting item that can be briefly mentioned in the fraud policy is discipline. Employee fraud necessarily has disciplinary repercussions for those involved, as long as it can be proved that the suspect is implicated. There should be a strong link between the fraud policy and the implications for staff who get involved in dishonest and unacceptable activities. The policy may include something along the lines of: "All employees found to be involved in fraud or irregularities shall be disciplined and dismissed if proven guilty." Ask staff to ensure that they follow the guidance on fraud set out in the policy, as this is the standard required by the organization. In short, the disciplinary part of the policy should make clear what is deemed appropriate and as a result, cover the facts that employees:

- Found to be involved in fraud will be dismissed.
- Conspiring to commit or assist the commission of fraud will be dismissed.
- Interfering with a fraud investigation will be disciplined.
- Should be aware of the indicators of fraud, reporting lines, and the fraud policy.
- Should inform management (or the responsible officer) about any suspicion of fraud or irregularity.
- Need to fully cooperate with any investigations carried out by the organization.
- Should observe the highest standards of confidentiality and never disclose information to people not authorized to receive it.

- Should never interfere with what could be evidence in a fraud investigation. This includes documents, computers, people, assets, and anything else relevant to the investigation.
- Understand the risk of fraud and ensure that there are adequate controls over this risk in their area of responsibility.
- Bring to management's attention any weaknesses in controls that could result in fraud or irregularity.

The actual staff disciplinary procedures will expand on these themes and give precise details of all matters relating to employee conduct and activities. In the fraud policy, employers only need to mention the preceding types of issues and make sure the material is consistent between both documents. Tackling fraud is a positive development in many organizations, although it is not always so perceived. Concentrating on the disciplinary aspects may create a view of the fraud policy as a negative mechanism to control and harass employees. Careful drafting should be used to avoid this problem and ensure that discipline is a fallback rather than a priority, and is put into action only as a last resort. Try to keep the policy lively and upbeat, based on managing a dangerous risk that is not always properly understood.

## Confidentiality

The fraud policy should make clear the need for confidentiality in all matters relating to fraud. Investigations of this nature delve into personal issues, motives, behaviors, and relationships. They uniquely involve many items of potentially great sensitivity. There is potential for slander and great damage to professional reputations. There is potential to spoil evidence and make what could have been good evidence inadmissible in court. There is potential to alert the fraudster and allow this person an opportunity to harass witnesses, conceal evidence, and generally disrupt the progress of the investigation. The reality is that the fraud investigation will eventually go public, or at least be known to all parties implicated. Nevertheless, there are crucial stages during which it is better to keep the work confidential until the time is right. Employees have an important responsibility to observe high standards of confidentiality and understand the importance of keeping things under wraps for as long as necessary. No information should be provided to colleagues, friends, family, associates, customers, or anyone else for that matter, unless there is a legal obligation to do so.

## Reporting

Deciding on reporting lines and who reports to whom, on what, and when, should be agreed beforehand, as it takes time to define protocols. Also, reporting arrangements should not be made up as a specific allegation is dealt with. It is much better to set standards in this respect before the need arises. Again, as has been said before, the final arrangements will have to suit the organization and the way people work together. Some of the issues that could be decided through the process of defining a fraud policy include:

- **Reporting suspicions.** The whistleblowing standard will cover this aspect of fraud management. The fraud policy should just remind staff that they must report all suspicions.
- **Detection sweeps.** Work through who gets the reports on detection routines and how the reports are dealt with by the organization. Detection searches tend to collect a lot of suspect items that must be checked out. Personal data appearing on these reports could cause great embarrassment if released to the wrong person or made public.
- **Reporting.** This includes the initial report on the problem and further ongoing reports as the investigation progresses. Again, the lines must be carefully drawn up to ensure that the right people are involved in making decisions as evidence emerges and starts to build into a picture of what is really happening.
- **External parties.** Reports to external parties, such as the police, federal and state law enforcement agencies, the press and other media, attorneys, and union representatives, have to be carefully prepared and presented. Only authorized persons should have contact with any of these parties, and the criteria for becoming authorized should be determined at the outset.

Much has to be decided on in terms of reporting arrangements and contacts. A great deal of this will be found in the standard on investigations, but it should also be alluded to in the policy document. Staff need to know who to report frauds to and, if they get involved in making inquiries, or are asked questions by outsiders, they need to know how to respond. In most cases it will be about redirecting the inquirer to the right party.

There have been cases in which legal representatives for the defense have directed phone inquiries to various members of an organization and used the inconsistent replies to strengthen their counterclaims against the employer. It helps if people know in advance who they can talk to.

Finally, a fraud reporting process may be installed, covering statistics on fraud cases, allegations, investigations, and results. These reports may be compiled by the compliance officer and go to the audit committee or other appropriate forum.

# THE FRAUD RESPONSE PLAN

We move now into a more difficult part of fraud management, that of responding to live allegations, suspicions, doubts, and concerns. The fraud policy is hypothetical in that it talks about preventing fraud and being on guard against abuse that may be concealed. A philosophy of zero tolerance and quick prosecutions may also be in place, but this is dependent on being alert and understanding the risk of fraud. Response plans are separate but linked to the general policy. The plan will be less general and more like a procedure for dealing with any concerns that could possibly turn into a real-life fraud. In many fraud cases, the initial suspicions do not reach the fundamental and significant abuse that is going on below the tip of the iceberg. Dishonest people motivated by an overwhelming desire for more and more material possessions will exploit any opportunity to the greatest extent, constrained only by the need to conceal their activities. If the response to an allegation or suspicion of fraud is inadequate, many powerful predicaments could result, which could in the extreme assist the fraudster in getting away with the crime. Problems arise because of the following possible indiscretions:

- An overenthusiastic employee may confront the suspect and cause the individual to sue the company for false accusation and even false arrest.
- An employee may investigate the alleged fraud and inadvertently breach the corporate procedures on conducting such investigations. A test of good investigations is whether they are in line with set procedures and, overall, are reasonable and fair. Breaking the company's rules is not the best way to start an investigation.
- The chain of evidence may be broken. Documents, computer trails, and physical items such as checks and invoices may have to be traced back to the suspect to ensure the success of the investigation. When

an inexperienced person (or someone not properly briefed) handles or accesses the evidence, the chain that indisputably links the evidence to the suspect may be broken. For example, if forensic documents are handled and placed in plastic wallets, any fingerprints may be affected by the chemicals in the plastic. The evidence may thus become inadmissible because direct links cannot be clearly established.

- The suspect may be alerted to the fact that the crime has been uncovered. This provides an opportunity to cover up evidence, concoct alibis, interfere with witnesses, or stop the activity in question. In extreme cases, all the evidence, particularly documentation, can be destroyed. Some fraud investigations are based on live evidence of the offense as it happens, so anything that stops the fraud in mid-track can lead to the transaction being unfulfilled. For example, if someone is stealing company checks and paying them into a bank account specially set up for the crime, the activity may be tracked via a specially set-up transaction. In this instance, the transaction has to be completed to prove the theft and conversion.
- The suspect may be given a promise that he or she will not be prosecuted. In fact, it may not be appropriate to make such representations, which could bind the company and blur the line between who is right and who is at fault.
- Irretrievable mistakes could be made at the start of the investigation. Witnesses may end up writing poorly constructed statements. Computers may be booted up and alter the data that should have been used to support the investigation and any resulting charges. In extreme cases, the fraud may be covered up by managers who feel it would be an embarrassment to have loopholes publicized. In this situation the response to fraud will be that if found, the perpetrator simply resigns, taking the funds that have been misappropriated. In some cases the fraudster does not even have to leave.
- Insurance claims for employee fidelity cover may become void if losses caused by the fraud are compounded by the actions of company representatives or their failure to act in accordance with agreed procedures. Claims against banks for paying forged checks have to be made within set time limits, and a verified schedule of losses has to be prepared to support any claims.
- Cases that should properly be put before the police may be held back and cause problems if referred too late to the authorities. It is

difficult to get the police to act on old cases where the evidence is stale, and the cost of prosecution has to be balanced against the value in bringing an old case to court.

- The constitutional rights of the suspect may be infringed. The rights to silence, to a speedy trial, to not be harassed, to provide an explanation on being confronted with the evidence, and other basic rights may not be observed by someone who has not been trained in handling such cases. The company may not only lose the opportunity to support a prosecution against the culprit, but may also lay itself open to a counterclaim in court if too many mistakes are made at an early stage in the proceedings.

- The workforce may feel humiliated and demotivated if people are implicated by association. When the response is unfocussed and unduly aggressive, the fallout can be catastrophic. Accusations may be thrown around the office, and a feeling of mistrust and fear could result from a mishandled inquiry that could take months to put right. Untrained managers who take on serious fraud cases tend either to underreact and try to get the problem to disappear, or overreact and assume that everyone is guilty.

A lot could go wrong if the initial response to an allegation is poor. This is why standards are so important, along with clear roles and proper communication among all parties involved. The issues covered by a good fraud response plan include the following, among other things.

## Importance of Proper Initial Response

Make clear the need to respond carefully to all allegations. The organization may be fined if it fails to behave in an acceptable manner. Management needs to act with due diligence in tackling employee fraud and to take effective steps to prevent further losses. Major problems will result if there is any suspicion of obstruction of justice or any failure to follow through on initial suspicions. All employees represent the organization in the way they handle wrongdoing, and this is one of the few occasions when an employee's response may well be scrutinized by authorities outside the organization. If an organization fails to discipline directors, officers, employees, or agents who are engaged in criminal activity, it becomes culpable. Much should be based around a sound compliance program. All employees should be aware of the fraud response plan, although they will not necessarily deal with the fraud themselves. Fraud should be handled in line with set procedures, which basically means reporting it to the right party in the most appropriate manner. The complicated nature of financial crime would be mentioned in the fraud response plan. The perpetrators typically stay one step ahead of the investigators, as they alone understand the scam and the way it is obscured from outsiders. As the investigators probe, the confident fraudster moves things around. It is like a stage play where one actor (the fraudster) knows the plot, the story line, and the props, while the other actor (the victim/investigator) stumbles onto the stage without any knowledge of the script. The person who first comes across the fraud needs to stand back from the scene and report exactly what was witnessed. All organizations experience employee fraud at some time and if they handle it well, they could come out looking effective and solid. If they handle it badly, the company's share price and its reputation could suffer tremendously.

## The Fraud Policy

The fraud response plan should make clear the adopted fraud policy. So, for example, a line in the plan may state that all allegations of fraud should be reported immediately, as it is policy to prosecute all crimes against the organization, without exception. The policy could also state that all crimes will be reported to the police department, again without exception. Sweeping the matter under the carpet leaves the fraudster free to go on and commit the same crime against a new employer. If a clean reference is provided for the suspected fraudster, the company could be liable for misrepresentation and be sued by the new employer.

## Notifications

Reporting arrangements should be detailed in the fraud response plan. Several points can be made as to the initial notification of alleged suspicions of employee fraud:

- The CEO needs to adopt an overview in the matter of employee fraud and should be notified as soon as possible.
- In turn, the CEO will have to decide whether the shareholders should be notified. This tends to occur when the investigation is completed and there is compelling evidence of a serious crime. Likewise, the audit committee may need to be apprised as the work progresses.

- The person who first believes there is evidence (or information) that a crime against the company has been perpetrated has a responsibility to notify the appropriate party. The fraud response plan must contain clear information on who should be notified. It may be the chief internal auditor, compliance officer, security manager, chief fraud advisor, chief finance officer (or nominated person), head of personnel, someone reporting to the CEO, or whoever the organization feels is the right person to start the investigation.
- It may be the policy to appoint an attorney right away if the allegation is relatively serious. The attorney will have client privilege and is a key part of the legal process. If this matter is worked out beforehand, the reporting line will be clearly understood so as to avoid wasting time.
- The response to serious employee fraud may be to establish a fraud panel consisting of key players who would be able to make competent decisions regarding the pace and direction of any ensuing investigation. Skilled people from personnel, legal, and audit, together with the compliance officer, may form a panel to oversee the detailed response and follow-up.
- In turn, a team of investigators may be appointed to carry out further detection, surveillance, and investigation work. Professional investigators are trained to gather and evaluate evidence and not judge the guilt of the suspect(s), which is the job of the courts. It is this calm, collected approach, with no emotional attachment, that makes for a good investigation, which is why managers in the area affected by the fraud should not try undertake their own investigations. Specialist investigators are trained in evidential requirements for criminal cases and how to gather evidence in such a way as not to jeopardize or contaminate the case.
- There should be one point of contact between the organization and the police department in the location where the alleged crime was committed. The fraud panel will agree on this process and monitor events and assist the police in their inquiries. The investigation of external fraud against the company depends mainly on the efforts of law enforcement agencies, unless it is a specialist area such as food stamp fraud or irregular insurance claims, where the organization may have a team of in-house investigators to call on. The police would like to be given a profile of motive and opportunity to help them understand the case and the evidence that is readily available.

They may also ask the district attorney for a search warrant to access relevant material.

- External reporting is a very sensitive issue. The external auditors may have to be advised when the fraud affects the final accounts and makes them unreliable.
- The local press may be given a release on the events and how the problem is being dealt with. The press office is important in handling media relationships, which could make the difference between maintaining a good reputation for the company and a public relations disaster. Addressing issues of employee fraud in a firm but fair way could enhance the standing of the company, if done well. The press will get information somehow—if not through the company, then from rumor and gossip. All press releases should be cleared by the fraud panel and the organization's attorney.
- The organization's insurers and any other parties against whom a claim might be filed, such as company bankers, should be properly notified. *Properly* means in accordance with the set procedures agreed under any contractual arrangements. Claims against company bankers will have to be made within a set time period, normally a year. Any forged checks that have to be frozen must be notified to the bank by meeting the bank's evidential requirements for not paying a check.

## Informing Staff

The response to an allegation of employee fraud may be to suspend the person in question and launch a formal investigation into the substance of the allegation. In this scenario, suspension must be handled very carefully, to ensure the due progress of the investigation and to be fair to all sides. This type of investigation is quite public and employee relations will have to be handled with some delicacy. The line manager for the area in question would need to confer with the fraud panel and company attorney to design a statement and method of informing staff about the investigation. The information should reinforce the objectivity of the investigation and the lack of assumption of guilt, and should be provided on a "need to know" basis. The fraud response should make clear the "scene of the crime" where there will be certain books, records, material, and representations that will have to be preserved, protected, and then made available to the investigating officers. The suspended employee is assisting in the investigation and is not a criminal awaiting prosecution and internal discipline. However, the fact that no communication should be had with the suspended person unless cleared by the organization also must be conveyed, but in a way that does not impair the reputation of the employee in question—not an easy task. The fraud response plan should make it clear that no other discussion should take place regarding the inquiries and that anyone found using what is now deemed classified material is in breach of the disciplinary code. This is what being firm but fair is all about: being able to balance things in a way that makes sense and is defensible. It is a different matter when the investigation is not public but is based on discreet research into the activities of the suspected fraudster. The need-to-know principle becomes paramount when any leaks could undermine the integrity of any inquiries and restrict the type of evidence that may be available. In this context, unauthorized disclosure of confidential information becomes a much more serious issue.

## Simple Error

One component of the fraud response plan is the need to show intent in any investigation into fraud. The plan should mandate that all steps should be taken to ensure that the allegation is not the result of a distorted interpretation, innocent mistake, or basic error. Management should search for an innocuous explanation of the irregularity. For example, if an employee has been paid twice for a claim for overseas travel, the first step is to make sure this is not just an error in the system or a misunderstanding that does not attach blame to anyone. There is no point suspending everyone in sight who had anything to do with authorizing or processing this odd payment. An overenthusiastic response may offend many staff members and possibly lead to civil action against the company. Being on the lookout for fraud does not mean assuming that anything that goes wrong is the result of a grand conspiracy. Some say that fraud is what's left over when all other explanations have been exhausted. But do remember that the experienced fraudster may have a selection of innocent explanations at hand. Perhaps a better picture to paint is that fraud is what is left over when all reasonable explanations have been judiciously checked out and exhausted.

## Confronting the Suspect

This aspect of fraud response can cause many problems. The empowered manager is used to dealing with all aspects of people management and has a role in recruiting staff, dealing with their orientation, and motivating them to achieve set targets. A lot is done through close teamwork, where close interdependencies are developed so that team members fit nicely into an efficient unit. These interdependencies are based on mutual trust and cooperation, and may even involve a degree of socializing during nonoffice hours. When the team relationship is threatened by an allegation against one of the team, the manager is tempted to swing into action and deal with the problem. It may be by issuing a warning, or by being firm and removing this person from the team and perhaps the company. Each of these options has hidden dangers. Representations, promises, forgiveness, instant dismissals, and requests to make good the losses are all knee-jerk responses that do not fit with standards that should be set out in a comprehensive fraud response plan. In other words, the empowerment concept should be put to one side when an offense has been alleged, so that the suspect is not confronted at the outset. We all have a constitutional right to confront our accusers, and this means viewing the evidence against us and being able to offer an explanation and defense. But this comes later on when the evidence has been compiled and all the facts understood and documented. At the initial stage, the fraud response policy should ask everyone to observe a number of standards. For example:

- Do not confront the suspects or indicate that an allegation has been made against them. Stay calm, make a full record of the allegation, and keep the record secure at all times. An unfounded accusation may result in a claim for defamation against the organization, particularly if the accusation is made in public and turns out to be wrong.
- Do not do anything to arouse the suspicions of anyone, including the suspect. It is never clear at the outset whether an allegation is well founded and whether others are implicated, directly or indirectly, in fraudulent activities.
- Think through any evidence that is under the control of the suspect and may be in danger of being interfered with or damaged, if not protected. Take any reasonable steps to safeguard the evidence, again without alerting the suspect. For example, if the allegation is that a purchasing clerk has been forging company orders, it may be possible to hold onto the file, as long as this is reasonable and will not make the suspect suspicious.
- Do not touch anything that can be deemed the personal property of the suspect, even if this property is in the office at the time the

allegation is made. If the allegation is that the employee is running a private business at work, using company computers and other resources, the company still has no legal powers to go through the employee's jacket and personal bags looking for a floppy disk. If the allegation is that the employee comes into work most weekends to run a private business, evidence of this person's presence at work on weekends, including attendance records, phone logs, and overtime claims, can be considered.

There is much that can be done before the fraud becomes common knowledge. In more serious cases, an investigation may be a race against time, as investigators try to get a good picture of what is happening before the knowledge goes public. There may be a frantic race to freeze the assets of the suspect before they get moved beyond the company's jurisdiction. The person who first receives the allegation can assist at this stage if no mistakes are made. A standard that simply says, "Do not touch anything, or say anything—just notify the responsible officer immediately," is a good start to a professional investigation.

## Quick Controls

A fraud response plan that essentially says "do nothing" has little real impact on managers who have misbehaving employees on their team. Although the hands-off approach is important in ensuring that the evidential chain can be established and developed properly, there are aspects of fraud response that come closer to the general manager's responsibilities. One such aspect relates to controls that have to be strengthened. There is a long and a short view. Both of these views are based on the premise that employee fraud happens because people are tempted into deceit and there are weaknesses in company systems that can be exploited. So, when a fraud occurs, what was an unknown risk becomes a real-life occurrence that must be addressed. The long view suggests that risk workshops should prioritize fraud in future, so that staff will be able to devise better techniques for fraud prevention. The short view is a little different, in that it asks management to consider stopping the fraud immediately. Employees have a fiduciary duty to protect the company and its resources; as soon as they become aware of an ongoing, or attempted, abuse of these resources, quick controls should be put in place at once. If a contractor is inflating bills fraudulently, a vetting procedure should be installed whereby all invoices against these types of contracts are verified before payment. When a problem comes to light, steps must be taken to minimize the overall impact. Meanwhile, the matter should be reported and thoroughly investigated.

## Crisis Management

Building on the idea of quick controls, there is the wider issue of damage limitation to be addressed. Crisis management is about putting contingency plans in place before a crisis so that a set plan of sensible action can be exercised. This not only saves time but also draws on thinking and planning that has been undertaken in a period of calm, when everyone is in place to add their views and expertise. For a significant crime against the organization, the fraud response plan will swing into action, and if effective will ensure that the crisis simply becomes a situation addressed by the contingency plans, rather than a nightmare. For example, if a fraud by a contractor arises, there should be provisions for dealing with conflicts with contractors, perhaps sending the problem to arbitration. Moreover, the fraud response plan should refer to contingency arrangements under which certain services, or people, are suspended while an investigation is initiated. In contract fraud, a consultant may have to be employed to act as an independent expert witness, if the case comes to trial in the future. Losses from frauds against the company will have to be recovered, and it is a good idea to think about this right at the start of the investigation. Restitution can be ordered at sentencing, if the case gets to court, so a schedule of losses should be compiled at an early stage to support any such claim. Crisis management procedures may have several set objectives based on maintaining the business against all the chaos and confusion that may arise if a significant fraud occurs.

## Fidelity Insurance

We have referred to insurance coverage for employee fraud. This insurance pays when the fraud causes the employer a loss and the employee in question achieves some kind of benefit. The fraud response plan will make clear who deals with the insurance claim; it may be someone from the legal team who will ensure that the policy does not become invalidated through negligence or basic mistakes. Although the insurer will tend not to get involved in the investigation itself, it will want the work done properly and may ask for proof of loss in a claim to be filed within set time limits (for example, 120 days). The insurer will also seek further information as the case progresses. It may acquire the rights of the insured and possibly sue the culprit at a later stage.

## Preserving Evidence

The fraud response plan could contain an outline of the importance of evidence and advice on preserving all material findings.

> In one fraud case, a husband started a fire to hide a fraud that was committed by his wife at her workplace.

In desperate times people will take desperate measures, particularly if the end result of a prosecution is restitution and imprisonment. A list of do's and don'ts may be used to highlight the types of measures that are important here.

> In another case involving the unauthorized removal of laptops, the investigation was hampered because the videos used by the closed-circuit TV system were being recorded over, and no reliable record was available on the movements of people around the offices during the day and evening in question.

A reconciliation that indicates funds are missing or cannot be accounted for may be used as evidence of a crime, and again the record of this reconciliation has to be preserved properly. In fraud investigations, everything relevant to the case becomes evidence, and this basic fact must be understood by all who come into contact with the evidence.

## Systems Profiles

Managers, supervisors, and team leaders become directly involved in profiling the system that has been abused. If an allegation comes to the attention of a manager, the right response is to report this to the appropriate party as directed by the fraud response plan. The problem is that the investigation team will be outside of the system that has been subject to the fraud or attempted fraud. It is much more helpful to provide some relevant information in conjunction with the reported allegation, in particular about the systems and procedures in question. This may be called *systems profiling,* where an account of the at-risk system is provided in a way that can be readily understood by anyone unfamiliar with the system.

For example, a finance manager receives an allegation that an accounts clerk is adding an extra $500 to all large expense claims and inserting forged vouchers to account for the extra item. This fraud may be hard to decipher. The finance manager responsible for the accounts clerk will, of course, report the matter to the right person—say, the head of an in-house fraud team. But it would help if the same manager were to prepare a brief record of the system for making expense claims and the role of the accounts clerk in this system. The systems profile in this case would record the movement of documents, the various authorizations required, and checks made on supporting documentation.

The profile may be in the form of a series of block diagrams, or a descriptive narrative with reference to any standard documents used in the process. In time, the note may become an official record attached to a formal statement by the finance manager, if the case is taken further and goes to court or an internal disciplinary group. In addition to the systems profile, other material may also be useful, such as an organization chart with an outline of each person on the team and their respective roles, or copies of any procedures manuals. The latter may also be used by the investigation team to work through the fraud and learn how it is being perpetrated. In terms of initial response, it may only be necessary to provide a brief description of the system in question, to help the investigators understand the nature of the fraud.

## Interviews

The fraud response plan may include a note on interviewing. At an early stage of an investigation, there may be a need to carry out initial interviews with potential witnesses and get some background to the problem. These interviews are best done by persons trained in investigative techniques, to ensure that they are carried out in accordance with best judicial practice. The response plan should ask that managers do not interview anyone to gather background information after receipt of an allegation of fraud. However, if an informant makes a personal appearance and wishes to give an account of the fraud, this person should be interviewed to find out as much as possible about the fraud and who is involved. Questioning should be done in private and an attempt made to discover:

- The identity of the information.
- The precise allegation.

- Whether anyone else has been told about this problem.
- How the fraud is happening and for how long.
- The extent of any losses involved and whether these are ongoing.
- Whether any other persons are involved, either directly or just that they also have knowledge of the fraud.
- Whether there are any documents and files that would reveal the extent of the fraud.
- Whether the person is prepared to make a formal statement in this matter.
- Whether there is anything else that might assist an investigation into the allegations.

The person receiving information of employee fraud may make a few discreet inquiries that do not impair the investigation or alert the suspect.

Someone calls the chief accountant and says, "John in payroll is processing false employees he made up last month and is banking the checks!" Following this, the chief accountant may check to see if there is a John working in payroll and whether any new names have been added to the payroll in the last month, before passing the information over to the responsible persons.

As we mentioned earlier regarding systems profiling, the chief accountant may also prepare a short note on the procedure for placing people on the payroll. There are things that can be done at an early stage of an inquiry and common sense will help direct people to these, with a little help from the fraud response plan.

## IT Sites

Fraud involving the use of a computer system is big business. It is a growth area directly in line with the growing dependency on computerized applications in business and the public sector. In the past it has been a fairly straightforward task to convince a jury that someone entered, or altered, data onto their personal computer during the commission of a fraud. A printout of the record in question and a confirming statement from the computer department was all that was required to have the printout admitted as evidence. Times have changed: A good defense team will kick unverified computer printouts right out of court, if there is any doubt at all as to the veracity of the evidential chain. This is probably where the fraud response plan has the most effect, in getting people to understand the sensitivity of computer-generated information. Suppose that the claim is that a senior loan manager is granting loans to his friends that otherwise would never have been accepted by the company and ensuring that they are subsequently written off, for a 50 percent fee. This allegation must be addressed. The loan manager may have a office PC where all the relevant data on loans granted and processed is stored on the hard disk, along with a great deal of potentially incriminating evidence that could be used to track the loans and bribes paid. Having been advised about the fraud by a friend who turned informer, the first reaction may be to turn on the PC and have a good look at the data in question, then maybe copy certain files, perhaps to a floppy disk, and look for any disks in the jacket pocket of the suspect loan manager. The loan manager's car trunk may be flipped open and the car interior searched for anything that can be used to establish the fraud. The desire to get hold of the evidence may be so strong that professional investigators are brought in only at a much later date to pick up the pieces. This type of situation would be disastrous. The fraud response plan has to take care of any foul-ups relating to the computerized environment. A good response plan may contain material along the following lines:

- Treat the PC workstation of the person against whom the allegation has been made as a "scene of the crime."
- Talk to people near the workstation and make a record of physical movements near or at the workstation. Formal statements can be taken later on.
- Do not touch anything or turn anything on. Secure the area, by 24-hour security if required. If the computer is switched on, the evidential trail will end with the last person who activated the machine, and it may be difficult to prove the integrity of data held on the PC.
- The IT forensic auditor will have to be called in to assist in these types of cases.
- Photograph all PCs and peripherals and mark which cables go to which machines.
- Ensure all fingerprints are checked at a later stage.
- Remove the hard disk and copy it using suitable data imaging techniques. Also, mirror-copy all floppy disks found at the workstation.
- Using the copy hard disk, undelete all deleted files and look for clusters of data from overwritten files and apply other software tests until all available information is retrieved.

- Get access logs from the systems administrator; look at Internet activity and any cookies and zip files left on the systems. Information on the server backup will also have to be extracted and analyzed.
- Demonstrate that the chain of evidence is intact and that all data has been stored and protected such that it cannot be interfered with at all. The success of the case may rest on this single factor.

There is a lot to remember, but the basic problem relates to being over-enthusiastic in getting evidence from the PC. If the PC is viewed as the dead person in a murder inquiry, it is possible to visualize all the activity that goes on around the body before it can be removed. Visualize the experts, photographers, sketches, fingerprint tests, and fingertip searches and questioning of people nearby, for an idea of the parallel situation that computerized records present. Some argue that the vast majority of real frauds (i.e., removal of value and then careful concealment) will be computer-related in the future. There is also a growing sophistication of criminals, who see automated systems as facilitators of fraud and who know that simply destroying the data, if it gets too hot, may foil any chance of prosecution. The battleground in the fight between fraudsters and targeted organizations is firmly set in virtual reality, where the key concern is the state of the chain of evidence.

## CONCLUSION—DRIVING HOME THE FRAUD POLICY

The fraud policy and fraud response plan have been addressed in terms of their content and coverage. When an organization has spent a great deal of time preparing a policy document that covers the subject in great detail, and has also arrived at a comprehensive procedure for responding to any frauds that come up, it has made a good start. What then has to happen is for everyone in the organization to understand the policy and how it affects them. If someone turns up at a remote office and reports a major fraud, the person receiving this information needs to know how to respond on the spot. There may be no time to double-check the guidance and make phone calls to security and audit, if an immediate response is called for. When a manager spots something odd on a computer screen used by a member of staff, effective action may be required at that instant. Herein lies the importance of getting staff to understand and use the fraud policy. This is also true for the material on fraud prevention: Front-line staff can represent the best guard against fraud, so long as they are alert and inspired to act. This calls for a level of awareness over and above just sending the policy around on the e-mail system. As a start, measure the level of understanding of the fraud policy around the organization. A simple exercise is to send out a short questionnaire to all staff that asks them to indicate the extent to which they know and understand the organization's position on fraud prevention, detection, and investigation. Some of the areas covered in such a questionnaire may include the following:

1. Are you aware of the corporate fraud policy?
2. Are you aware of the corporate fraud response plan?
3. Could you access these documents readily?
4. Are you clear about your responsibilities with respect to fraud prevention, detection, and response?
5. Would you know how to react if you received an allegation of fraud? Describe what you would do.
6. Would you know how to react if you suspected that a member of staff was involved in a fraud? Describe what you would do.
7. Are you aware of the aspects of your business that are at risk of fraud?
8. What steps do you take to manage the risk of fraud?
9. Does your staff have a good understanding of fraud and the corporate fraud policy?
10. Can you suggest any steps that can be taken to ensure that the fraud policy is properly understood throughout the organization?

A Likert scale that gives a range of responses, from "None at all" to "A lot," or "Never to Always," can be used for some of the questions. It is best to pilot-test the questionnaire in parts of the organization first. A small buzz group can also help here to provide feedback to the questionnaire designers. Once the questionnaire is finalized, the idea of taking time out to answer the questions has to be sold to staff before it can be sent out. It may be a good idea to send it to all senior managers for them to pass it on to their staff. Check through the resultant returns and follow up any inconsistent information to ensure the results are reliable.

The returns can then be analyzed. The bottom line will be a statistical view of awareness and understanding across the organization by grade and section, which will provide a picture of how well the fraud policy has been implemented. The exercise can be repeated annually; as a follow-up, targets can be set to increase the level of understanding in parts of the organization that do not score well. When there are particular problems indicating that the policy has not reached certain sections and teams, various development initiatives, such as workshops, seminars, and targeted circulars, may help reinforce the message that the risk of fraud has to be realized and addressed by all. It is also possible to set performance targets based around increasing awareness among staff. Look for returns that display a poor appreciation of controls for combating fraud and consider whether to commission independent reviews in these parts of the organization, by internal audit or the compliance officer. Summary reports based on the returns can be presented to the audit committee on an annual basis, or more often if the questionnaires are sent out more frequently than once a year.

If the CEO wishes to drive home the antifraud message, there must be a way of assessing whether the message is getting across. There must also be a mechanism for responding to suggestions that more should be done. The best way to ensure effective measurement, review, and action is to get a responsible person in a post such as chief fraud advisor. The act of making a person responsible for coordination and monitoring of all aspects of fraud management allows a better chance of success. Without this single point of reference, the various models of detection, investigation, reporting, and discipline become disparate and maybe even inconsistent. Chief fraud advisor may be a role that would suit the compliance officer, as long as it is strategic in nature and looks at the big picture in involving everyone in the fight against fraud. We go further and argue that a fraud advisor should be appointed in each department, again under the overall direction of the chief fraud advisor or compliance officer. The fraud advisors need not be dedicated positions, but simply someone in each section who is given this responsibility for that designated part of the organization. Fraud management is a policy issue, but should result in a proactive battle in line with a set of carefully prepared standards. It is also about having the right culture in place and a vision of the future so that problems can be anticipated and tackled. A sense of direction and coordination is essential in this kind of environment, as is the ability to measure and judge progress so that those at the top can tell if fraud risks are being addressed intelligently.

# CHAPTER 6

# Investigations

*A cat in gloves catches no mice.*

## INVESTIGATION STANDARDS

We now arrive at the investigation into an alleged fraud. Having discussed the whole spectrum of fraud awareness and the need to detect and respond properly to allegations of misconduct, we need to deal with the actual process of launching and managing a formal investigation. Fraud investigations are primarily about gathering, documenting, assessing, and presenting evidence relevant to the allegation in hand. Therefore, we will discuss the objectives of an investigation, methodologies, interviewing, evidence, and reporting of results. The starting place, however, is to consider standards for conducting fraud investigations. Each organization that commissions an investigation into fraud should ensure that the investigation is carried out in line with set standards, ideally documented in an investigation procedures manual. The work can be undertaken by external consultants or an in-house team. If outsiders are used, they must be contracted to perform the work in accordance with professional standards. If reliance is placed on an in-house team, they should apply the procedures manual for this type of work. In turn, the applied standards have to be monitored so the organization is happy to stand by the results. Fraud work is one of the few services that may be examined in detail by external parties, and it may be examined in a way that seeks to undermine the reliability of the work. The work is unique in that there is likely to be an adversarial response to the results of the investigation. It is the duty of defense counsel to challenge the findings of the investigators and probe all possible gaps, inconsistencies, and questionable items. In contrast, it is the duty of the investigators to be sure of their ground, because their findings may affect someone's career, finances, and liberty. In terms of standards, all fraud investigators need to:

- Base their work around accepted best practice, which is updated to reflect this point.
- Promote due care in the way evidence is gathered and deemed to be admissible.
- Ensure that documentation is properly secured, protected, and indexed and that there is a firm audit trail in place.
- Ensure that the rights of all employees are understood and observed at all times.
- Realize that the burden of proof rests firmly with the employer/ prosecutor in terms of staff disciplinary/criminal cases respectively. The burden of proof for criminal cases is beyond a reasonable doubt; for civil cases, it is the preponderance of the evidence.
- Capture the essence of the investigation and meet all time-critical targets.
- Cover all key aspects of investigations work, including planning, evidence gathering, interviewing, third-party contacts, confidentiality, observing protocols, documentation and recordkeeping, police involvement, legal obligations, supervision of the work, and reporting requirements.

In this way, the set procedures should help guide and direct the way frauds are investigated and the ways in which investigators are trained, developed, and encouraged to meet professional standards. Standardized formats for records, such as interview forms, witness statements, surveillance records, employee profiles, and so on, can also be designed and used to ensure that these standards are met.

# KEY OBJECTIVES

Before launching into a major investigation, it is best to work through the objectives of the project. Bringing in teams of specialist people and making provisions for security, detailed document control, and even storage of physical evidence create a major commitment for the organization. It also sets into motion a train of events that may hurtle out of control and perhaps end in costly lawsuits, if not handled adequately. In short, ensure that a clear objective is framed for the investigation, while realizing that objectives will vary according to the organization and type of inquiry in hand. It is true that all frauds are different. They involve different types of people and different situations. In one case, an opportunist spots a gap in the system and leaps in quickly, with perhaps only a crude attempt at concealment. Other frauds are much more sophisticated, when someone has studied the system, gained a degree of trust that is abused, and hides the fraud from view. The fraud may be perpetuated by an entire organization; for example, when damaged goods are sold to an unsuspecting public. We spent a great deal of time discussing this issue in Chapter 1, noting that the variety and scope of both internal and external frauds being carried out is staggering. Notwithstanding this, there are still possible objectives that can be set out as a checklist when starting an investigation. The objective may be to:

1. Discharge management's fiduciary duty to protect organizational resources. This overriding objective relates to the legal obligation of management to look after the business on behalf of the owners. It is difficult to defend a position that ignores or simply tolerates employee fraud when that fraud has an impact on the business.
2. Examine, gather, and assess sufficient and relevant evidence. Many see investigations as simply a process of gathering evidence. The focus is on establishing the rules of evidence and ensuring that these rules are observed and that the right evidence is secured. This approach brings in the concept of forensic evidence—that is, material that will stand up in court—and therefore the need to apply proper expertise to the task.
3. Protect the reputation of employees by determining who is innocent. Investigations into employee fraud can be very disruptive and damage the team spirit that binds the workforce together. When

there is no obvious suspect, all employees in the area in which the fraud occurred may fall under suspicion. A good technique is to present the investigation as a way of protecting people who might initially be tainted by the allegations. In this way the investigators seek to gain cooperation from all who may be able to provide relevant information.

> In one investigation about a missing cash bag at a cash collection site, the cashiers were encouraged to cooperate with the investigators as a way of finding out who had impaired the reputation of all the cashiers. The idea was to prove who was innocent rather than who was guilty. A bonus is that after the innocent people are ruled out, attention can be focused on any suspects.

4. Find and secure all records relevant to the investigation. A great deal of evidence in financial crime work comes from documents that link the crime to a person. If a large amount of paperwork has been used to conceal the fraud, or if the fraud itself can be isolated through the documents available, the investigation may focus on making sure that records are kept intact. The main objective may be to get hold of the appropriate papers before they disappear or are destroyed. This type of investigation involves securing the work area and analyzing large quantities of paperwork. Much of the work may be fairly unskilled, like classifying and filing papers or perhaps linking various documents to associated records and looking for inconsistencies.

5. Find and recover all losses from misappropriation. When large amounts of funds have been diverted, the main theme of the work may be chasing the funds. One view of fraud work holds that if there are no real clues as to who committed the crime, the audit trail for the missing funds should be tracked to discover the truth. The work also involves freezing assets, obtaining search warrants, and involving law enforcement and company attorneys to obtain a legal claim to the missing funds. Meanwhile, the investigators will be concerned with compiling a schedule of losses to support an order for restitution during any resulting prosecution.

6. Ensure that all persons, including the suspect, understand the terms of reference of the investigation and are willing to cooperate. This type of investigation is best done as a public inquiry, where a formal panel of respected people from the organization is set up to hear any forthcoming evidence about the fraud. This approach tends to

be useful for widespread corruption cases in which covert inquiries have been exhausted and help is sought from all those who have an idea of what is going on. Far-ranging, in-depth inquiry into endemic problems tends to benefit from the open inquiry process.

7. Make sure the perpetrator pays for the crime. There are two versions of this approach. One is to label the offender by going for full prosecution whatever the cost, even for smaller offenses. The idea is to put the person out of circulation and warn the public that he or she has committed a crime and has been duly convicted (a zero tolerance policy). The other version is to get the culprit to pay back the funds involved and then resign. The latter is a way of sweeping the matter under the carpet, but is defensible on the basis that any monies lost have been paid back. The investigation here concentrates on negotiations around respective positions.

8. Get rid of all employees who commit crimes against the organization. Like the previous objective, the main aim of the work may simply be to get rid of a bad apple. The approach here is to compile a huge file of evidence and scare the alleged offender into disappearing under the weight of this evidence. The contrasting approach is to ensure that the evidence is carefully presented so that a disciplinary case may be brought against the person in question. This takes precedence over any criminal case.

> In one fraud case, three senior managers were dismissed because of their systematic misappropriation of valuable assets. The police case proved more difficult and in the end floundered. Years later, when the police officer involved in the case was asked about the lack of success in bringing a criminal prosecution, he pointed to the fact that the company had been able to get rid of the crooked managers, noting that this in itself constituted a success.

Taking a pro-organizational stance, it could be argued that the most important thing is to ensure that the employer parts company with fraudsters, even if the case does not come to court.

9. Ensure that the organization suffers no further depletion of its resources. Fraud causes a loss to the organization and at times there is little that can be done to recover losses or identify the offender. One approach is to frame the investigation around the need to stop further losses and close all known loopholes. The work is centered around new procedures that must be quickly put in place and

arrangements for enhanced security. "Smash and grab" cases, where the crime is not concealed and the perpetrator is either not obvious or has disappeared, call for a quick response. This is based on righting the weaknesses in controls that led to the fraud in the first place.

10. Decide how to progress the investigation and whether to limit or widen the scope of work. Some fraud investigations are tentative in nature. They are designed to look into a problem (for example, larger than average levels of inventory wastage), with a view to probing until the work comes to a stop or there is good explanation for the apparent discrepancy. This type of investigation will tend to creep along and collect all material that could point to the cause of the problem. It may stop when it runs out of steam or is overtaken by a new and more urgent task.

11. Carry out an investigation in line with set standards for this type of work. A more mechanical approach derives from working through the standard response to an allegation of fraud. It is not only done by the book but also through a set of rigid routines. Investigators may work through a set of standardized forms on the fraud, potential suspects, losses involved, list of key witnesses, documentation logs, and so on. The emphasis is on following documented standards and not making mistakes anywhere along the line. This objective is paramount when the organization has suffered a series of embarrassing incidents where such work was not done properly in the past. Close adherence to set standards should not be a key objective as such, but a method to achieve the set objective.

12. Provide regular progress reports to help frame decisions for the next stage in the investigation. Many fraud investigations are iterative, in that they delve deeper and deeper into a certain problem and flex to fit the problem as it changes shape and evolves. It is like the tip of the iceberg as slowly what is really happening in a particular part of the organization is uncovered. Bid rigging may fit this scenario, where many more people and vendors are implicated as work progresses on the way the bidding system is being operated and what aspects are in fact illegal. A well-informed fraud panel will need to receive regular progress reports and make decisions about the shape and form of the investigation as, armed with more information, it gets wider but hopefully more focused. Consultation, discussion, and weekly presentations are the trademarks of this type of response to fraud.

**13.** Ensure that the perpetrator does not leave the jurisdiction of the investigators before effective action can be taken to remedy the situation. Shoplifting is a physical crime where goods are hidden about the person and security staff try to hold onto the culprit once it becomes clear that a crime has been committed. Most employee fraud investigations do not have this characteristic, as the identity and contact details of staff are known. There are times, however, when there is a real danger of the person in question disappearing; larger frauds, involving readily convertible items, have this trait. The focus of the work may be around finding the persons involved and ensuring that they remain within the legal jurisdiction of the city, state, country, or world region so that action may be taken against them.

**14.** Gather as much sufficient admissible evidence as possible, with the minimum of resources and disruption to the business, in line with what is in the best interests of the organization. This objective recognizes the balance that must be struck in any fraud work. An investigation is simply a project that involves sensitivities and deceit. Like all projects, though, there must be a business case for putting resources into the tasks and efforts involved. Projects involve direct costs for the staff and equipment employed, and indirect costs of the overhead to support the work. Also, there is the impact on the business of the inquiries, disruption, and information needed to get to the truth. The entire exercise has to be seen as worthwhile and investigators may have to work under defined time restrictions. Perhaps a decision will have to be made on whether it is worthwhile traveling abroad to interview an ex-employee who has knowledge of the fraud. The costs of putting manual records onto a computer database, to run a complicated interrogation package against the suspect data, would have to be calculated. This type of investigation is closely monitored and works around strict budgets and control reports. In other words, apply the accepted principles of good project management.

**15.** Obtain a fair view of the fraud and come to a balanced decision on the most appropriate action to take. A linked aim is to deal with the investigation objectively. Fraud investigators should be top professionals, with a clear degree of independence; their reports should be formally reviewed before action is considered and taken. Evidence that both supports and contradicts the case for the employer should be properly recorded and made available to the employee or the employee's representative. Decisions must be made on the basis of good business sense. The motives of the suspect and any mitigation may also be taken into account, along with the behavior of line managers who may have condoned the activities.

16. Explore the allegations in sufficient depth to provide an adequate response. Investigators are obliged to work through an allegation to make sure it fits with their knowledge of the case. An investigation that builds this objective into its terms of reference does not take material presented to it at face value. The idea is to drill down into the matter to ensure that the evidence as received is reliable. It is wrong to launch a major investigation when the allegations derive from an internal dispute in a tit-for-tat disagreement between two employees or an employee and the line manager. The focus is on the context of the allegation and whether it needs to be taken seriously.

17. Ensure that employee morale is preserved during the investigation. If staff morale is important to the organization, then it should be built into the terms of reference, or form part of the professional standards, that underpin the investigator's work.

18. Protect the good name of the organization. Somewhere along the line, the impact of the fraud on the organization's image will have to be considered. A fraud against the organization, either from within or externally, always raises the question of negligence and/or culpability. This has already been addressed in earlier chapters, which advised that a named person be made responsible for handling the public relations aspects of the work. Also, the investigators and decision makers need to be aware of the potential fallout from any mistakes or poorly communicated practices of the investigators.

19. Observe any legal obligations regarding due diligence and claims against third parties, such as company insurers. The investigators need to have one eye on the investigation and the other eye on third-party obligations. The entire exercise must withstand the test of due diligence. It must also comply with the claiming procedure under any relevant insurance policy. It is good practice to set these items within the scope of the investigator's brief to ensure that they are duly considered and acted on.

20. Carry out the investigation in such as way as to observe all ethical obligations. People understand legal obligations and the fact that, if ignored, the repercussions may be felt by them personally. It is more difficult with ethical obligations. Fraud investigators tend to be given

a wide berth in the way they operate and secure evidence. Any reluctance to accept the investigator's work methods is generally seen as a sign of guilt or conspiracy with the suspects being investigated. That is why investigators are not normally challenged or questioned during their work. Unfortunately, an absence of critical inquiry also breeds the potential for contempt and a disregard for the rules of fair play. This is why the need to adhere to corporate standards, such as respecting others, valuing views, not bullying staff, and so on, should also apply to investigators. The investigation should be done in accordance not only with good operational standards but also with acceptable standards of conduct.

21. Identify the perpetrator and establish intent (malice aforethought). The intention is to go straight for a criminal prosecution and secure all the evidence needed to prove the case beyond reasonable doubt. A secondary objective is to present the case to the law enforcement agencies in a way that encourages them to seek prosecution. A main feature would be a wish to get the law enforcement agencies involved and support a full-scale police investigation with search warrants, subpoenas, and referral to the prosecutor's office. This requires an all-out effort with full publicity and fits well with a zero tolerance policy.

22. Secure sufficient evidence to determine whether misconduct has been committed by the employee. A different but parallel approach involves getting charges proven at a disciplinary hearing on the preponderance of evidence. This case revolves around the civil process when an employee has broken the mutual trust that must exist for the continued presence of the employee in the workplace. The police case here is a secondary issue to the disciplinary machinery.

23. Identify unacceptable management practices or negligent behavior that led to the problem and take appropriate action. We come now to a very difficult objective to handle. Employee fraud results from poor controls. The culprit has spotted a loophole and is of a mind to deceive the employer, and controls are bypassed, ignored, or abused by the fraudster. It may be that no real safeguards are in place to prevent the wrongdoing in the first place.

> A purchasing clerk is able to secure bribes from company vendors on a regular basis and has bought a large beach house with the proceeds. Having received an allegation to this effect, the company may launch an inquiry to seek evidence to support the allegation. One

question that quickly comes up is this: If this fraud has been going on for so long, why didn't the purchasing management discover it or establish controls to prevent it? When this question falls within the scope of the investigation, a different type of examination results. The managers and colleagues in the section in question may be subject to sanction, warnings, or even dismissal if they are found to be culpable in any way. Not only is there a suspect to investigate, but managers and staff are also in the frame, and it becomes much more difficult to obtain their cooperation. People may have to be dismissed and the fallout could be severe in terms of emotional distress and business continuity.

Some investigations have two stages. The first is about the allegation and the activities of the suspect. The second stage then looks at the behavior of others in terms of negligence and delinquent behavior.

24. Maintain suitable confidentiality and ensure that the organization is not vulnerable to a suit for defamation of character. The storm-trooper approach will probably motivate the investigators and draw clear lines of attack, but it may lack subtlety and sophistication. The bottom line is that everyone is innocent until proven guilty, and the investigation is essentially about maintaining confidentiality and protocols.

25. Identify the witnesses to the fraud and ensure that they provide reliable evidence to support any charges that may be brought as a result of the investigation. Some investigations focus on the witnesses, on the theory that someone must know what is going on. Concealment by the fraudster in this environment can consist of intimidation and blackmail of potential witnesses. An investigation taking this line will need to manage the reluctance of witnesses to speak and make formal statements. It may be necessary to offer some form of protection and also to reiterate the requirement that all employees cooperate with formal investigations undertaken by the organization. The important point is to be able to recognize any reluctance and have a strategy for managing the problem should it arise.

26. Provide recommendations regarding the way the risk of fraud is being managed by the organization. The long view of dealing with fraud is based on good risk management. When frauds happen, justice must be done and the perpetrators identified and made to pay for the crimes. When management has been at fault, this issue must also be addressed. Losses have to be recovered and the corporate

reputation held intact. These are all defensive responses to a problem that hopefully has been dealt with by the organization. A more positive response is to ask why the risk of fraud is not being managed properly, and then put this right through constructive development across work teams in the organization. The investigators may have an idea of ways to move forward, although this creates wide terms of reference for the investigation and may be better addressed when the dust has settled and the level of emotion in the debate has subsided.

It is clear from the preceding that many and varied aims can be set for the investigators; much will depend on the organization, type and materiality of the fraud, and the culture in place. The onus is on top management to review the list of options and approaches and give clear direction on what is required for the investigation at hand.

## OBSERVING RIGHTS AND
## MAINTAINING STAFF MORALE

An investigation into employee fraud delves into the activities of people implicated by the evidence gathered. These people may be witnesses, suspects, or just those who have information that may assist the investigators. Employees are generally required to cooperate with an internal investigation and may be asked questions about their movements, work, views, and anything else that is relevant. At times little or no information is available on the actual terms of reference for the investigation, and most of the information obtained by the investigators is deemed confidential. The inquiries are often done with a great deal of secrecy. In this environment some of the normal rules of communication are suspended. An employee may be grilled for several hours by investigators and not be able to seek advice from the line manager or colleagues. Phone conversations may be recorded and played back to the investigation teams and analyzed along with a log of phone calls made by the employee. All interaction with computerized systems may be logged and analyzed for later review. In parts of the organization, closed-circuit TV may be used by security personnel. All this represents efforts by the organization to ensure that only authorized business is transacted and that any improper activities are identified and addressed.

Meanwhile, every individual has constitutional rights that supersede all other legal provisions and must be observed. Breach of these rights means that any evidence obtained inappropriately is likely to be dismissed by the trial judge. Not only is it best practice anyway to observe employee rights, but it also ensures that the investigation is not ruled out of bounds when the case comes to trial. The many basic rights provided by the Constitution and federal and state law, in terms of employee fraud investigations, include:

- The right to remain silent and not to have to give evidence that may incriminate the individual (Fifth Amendment). Employees have a fiduciary duty to cooperate with the investigation as long as it is reasonable and relates to their responsibilities at work, but generally speaking, not to the detriment of their right to silence.
- The right to a speedy trial in front of peers.
- A right to confront the accusers and present a defense (Sixth Amendment).
- A right to have all investigations carried out with regard to due process.
- The right to advice from legal counsel.
- A presumption of innocence until proven guilty.
- A right to have the government prove the criminal case beyond reasonable doubt.
- The right to have the burden of proof rest with the government.
- The right to have all searches and seizures be reasonable (Fourth Amendment). Homes and personal property can be searched without permission only when a search warrant or subpoena has been obtained.
- The right to protection when disclosing information relating to a criminal act.
- The right not to be dismissed for failing to cooperate with an investigation (for public employees).
- A right to privacy where there is a reasonable expectation of privacy (a lot depends on company policy regarding this and what has been relayed to staff).
- A right to access restriction and security for records containing personal details. Employee records are covered by federal and state laws and regulations, and an organization can access them only for an authorized purpose and with approval from the head of personnel.

Senior managers can access records as a normal part of their operational responsibilities, and much will revolve around ownership issues and corporate policies.

- A possible right to union representation under a collective bargaining agreement.

Private sector companies may use polygraph lie detection tests (under the Employee Polygraph Protection Act) when the investigation relates to matters of economic loss, but it is difficult to discharge someone for refusing to take the test. Some states have laws that make these tests a potential invasion of privacy.

There is a lot to consider when dealing with employee rights, and there is scope for mistakes during any part of an investigation. Respect for these rights should be built into the way investigations are carried out generally. Sometimes good legal advice is required on a particular proposed practice for an investigation. An employee may refuse to cooperate and may also dispute the evidence gathered. Recorded phone conversations can prove troublesome, particularly when the person making the record is not party to the conversation, and it is important to get legal advice as to the current thinking on privacy versus the ability to investigate and check on people. At times there is a tension between the legal rights to access the information and the reasons and use of the information gained as a result. Much can depend on whether the reason for accessing the information was for an authorized use. There will always be a balance between an individual's freedom and security measures that sways over time from one side to the other and between different countries, business sectors, and states.

The other issue in many investigations is the impact on staff morale as illustrated in the following.

A worker is suspended and disappears from sight. The coworkers are warned not to communicate with this person and are then asked to attend a formal interview, where they are grilled for hours by two grim-faced external fraud specialists. They are asked about their association with the suspended party and whether they are aware of any wrongdoings, and are also asked to explain their work roles through a series of probing interviews. The local gossip suggests that thousands of dollars have been misappropriated from the company. Meanwhile, the family of the suspended person is trying to contact the same coworkers to find out what is happening to their relative, who is becoming increasingly depressed. The team manager is swept away from time to time by the fraud investigators and comes back looking worried and upset. Several police officers are spotted in the building and appear to be visiting one of the senior directors. There is a rumor that other workers will be suspended in due course. The team leader has e-mailed all staff and told them not to discuss the case and explains that to do so would constitute a disciplinary offense.

This is not an unusual scenario and the events described can result from a well-planned and well-organized fraud investigation. The problem is that no one thinks about managing the emotional fallout from the situation. Investigators are trained to get the facts from anyone who can contribute, and more often than not are reluctant to say too much about what is a confidential inquiry. Thus, people are told to cooperate with an investigation as part of their work duties, but are not really told what it is about. The group will come to a consensus on whether the entire process is fair and acceptable, and its final verdict will depend on a number of things. Before we discuss the influencing factors, though, we need to list the negative effects on staff of an investigation into employee fraud:

- The investigators are seen as the enemy and anything that is told to them is guarded and restrained.
- The team manager will be asked to choose sides—the team or the investigators.
- A climate of fear will permeate the team; people will take time off sick and find it hard to concentrate on their work.
- The organization will be seen as unfair and the more able team members may well seek alternative employment.
- Some coworkers will break the rules and talk to the suspended person.
- People who have valuable information may fail to come forward with it.
- Some will view the matter as part of a wider agenda to pick on staff who are disliked by senior management.
- Severe emotional distress can be created in a suspect, which is grounds for a legal complaint.
- Overall, the investigation will become difficult and the lack of good cooperation will impair progress.

It is against this background that the effects on staff of the investigation need to be considered. Terror, fear, apprehension, whispers, and rumor will dominate the office while work takes a back seat for a while. Once damaged, staff morale may not fully recover even with time, and there will be some impact on work productivity. There is no single answer to this problem; as we have already said, even a well-run professional investigation can still have negative repercussions.

A staff impact strategy attached to the investigations strategy can be used to anticipate and overcome the problems. There is no one model for managing the impact on staff, but there are a few points that can be considered:

- Make clear that any suspension is to ensure a fair investigation for all concerned. Suspension does not presume guilt and the investigation will be as much to clear people as it is to find out who is responsible for the irregularity. In fact, the term *irregularity* can be used to overcome the emotional impact of stronger words such as *fraud, crime,* or *deception*. If there is a need for internal discipline again, softer terms such as *irregularity* or *breach of procedure* will be more appropriate than terms denoting a criminal offense.
- Make clear the need to cooperate. If the investigation is seen as important to clarify things for everyone, the need to cooperate may be more obvious to staff.
- Ensure that the investigation is about getting to the truth and nothing more. People generally accept that finding out "the truth" is a commendable objective no matter how uncomfortable the process. Tell staff that outsiders are being used because the investigation has to be professional and objective.
- Make sure the investigators are good "people" people. They need to be skilled in dealing with a diverse set of individuals and not impair the smooth running of business. All incoming members of the team of investigators should be interviewed by personnel to check their interpersonal skills and those that do not fit sent back. In-house teams need to put "people" skills firmly into the core competencies for recruitment and development purposes.
- Get the workers together in a group meeting and talk through the previously noted issues. A senior investigator may attend and answer questions. At the same time, be firm about the need for confidentiality.
- Make clear that the investigation should not become mixed up with grievance issues, where staff use the investigation to air mundane

management issues that have nothing to do with fraud. Larger teams tend to split into subgroups where some support the investigation, some oppose management's treatment of the suspect, and others have no particular view. It can get more sinister when the prime suspect actually has a team of coconspirators who are in some way implicated in the fraud. Make clear that general management issues are not part of the investigation.

- Make no promises ruling out further suspensions of other team members. This is a common-sense response, in that the investigators have to be firm but fair. Investigators work on evidence, not innuendo, and no one will be affected if they have done nothing wrong.
- Provide some kind of pressure relief valve where staff can talk through anything that worries them about the investigation. Get the workers used to individuals having private meetings and then not talking about the matter to their coworkers. Explain the need for privacy on the ground that each statement is a personal document, written by the individual rather than the group.
- Make sure actions deliver what has been promised. Provide a facility where staff can complain about the investigation and receive a considered response, particularly when a complaint involves a perceived breach of constitutional rights.
- Explain the need to keep to business targets, notwithstanding the activities of the investigation team. If the investigation can be completed quickly and efficiently, not only will the air be cleared, but people can also get back to a full-time focus on business goals. If employee fraud is not addressed, eventually the business will suffer. If staff have any suggestions on improving controls, these should be considered.

Build these strategies, or whatever alternatives work best, into the profile of the investigations team, or get someone to join the team and take responsibility for staff impact issues. Whatever the approach, a formal assessment of potential problems and some kind of plan must be devised and put into action for addressing these concerns.

If the investigation starts as a series of covert inquiries and there is no suspension until later on, the scenario becomes a little different. Work is carried out from outside the area of the problem, and profiling of the fraud, determination of how it was carried out, and compilation of a list of potential suspects are done without alerting anyone outside of the investigation team. In this situation there is no staff fallout because they do not actually know about the problem. The investigation will come to light at some stage, but much of the work is a fight against time to gather live evidence before it goes public.

# WHAT ABOUT EVIDENCE?

We have already said that fraud investigations are primarily about gathering evidence. The term *evidence* is somewhat abused in today's society, but generally means compelling material that would convince a reasonable person. In fraud investigations, this definition becomes much tighter because of the following factors:

- The evidence should either engender a guilty plea from the defendant, or be subject to rigorous examination by representatives of the defendant. Any confession by the suspect must be entirely voluntary.
- The evidence must comply with various legal rules regarding admissibility. If it is misleading, prejudicial, or wastes the time of the courts, or is just mere speculation, it may not be legally admissible. For example, claims of entrapment should be avoided. This is when the crime would not have been committed without efforts to tempt the person.
- The defendant may prepare a case that seeks to refute or discredit the evidence presented by the prosecution. In fact, defense has discovery rights to the evidence used by prosecution, and the Federal Advance Disclosure Act requires that certain basic items be provided to the defense even if they are not asked for. This is to ensure that the defense knows what evidence is held and is in a position to request copies when required. At the start of an investigation, if an attorney is employed, the material will be confidential under attorney-client privilege, at least for a while. If the evidence is given to a third party, this privilege may be lost.
- It may be in the interests of the defendant to ensure that any evidence supporting the prosecution case is not readily available or forthcoming. This also applies to potential witnesses and documents in the possession of the defendant. It may be necessary to agree to admissibility with the defense beforehand and save time in courtroom debates.

- The standard of proof for criminal cases is beyond a reasonable doubt; that is, the prosecution must convince a jury that there is no doubt that the defendant is guilty.
- Evidence costs money to acquire, maintain, and present. It also takes time, and the value of the evidence and its impact on the case have to be weighed against the costs before adding it to the case for the prosecution.
- The onus is on the investigating team to ensure that the evidence is sufficient, relevant, and reliable. If the evidence is simply someone's opinion, it is unlikely to be heard unless that person is an expert witness. *Hearsay* is evidence that has been told to a third party because the prime witness is not present to give the evidence and so cannot be cross-examined by defense. As such, it is generally disregarded.
- If there is any break in the chain of evidence that links the crime with the defendant, the evidence may be deemed unreliable and disregarded by the courts. The evidence itself may be sound, but the way it was obtained, stored, and presented may impair its reliability.
- If the rights of the defendant are violated in the process of securing the necessary evidence, that evidence may well have to be abandoned.

There is a lot at stake when collecting evidence to support a case, and that is why specialist fraud investigators tend to be used for this type of work. The objectives of an investigation, as mentioned earlier, may include obtaining evidence of past, present, and future crimes, and working out who did what and why and when and possibly how (the modus operandi). The state of the evidence is crucial, as a case may go before a grand jury to see if there is probable cause to believe that an offense has been committed. The grand jury may decide to indict the person in question, after which an arrest warrant may be issued. All of this is based on a consideration of the available evidence. *Evidence* is anything that can be presented to the courts to prove a case to the satisfaction of a jury. Legal evidence tends to prove or disprove any facts in question and it is these facts that are argued in the court or at an internal staff disciplinary hearing. There are a number of attributes of good evidence:

1. **It is relevant to the case in question.**   Relevancy means that the evidence helps to prove or disprove the facts in issue. Prosecutors will need to prove that an offense has been committed and that the defendant committed the offense. A case of misappropriation can-

not be based on the fact that an employee is addicted to gambling and spends a lot of money on the horses or in casinos. This fact may make the person a suspect who is added to a list for purposes of the investigation, but the evidence must link the person to the crime.

2. **It is competent.**  Information gathered from personal records, such as medical, financial, criminal, and driving records, may be examined by the defense to ascertain their accuracy and authenticity. Anything other than testimony should be verified. Here the documents or tangible objects, such as video recordings, must be shown to be reliable and their source, ownership, and accuracy ascertained. Documents that come from business processes should be authenticated by the documents manager and shown to derive from the normal course of business activity. Computerized records must also pass this test, as the audit trail will be rigorously scrutinized by the defense team. Competence relates not only to the accuracy of the evidence but also to the way it is presented. When the investigators' working papers are clearly laid out, show the findings (cross-referenced to the evidence), and detail the decisions made, this will help everyone understand the case. Typed, well-presented reports and summaries can assist the credibility of the investigation in the eyes of judge and jury. If the working papers address matters of fact and do not contain opinions on the character or guilt of the defendant, they will be much better received by all parties to the case.

3. **It is sufficient.**  We really need to show that the offense has been committed and that the defendant had both motive and opportunity and intended to commit the offense. Thus, the evidence must be compelling, not only in its accuracy but also in its sufficiency to support the case for the prosecution. Some cases generate a great deal of material, and the way the documents and exhibits are dealt with should be seen as a document management project in its own right. If anything is missing, is contaminated, or is misclassified, the mistake will cast doubt on the entire case. Meanwhile, the court will not be impressed by excessive amounts of evidence that may confuse the jury, blur the issues involved, and waste a great deal of time. There needs to be a clear focus on the way the case is presented; the use of visual aids, summaries, and diagrams, together with a chronological ordering of documents, can help a jury understand the case. This is particularly relevant for fraud cases, which can become so complicated that reasonable doubt arises from complex material that overwhelms the jury.

## Types of Evidence

The evidence obtained during an investigation may be directly derived from the fraud or it may be circumstantial. A signed statement from a person who saw the suspect remove a company check and place it in his briefcase is direct evidence of the theft of that check. The suspect's presence in the building at the time funds went missing is only circumstantial evidence and has less of an impact. Involvement in fraud may only be deduced from the presence of the suspect. If the returned check was paid into the suspect's account and has the suspect's fingerprints on it, this helps prove the case. Attempts at showing that the suspect is of bad character tread on less solid ground. The courts generally do not classify defendants as good or bad, although witnesses may be assessed for characteristics such as reliability and honesty. There are many and varied sources of evidence, including the following:

- Witness statements. These are generally acceptable unless the witness has been impeached because of bias, conviction of a felony, or for making inconsistent remarks.
- Circumstantial evidence relating to unaccounted income. This is interesting because of the presumption that such income is from unrecorded and fraudulent activities. An analysis of income can support a claim that the suspect is in receipt of illicit income. The person's assets and liabilities are established along with income from official sources, less known expenses. The difference between the net income from known sources and actual income is income from unknown sources, and the inference from this fact is used to support the case against the defendant.
- Financial reports on the suspect. These may be obtained from a company that specializes in providing this type of information. Investigative consumer reports involve a great deal of research, such as questioning friends, neighbors, and associates, to form a view of the person's reputation and way of life. These are generally not admissible unless the suspect has previously agreed to this type of research.
- Physical evidence. This may consist of maps, photographs, and actual objects and is sometimes called *real evidence.*
- Documentary evidence. This type of evidence is varied and includes things such as invoices, computer printouts, letters, the contents of files, and legal documents.

- Financial reports and operational data from the company that has been derived from normal business processing.
- Demonstrative evidence. The investigators may compile evidence for the court, perhaps in the form of a written report on the case created by the team of investigators.
- Analytical data. The investigators may carry out analyses to assist their case, which may then be presented to the court as evidence. If a cash count is made and analyzed to show that the employee in question had been underrecording sums of money over a defined period, this schedule could become a court exhibit. If the analysis contains any errors at all, it may cast a shadow of doubt over the entire case. Data mining of (for example) refunds per supervisor, amount, and customer can be used to identify strange relationships, but again each suspicious item must be checked to provide evidence of a fraud.
- Testimonials. These can be derived from interviews and are made by witnesses under oath. Interviewing is dealt with later on.
- Secondary evidence. Whereas original documents may be seen as primary evidence, certified copies of documents, with a suitable explanation of why the originals are not available, may be accepted by the courts.

## Why Is Evidence Important?

In most crimes, evidence is simply material that links the criminal with the crime. In fraud cases it can get really complicated. At times there may seem to be no real crime. Someone taking kickbacks may not create a loss for the employer, and the vendor paying the bribes may have written them off as "consulting fees." In fraud cases, there is generally some camouflage where transactions go round in circles, or recorded transactions are not actually present to be gathered as evidence. If the company is making healthy profits and the workforce and shareholders are receiving salaries and dividends, there may be little incentive to engage in a long, drawn-out search for evidence to bring the case to court. Some frauds are so simple and well hidden that it is hard to know where to start. Skimming involves the removal of cash before it hits the books, with the only evidence being some wastage on inventory. A customer who conspires with a checkout operative to pay less for the goods, and then split the money later on, may leave no trail that can be followed by investigators. The warehouse or basement staff may become suspects when the figures suggest that stock, rather than cash, is missing. The main response is to set up video cameras and reconcile the goods taken to the cashiers with the amounts rung up on the till—not an easy task through CCTV links. Price fixing by major players in a luxury goods market is even harder to identify. Much of the evidence may be strictly circumstantial in nature, such as remarkable similarities in price ranges, but it may be hard to prove wrongdoing beyond a reasonable doubt. A worker who steals checks from the mailroom is committing mail fraud and theft, but it is hard to pin down nonreceipt of checks, as the books suggest they never got to the company in the first place. This is compounded by the fact that mailroom personnel may be low-paid temporary workers, for whom little vetting was done when they were taken on. When recoverables have been written off, there is no expectation of receiving the monies due. A clerk who is able to get debts due written out of the books is in a position to carry out the perfect fraud against income received thereafter. A statistical analysis may provide circumstantial evidence, but we would have to confirm that the debtor paid up and that the funds went to the employee's account. The police may have to be informed to get this case to court. The bottom line is that a fraud is not a fraud unless and until there has been a conviction in the courts for a related criminal offense—and a conviction is possible only when there is sufficient, reliable, and relevant evidence to submit to a jury and convince them that they should convict.

## INTERVIEWING

The best way to find out something is to ask someone in the know. This rule applies to all types of investigations, including work relating to employee fraud. An interview is a formal exchange of information through a series of structured questions and answers. The interviewer is in charge of the situation and should retain control over the way the communication is carried out, and should use clear questioning to secure information that fulfills the objective of the interview. When starting a fraud investigation, interviewees may be divided into distinct categories, which may change as the investigation proceeds:

- **Representatives of management.** In many cases top management will have called in the investigators to look into a particular irregularity. These managers are responsible for the systems and controls that have been breached during commission of the fraud; interviews with them will focus on finding out about the system and how the fraud was perpetrated. Management may be further broken down into three general groups:

1. The first group will have reported the fraud and will be asked about their knowledge of the fraud and whether they know anything that would be of use in helping direct the investigators.

2. The next group is not a group as such, but the senior official who is responsible for the area where the fraud occurred and who will go on to represent the organization in court, if it comes to that. It may be the director for the section in question. The investigators will want this person to tell exactly how the fraud came about and how any controls were overcome, and provide a formal statement to this effect.

3. The final group tends to be less senior people who actually supervise the area and people in the affected area. Interviews here would consist of information about the systems and the suspect, if there is one.

> A fraud involving false insurance claims fabricated by an insurance clerk is reported by another insurance clerk who realizes what is going on. The director of the insurance claims department then advises the CEO, calls in the investigators, and represents the organization if the case is heard in court. Meanwhile, various insurance managers are interviewed to find out how this could have happened and what parts of the system have been abused.

- **Witnesses and potential witnesses to the fraud.** Most of the interviewing will be of people who can provide direct information that supports the investigation. Much of this information will constitute formal evidence that is forwarded to the police department involved in the investigation. Witnesses are interviewed with a view to providing evidence in the form of signed statements; any material attached to their statements will be included as exhibits. A person may start out as a witness but end up a suspect as the weight of evidence starts to point in his or her direction.
- **People with general background information.** Another group of interviewees consists of people who have background material. If the fraud involves people who are not employed by the organization

appearing on the payroll (ghost employees), the personnel manager may be interviewed to find out how newcomers get onto the payroll. Meanwhile, the payroll manager may be a key witness against a member of payroll staff who have decided to put nonexistent people into the system.

- **Experts, specialists, and third parties.** Investigators may need to interview various experts who have been called in to form a view on matters crucial to the case.

  > Continuing the example of false insurance claims, an expert may be called in to examine a car that is supposed to have been damaged and repaired, to assess whether this has in fact happened and the claim is valid. This expert will issue a report and provide a statement to document the work carried out and opinion arrived at. The expert will probably be interviewed to ensure that the evidence can be used. Other interviews may include the garage in question, the mechanics, and anyone else associated with the problem at hand.

- **The suspect.** This person tends to come last in any list of interviewees; the usual scenario is to present the suspect with the evidence gathered during the investigation and ask for an explanation. The suspects may make a formal confession, if this is seen as appropriate, or dispute the facts presented. Alternatively, they may refuse to cooperate or simply lie. They may also offer an irrefutable explanation that immediately clears all allegations against them. Some suspects become too emotional to continue and ask to be excused from the interview.

Others may come forward and need to be interviewed because they have knowledge of the fraud. It may be a subcontractor who has knowledge of other scams carried out by a vendor being investigated. It may be an informant who reported the fraud anonymously but now has more information. The CEO may need to be asked about the corporate policy on things like employees having their own private consulting practices. A cleaner may have knowledge about the early morning activities of someone who is suspected of unauthorized access to computer systems for the purposes of defrauding the company. The list goes on and on. The point is that investigators must master the skill of getting information from people quickly, clearly, and accurately, without alienating respondents. Good interviewing technique comes close to the top of key skills required for carrying out fraud investigations.

## The Interview Process

Having established the wide variety of situations that fall under the general purview of interviewing, it should be clear that a flexible approach to the task is needed—flexible and responsive to the actual circumstances the interviewer is faced with. Each interview will be entirely different in context and content, although standards may be set for the key stages of the interview. Keeping the framework general, the main stages to the interview are as shown in Figure 6.1. Each stage in Figure 6.1 is explained here.

**Preparation.**   Before the interviewee is contacted and the meeting set up, there is much work to do. Think through why the interview is required and what you want to achieve. Write down what is already known and what more is needed. Determine the right approach to the task, which may mean thinking about the time, place, and interviewer. There tends to be a better response to a request for an interview when someone is asked in person rather than over the phone. Choose the location carefully, as sensitive material may be best obtained offsite, but it should not look like a clandestine meeting between coconspirators. Factfinding interviews may best be done in the office of the respondent, so that there is instant access to relevant files and records.

The style of interview should also be considered. It is probably best to adopt the style that comes most naturally and not assume a false persona for effect. Some argue that the style may be rehearsed to achieve the most

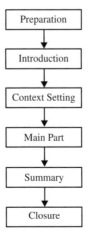

**Figure 6.1**   Stages of the Inteview

impact—say, aggressively searching for the truth or being apologetic for the inconvenience. Others feel that the interviewer should be cold, calculating, and severe, to bring home the seriousness of the matter. Some are jovial, because they feel that creating a sense of fun and adventure helps people relax and drop their guard. Again, it is partly personal preference and partly what best fits the circumstances. Although interviews should be natural, it is useful to have different styles available to ensure flexibility in responding to the attitude and stance of the respondent. Most detailed interview theory considers dealing with the suspect the most important part of the investigation. In many interviews, there is less call to play cat and mouse.

Reference should be made to the employee handbook and the procedure for getting information from staff. Problems, up to and including claims of false imprisonment, can arise when the employee is forced to attend and is not allowed to leave the room. An excessive number of interviewers and an aggressive interview style can lead to extreme and unacceptable duress. Also, it is important to make provision for coffee breaks and time out. The rules get really strict when the respondent is a suspect.

**Introductions.**   Rapport should be established and the objective of the interview made clear. In one sense, these two requirements create a degree of conflict. Building rapport is all about making contact with the respondents and getting them to cooperate. However, the aim of the interview will be to uncover the full facts behind fraud and deceit, possibly by a colleague of the respondent, which may make people feel uncomfortable. Bearing this in mind, official introductions of all those present should be provided. Some investigators argue that there should be two interviewers present when the matter is sensitive (for example, a key witness to the fraud). Explain the purpose of note taking or the use of a recording device, if appropriate. Make it clear that this is standard practice for all interviews apart from short and informal meetings, and try to get the consent of the respondent. Make verbatim written notes of parts of the interview that are key to the case. Notes are less about recording the impressions of the interviewer and much more about getting the facts down in terms of the various questions and answers. If the respondent is unwell, distressed, or possibly intoxicated, it is probably best to postpone the interview. The most important point to note at this stage of the interview is that everyone has self-esteem that should be respected at all times. The instant the parties meet, the question of respect will subconsciously arise. No real communication is possible without mutual recognition of each party's self-esteem.

**Context setting.** The objective of the interview should be stated with a brief note as to the wider investigation and where the interview fits in. Stress the need for good cooperation and full disclosure of all relevant information. Remind the respondent about the need for confidentiality, although the interview record may be viewed by external parties. People are more likely to feel part of a process if they understand what it is about and their role in it. Tell the respondent that the interview will assist the investigation and is in search of facts that are material, reliable, and related to the matter at hand. Encourage the respondent to think about other sources of information that confirm the facts. Restate the importance of getting the facts straight before answers are given, as there is no time restriction for important detail. Ask whether there are any questions at this stage and try to answer them as fully as possible. It is important to get the context right before embarking on the actual questions.

**Main part.** This is really the question-and-answer session. Remember, the Fifth Amendment means that employees should not be forced to answer questions that incriminate them, under threat of disciplinary action. The questions should be designed to obtain specific information relevant to the fraud, and they may be referenced to the file of evidence that is available so far. The questions may also relate to the behavior of the person being interviewed, to ensure that he or she falls outside the problem zone and is not culpable. A great deal rests on the listening skills of the interviewer and this can make the difference between a good and poor session. Listening is about showing an interest in the answers, probing unclear points, summarizing, encouraging, and responding positively to signals sent by the respondent. It is about showing that there is no prejudice in the mind of the interviewer and keeping to the point. Listening can be about interrupting to explore an answer or asking for time to take something in. In other words, it is not just about staying silent and looking interested—it is about positive listening. The types of questions that can be asked to get a rounded view of the facts include:

- **Closed questions.** These questions require a yes or no answer. This is to get basic information and start the process off. Some details are important to get right and short, closed questions can help. The problem can be that initial reliance on closed questions can set the tone for the whole interview, such that the respondent finds it hard to open up when the questions seek a fuller answer.

- **Open questions.** These are designed to elicit a descriptive response. "Tell me about your duties at work?" should encourage a detailed reply. Although they are very useful to get to the facts, an abundance of open questions can lead to some conversation drift, where the direction and focus get lost and the interview turns into a loose discussion. An occasional interjection from the interviewer may be required.

- **Complex probing questions.** These seek to gather the facts required to meet the interview objective. When the issues in question are complicated, one technique for getting a result asks the respondent to think about the matter and get the key dates down on notepaper. Then allow time for free recall, during which the respondent can marshal the facts and try to get them in chronological order, perhaps with help from a diary or rough notes. The facts are placed with the dates and associated detail with no time frame attached. Encouragement and time out are used to get the facts in the right order and see whether they elicit further details that may help clarify things. When this process is completed, the question is asked again, with (one hopes) a better response. The interviewer becomes more of a facilitator and guide than an inquisitor. Some argue that people who do not instantly remember past events are more likely to be honest.

- **Confrontation of the suspect.** We move into really difficult territory when the evidence implicates the suspect. The interviewer has a right to ask questions, accuse the suspect, and seek explanation or a confession. In fact, in some long-winded fraud cases, when the investigators finally get around to interviewing the suspect, the person admits the offense almost with relief. However, investigators who mainly rely on confessions will arguably perform substandard work and will probably put their efforts into harassment, inducement, or emotional blackmail. This is not really a professional approach to important work. Before questions are posed that implicate a person in a criminal offense, a number of protocols must be observed, including informing the person of the right to counsel, the right to due process, and the right to call in a union representative. Suspects should be given the charges and evidence and allowed the opportunity to explain their position or decide not to respond. Suspects should be told that the information is required to complete the investigation into work-related matters and that the case may lead to disciplinary action. Ask for full disclosure of all matters relating to work but not the respondents' private lives. Meanwhile, all matters discussed should be kept confidential; the suspects should talk only to the union representative (or lawyer), but the employer may relay the information to the police and company insurers. Work from the general to the specific, from the less important to the significant, from the hypothetical to the actual, from easy to tough questions, from general viewpoints to specific facts, from the known to the unknown. Offer opportunities for the suspect to reveal all, including any explanations and justifications. Investigation is not about accusing or passing judgment, but simply trying to make sense of the evidence. In one sense, the interviewer is aligned with the suspect in wanting to understand the explanations and motivations involved. If a confession is forthcoming, make sure it is properly recorded and supported. Get the facts, the circumstances, the evidence, the losses involved, any conspirators, the method used, and anything else that supports the case—and get it in writing. *Defamation* is release of incorrect information that impairs someone's reputation to persons outside the interview format. As soon as a point makes sense and is agreed with the interviewer, make sure it is written into the interview record.

**Summary.**   The interviews described here can be quite exhausting for both sides, even with breaks. A further break may be advisable before summarizing. After the question-and-answer part of the interview, take stock of what has happened while emotions are allowed to subside. The summary part of the interview can actually be quite involved. Check what has been said and look for inconsistencies and gaps. It may be that a question was asked several times but not properly answered, or the answer may lead to another key question that was not clearly posed by the interviewer. Any denials may have to be clarified, and answers given may call for further explanations. When a witness has made an important claim, make sure it has been properly recorded and linked to any confirming evidence (which will be assessed at a later stage). The respondent may wish to add further information and some more clarification. The most important part of this stage is consideration of whether a formal statement is required, cross-referenced to specific exhibits. Think about the courts and what they will make of the statement, representation, confession, or denial.

**Closure.**   Professionalism means observing some basics before leaving the interview. Remind the respondent about confidentiality, and explain clearly what happens next. There is no need to draw things out unnecessarily, but the session should end with thanks, handshakes, and the promise of a written copy of the record (or tape). Even if the interview has not gone particularly well and the respondent has not been very helpful, a note of thanks should be expressed. An interview is an imposition on the respondents and uses their precious time. It is surprising how much respect can be commanded if professionalism is retained, even in the face of conflict.

## Nonverbal Communication

Most communication between two people occurs nonverbally. If there is a conflict between what is being said and what is being conveyed through unspoken signals, most will believe the nonverbal signals. If you ask a friend whether she is okay and she gives the standard "Fine'" reply, it is easy to know whether this is true or not. There are many signals attached to the reply that will tell you to probe this answer or accept it as more or less true. In fact, if you fail to follow up a grudging "Fine'" that is delivered with a shrug of the shoulders and a sour look, your friend will probably feel aggrieved.

A good understanding of nonverbal communication (NVC) allows the interviewer to probe difficult areas, to explore more sensitive topics, and to follow up answers that may be concealing the truth. The conversation can move from the official agenda to the real agenda that lies underneath the surface. A possible witness to a major scam by management may be very reluctant to reveal the way managers are distorting monthly performance figures to earn large bonuses. The respondent is an innocent bystander and will tell all if this is clearly required by the interviewer, but will not "squeal" on colleagues if this can be avoided. The official interview revolves around the respondent's work and understanding of the performance bonus scheme, but the real agenda is to find out who is involved in the fraud. If the official answers suggest that the respondent does not know about the scam, the underlying feelings expressed through NVC may be probed. Changes in demeanor, language, tone, facial expressions, or anything else may give a clue that there is something more behind a one-word denial. Probing these and providing a platform for the truth is one way of getting to the whole truth. There is an entire range of NVC, including:

- **Spatial factors**.   The physical distance that is maintained between interviewer and respondent can be determined by cultural factors. Think about the implications of invading the space of the respondent and the effect this may have on the proceedings. The position of the desk and chairs can also create an impression of formality, informality, barriers, sharing secrets, and other concepts. The interviewer has a lot of control over this factor if the respondent is being questioned in a place chosen by the interviewer. There is more scope to observe body language when there is no desk between the two parties, and sitting side by side may encourage the sharing of secrets. Positioning can also depend on the expectations of those involved. It can be useful to be able to move closer to the respondent when an important issue is being explored. At the same time, ensure that there is no perception of harassment, coercion, or intimidation.

- **Body language.**  Gestures, stance, and the movement of limbs can be signals for the interviewer. A person may appear stiff when under pressure and adopt a more relaxed posture when answering questions that are easier to deal with. The same person may look toward the door when a question appears to close in on her and she feels trapped. A shift in posture may indicate agreement or disagreement with what is being said by the interviewer. Nervous reactions such as placing a hand over the mouth can mean that the words coming out are being pushed back in or filtered. Crossing legs and arms can be interpreted as a defensive gesture against a perceived threat from the interviewer.

- **Facial expressions.**  The eyes, eyebrows, mouth, and jaw muscles of the respondent can say a lot about the level of stress, anger, surprise, concern, uncertainty, and a whole array of different feelings being experienced at the time. The degree of eye contact can indicate comfort, discomfort, and avoidance.

- **Silences.**  Pauses, looking away, looking unsatisfied, not answering, and other uses of silence can be quite effective in getting the right information from the respondent. Silence can mean the interviewer is not happy with an answer or is simply thinking about the answer that has been given. It can also be used to drill down into the inner thoughts of the respondent—the so-called hidden agenda of truth.

- **Voice.**  The tone and pitch of the voice can suggest much. Stress, hesitation, and tremors can all indicate areas that should be probed further by the interviewer.

- **Language.**  The words used can give us a clue as to the thoughts behind the answers. Some argue that people distance themselves from subjects that incriminate them or reflect badly on them. For example, a purchase order that has been altered by someone in an office is referred to as the "office order," to suggest that everyone in the office had access to it and so anyone could have altered it. Forensic statement analysis is a useful technique that is described and illustrated in Appendix A.

The interview is not a process through which the respondent is pressured into giving the answers that the interviewer wants. It is not a process to trap people into admitting knowledge or actual participation in a crime. The interview is a process to establish the facts in issue as a contribution to the efficient completion of the investigation. The facts in a case are what is true or thought to be true in the mind of the respondent. Thus, the interview is about searching for the truth, but in a way that respects the rights of the respondent and recognizes that people have different perceptions of reality. It also recognizes that people cannot be forced to speak.

NVC is very useful in helping to distinguish the truth from hesitation, lies, and concealment. If the interviewer understands his or her own NVC, the respondent may open up in response to positive encouragement. Effective communication between two parties is based mainly on a degree of mutual trust between these parties. Mutual trust derives from signals between the parties that are understood and accepted.

It may be necessary to know whether the respondent is providing the whole truth. An NVC baseline may be established by starting the question session with nonthreatening questions, the answers to which are already known to the interviewer. After a while, the normal actions of the respondent can become a form of standard. For the more difficult aspects of the interview, watch for divergence from the previously set standard. The pitch of the respondent's voice may change when asked about the missing funds and whether the respondent knows who had access to the account in question. The change in voice may indicate knowledge that has not been revealed to the interviewer. It needs to be probed and examined. The question has to be reframed to take out any threat and emphasize the duty of all staff to help uncover the truth. The question will end up as both threatening and nonthreatening by giving the opportunity to help protect the organization but with a baseline that this is what is expected.

When interviewing a suspect, the norm is to present this person with the evidence secured through the investigation. There should be less concern about uncovering lies; the suspect will probably lie anyway, as this is the nature of deceit. This should not be an issue, as the evidence—it is hoped—will speak for itself. Accept any lies told, but probe any explanation given for consistency and reasonableness. Only when the case is weak or poorly conceived will efforts have to be directed at exposing the suspect as a liar, to avoid an embarrassing failure in the investigation. Professionalism is about having standards and ensuring that these standards are observed; this applies equally to formal investigative interviewing.

# OTHER INVESTIGATIVE TECHNIQUES

The investigation team is in place and the workforce may or may not know that the inquiry is happening. Meanwhile, the investigators may or may not have a suspect at this stage. We come now to the type of work that may be carried out by the investigators. The strategy for conducting the investigation will depend entirely on what is being investigated, with a key driver being the question "What evidence do we need, and how do we get hold of it in such as way as to support the case in a reliable and robust manner?" Evidence was discussed earlier, but we need to list a few of the techniques for getting good evidence.

## Analytical Review

A comparison of figures, over various periods or between departments, may turn up inconsistencies that can be examined in some detail. If the allegation is that expensive goods are disappearing from a particular branch and the stock figures are being forged to hide the fraud, the problem has to be investigated. The figures at the branch may not be reliable, although these will have to be tested at some stage. The movement of spending on inventory over time and as a ratio of sales may be studied. Discrepancies that cannot be explained can be investigated. If the branch in question has a different ratio of stock turnover to sales than other similar branches, then again this can be explored further. Evidence from such a review is only circumstantial, but can lead to more direct evidence of the actual fraud itself. In this instance, it would be nice to see the goods disappear and perhaps take a photograph or recording to capture this event.

## Surveillance

When an investigation is not yet public and no one has been suspended, surveillance becomes a possible technique. Surveillance is about structured observation of events so that, unknown to those involved in the fraud, good evidence may be secured as part of the investigation into the fraud. Covert operation is more complicated and can involve getting someone to infiltrate those involved in the scam to get inside information, again as evidence for the investigation. There can be much personal risk to the person who is acting undercover. Physical frauds, such as the unauthorized removal of goods, checks, equipment, and so on, are well suited to surveillance exercises, as are frauds that involve the association of two parties (for example, when kickbacks are being taken). If the removal of valuables can be observed, or an inappropriate liaison spotted, this helps in proving the fraud.

> One scam, whereby excessive overtime was being claimed by key workers, was investigated through surveillance that recorded finish times and compared them to the overtime claims being made.
>
> Parking scams can be broken by observing the time cars spend in the parking lot and comparing this to the income accounted for by the operatives.
>
> People working while on sick leave, or claiming injury compensation while obviously active again, can be discovered through basic observation.

Simple frauds can be tackled through simple techniques, although the more sophisticated schemes involving senior people are less susceptible to easy discovery. Having said this, there are many reasons why surveillance can be difficult:

- Surveillance must be planned very carefully. Most such exercises are based on good intelligence when there is a suspicion that something is happening, that can be pinned down to a particular person, location, item, or destination. Good background details are required to do static surveillance, which becomes mobile when the suspect is followed. Not only should the exercise be planned carefully, and the team fully briefed (and kept in contact), but there should also be formal authority to proceed, probably from the CEO.
- There may be problems regarding breach of rights when there is a reasonable expectation of privacy away from the workplace. Tapping phones, recording conversations, taking photographs, and using eavesdropping devices are all methods that could violate someone's rights, if not used carefully. Eavesdropping devices are banned in most states.
- There is some danger of getting caught up in a difficult chain of events. Neighborhood watch schemes, suspicious local police officers, people who question strangers in an unusual location, others who

resent stalkers, and a suspect who discovers a tail can all cause tremendous problems for the investigator. A well-rehearsed cover story is essential in such a situation, even including made-up documentation if this is possible and legal. It is best to notify the local police and ensure that they are okay with the investigator's planned conduct.

Surveillance can draw very heavily on resources and time after time can lead to no real results. The wrong place and times may be chosen, or the suspect may have been alerted to the exercises, or maybe the suspect is simply suspicious or cautious. It is frustrating and a little embarrassing to take out a team and return with no proper evidence or leads as the cost of the exercise starts to stack up. Careful planning is important to ensure some degree of success at an early stage. There should be an original plan, a fallback plan, and a response strategy for developments that break very quickly. When briefing the team, go through a form of brainstorming on what may happen and how best to respond in each event. It is a little like risk management: What are the risks? How likely are they? How can these risks be minimized? How do we plan to deal with them if they arise? These considerations are well worth a half-hour briefing session. Investigators need to get tooled up—that is, trained, prepared, and equipped with the right communications, recording equipment, and suitable visual aids. One word of warning about going undercover:

> An undercover police officer stripped down to his socks and danced on the table at a strip club to ensure that he fitted in with the other members of the club. Witnesses claimed he was intoxicated.

Nonetheless, we can still think of surveillance as useful in certain circumstances.

> The ACFE reported one fraud involving truckers underdelivering expensive steaks to restaurants that did not bother to check the deliveries, and then selling the extra meat to restaurants that paid cash for the delivery. This scam would have been almost undetectable without observing what was happening and recording the exchange of meats and cash outside of normal practice.

### Examination of Audit Trails

Most fraud investigations involve a lot of paperwork. Frauds that abuse financial systems and attack funds as they are moved between accounts tend to leave a paper trail. There is a record of the underlying transactions that traces the movement from start to finish—the finish presumably being to an account controlled by the offenders or their associates. One technique is to use this trail to document the fraud as it progresses through the systems and display the interactions by employees, both innocent and those implicated in the loss. Trails can result from documents, computer interactions, phone records, attendance records, and anything else that traces the movement of people, information, transactions, and resources.

## Document Analysis

Documents may be analyzed to determine whether they can be used as evidence of fraud. An invoice may be a forgery, seeking payment for goods or services that never existed. As part of the investigation, the invoice will be subjected to forensic examination to ascertain:

- How it was produced.
- What equipment was used to produce it.
- Whether it contains any distinguishing marks, including fingerprints.
- How it was processed.
- What inside information was needed to undertake the fraud.
- What the details on the invoice can tell us.

Computerized documents can be examined using stylistics, where the style of the writer is determined and an assessment made of the likelihood that a document was written by a particular person.

## Verification

Verification involves finding and checking out something. It can be applied to real assets, to check that they exist and belong to the company. If the allegation is that an employee is running a private company using the employer's resources and contacts to gain business, the offices of this private company may be visited to verify that it does in fact exist.

## Reconciliation

Accounting systems are designed to be in balance. As a transaction is made —say, a transfer of money from the company bankers to the company—the funds will be debited to the company's bank account and credited to the banker as payment received. These accounts will be in balance as funds moving around the organization and between external parties are properly accounted for. Regular reconciliations should be carried out to ensure that accounts balance. The amount in the bank account should agree with the bank statement, taking into account checks due to be paid and income due to be credited to arrive at a reconciled bank account. Fraud involving financial systems may throw off the real figures so that they fall out of balance. It is by carrying out a reconciliation that the fraud may be discovered. *Lapping* is a type of fraud that involves timing differences in receipt and banking receipts to cover up the theft of an earlier receipt. Lapping can be isolated by analyzing the income for any timing differences.

## Using Expert Witnesses

Witnesses give evidence in court in response to questions that they answer factually, and are generally not allowed to express their opinion. An exception to this rule relates to evidence given by an expert. A forensic examination of documents may be commissioned to look for forgeries or alterations, or even a DNA assessment of, for example, stamps that have been licked by the suspect; such tasks must be done by experts. Handwriting can be checked to assess the likelihood of a match with other known samples of writing. Photocopies can be checked for a match with a particular copying machine to establish important links. Experts are required to express a professional opinion on matters that fall under their area of expertise and, after having carried out their examination, they will issue a report and present this to the court as evidence. An alternative explanation may be presented by the defense's appointed expert, particularly when the matter is complicated. The experts are employed to apply special knowledge to the case. They should make sure that they consider the following matters:

- Experts work with the facts and should be able to form an opinion based on these facts.
- They should classify the evidence to support the facts, and this evidence should be properly handled and filed.
- The work carried out by the expert is subject to discovery and can be examined by the defense team.

When presenting evidence in court, the expert needs to make sure the answers are clear, concise, specific, considered, and free of jargon, and that a professional demeanor is retained even under rigorous cross-examination.

## Third-Party Confirmation

Most evidence of employee fraud will come from within the organization. There are, however, times when we need to step outside and talk to third parties. In this case, an official statement obtained from the third party can be added to the store of evidence.

> In one fraud, a senior officer was accused of accepting excessive levels of free samples from a major vendor and making inappropriate procurement decisions on that basis. The vendor was happy to give official confirmation of the gifts it provided for the officer and correspondence on proposed new purchases, on the basis that it wished to retain the company's business.

When any external party provides information, that party should sign a formal statement, cross-referenced to documents used as exhibits.

## Data Interrogation

Investigators may make good use of computer interrogation as part of the investigation. There is readily available software that can be used against downloaded data to analyze, assess, and extract records that fit the criteria set by the interrogation exercise. The payables database may be searched for the year to look for all invoices that match the profile of suspect items set by the investigator. All items that match will be sorted and reported so that the supporting paperwork can be extracted and examined. It may be necessary to flag items going to a certain expenditure code, or for certain types of spend items, or for vendors with a certain contact cell phone number, for careful scrutiny; the interrogation software may be used for this task. In fact, the investigation of any frauds that involve large financial systems may benefit from the use of data interrogations, including data mining (see Appendix B).

## Personal Profile

Another good technique that can be used to guide the investigation is personnel profiling. A database may be compiled from information relating to employees who are implicated in the fraud. A great deal of information can be extracted from internal sources, such as:

- Personnel.
- Payroll.

- Expense claims.
- Invoices paid.
- Phone logs.
- Computer logs.
- Staff performance reports.
- Documents authorized by the subject.
- Car parking permits and records.
- Correspondence.
- Phone messages.
- Office diaries (and automated calendars).
- Fax messages.
- Internet searches and e-mails.
- Incoming mail (but watch out for mail fraud).
- Desk searches.
- Searches of wastepaper baskets.
- Other internal databases and records.

External sources may also be used to further build this profile. A wide variety of potential information is available from:

- City health departments.
- Tax authorities.
- Regulatory agencies.
- County registers of voters.
- County courts.
- Registered corporations.
- Professional bodies such as for accountants, doctors, and dentists.
- Credit rating bureaus.
- Federal Inspector General.
- Securities and Exchange Commission.
- Dun and Bradstreet.
- Chambers of commerce.
- Better Business Bureau.
- Interpol.
- National Crime Information Center.
- Western Union.
- State and national directories.
- Banks, via search warrants or subpoenas.

Each state has legislation on what personal records may be maintained and rules on access restrictions and which records are public. Such statutes are usually a version of the federal Freedom of Information Act and Privacy Act. Armed with an abundance of information, it is possible to build a comprehensive profile of suspects, known associates, and any business contacts, to be used to assist the investigation. The information may help ascertain whether the suspect is implicated in the fraud.

## Informants

Another weapon for investigators is to employ informers to provide inside information on the scam and give insight into ways that it could be tackled. Some informers are motivated by the small amounts of money they receive for their information; others are driven by a desire for justice or status, or simply a desire to deflect attention from their own questionable activities. The legal system frowns on inducement, although it is quite right to acknowledge the assistance of people who may be implicated on the periphery of the scam. There is an art to managing informants, especially when they may have somewhat undesirable lifestyles and are able to get close to the criminals. When a gang of career criminals are involved in, say, credit card fraud via the Internet, investigations can become very seedy. If investigators get too close to an informant, they can become implicated in crimes that they have knowledge of. If an informant comes to any harm, the investigators may share some responsibility. Complicated "sting" exercises using people placed in delicate situations must be left to the professionals, as they require a great deal of preparation.

The information provided by informants should be thoroughly checked out before it is placed in the file of evidence. Things can become even more difficult when the informant has broken laws in the pursuit of information. The final point to consider is whether the informant would make a good witness or whether he or she would have to attend a court hearing as a result of the investigation. This point is relevant to all investigations. At times good evidence is obtained through confidential sources and covert techniques. If the case comes to court, a decision has to be made on whether to continue and reveal those covert techniques and sources. If this point is not considered at an early stage, the case may have to be dropped because of important sensitivities. When selecting investigators to carry out a particular task, make sure the persons chosen will make competent and credible witnesses. If not, do not use them.

# A MODEL FOR INVESTIGATIONS

Employee fraud should be investigated in a way that suits the situation, by people who can best carry out the work. In practice, it is possible to set some kind of procedure for carrying out such an investigation, based on the standards we mentioned at the start of the chapter. We will keep this procedure general, as each individual fraud will be different. For employee frauds, whenever possible, the 14-stage procedure set out in Figure 6.2 may be applied:

1. Allegation

2. Background Research

3. Preliminary Report

4. Investigation Plan

5. Support

6. Definition of Barriers

7. Strategy

8. Full Investigation

9. Interim Reports

10. Witness Statements

11. Suspect Interview

12. Final Report

13. Action

14. Review

**Figure 6.2**    Procedure for Investigating Employee for Fraud

## 1. Allegation

Most employee frauds come to light because of information provided by an informant, the suspicions of people working in the section that is affected, or reports of an actual unexplained loss. We dealt with detection in Chapter 4, but here we want to reinforce the need for a process to capture all allegations and ensure that they are given due consideration. A document should be used to detail the essence of the allegation and record the decision on whether or not to investigate the matters alluded to. All allegations should be conveyed to a nominated person and recorded in a database of reported frauds. This starts the investigation process.

## 2. Background Research

Having received an allegation, the next stage is to carry out some basic background work. The main question is whether there is a real problem. When there is a clear loss—say, a large amount of money that should be in the company pension fund appears to be missing—further action is required. A specific allegation against a member of staff will likewise have to be checked out. This stage of the investigation will indicate the scope and scale of the problem and whether a full-blown investigation should be launched.

## 3. Preliminary Report

The next stage is to write a first report of the matter that will go to nominated parties for consideration. For example, an allegation of kickbacks on contracts is made to the purchasing manager and then passed on to the compliance officer or chief fraud advisor for consideration. After carrying out some basic checks, the compliance officer should prepare a preliminary report covering:

- Introduction—the allegation and any information on hand regarding the informant or suspicions.
- Work done—the basic checks made to substantiate the allegation.
- Conclusions—whether the allegation is well founded and initial checks are consistent with the reported problem.
- Recommendations—is there a the need for an investigation? If so, the focus and resource implications of a decision to go ahead with further work.
- Police involvement—appropriate at this stage?

Chapter 5 discussed the need for some form of chief fraud advisor and a high-level fraud panel that will oversee any investigation. Whatever the format, there should be a formal procedure to approve a full investigation. The preliminary report should be presented to the fraud panel by the chief fraud advisor (or equivalent) and discussed in confidence in some detail, with formal minutes taken. Based on the findings to date, a decision should be made, taking into account the best interests of the company. Possible involvement of local law enforcement should always be on the agenda, and the decision should revolve around timing so that the police are approached when there is a good case for examination. The chief fraud advisor should be asked to put together an investigation plan to cover the initial work required to conduct the investigation.

## 4. Investigation Plan

The fraud investigation will start to take shape with the formulation of a plan. The plan will be put together by the chief fraud advisor and cover items such as:

1. **The lead investigator.** Someone has to be in charge of the investigation, and this should be determined at the outset. It may be an appointed external specialist from a respected firm; if so, the contractual details must be properly organized. The chief fraud advisor should oversee the entire exercise and act as the liaison between the fraud panel and the lead investigator.

2. **The attorney.** For larger investigations, an attorney should be appointed to take charge of the work. This allows the attorney-client privilege to protect information from disclosure, at least for a while.

3. **The terms of reference.** A clear objective should be set for the investigation (possibly based on the items listed at the beginning of this chapter). The investigation should be conducted in line with the fraud policy and standards for this type of work. An organization that sets a clear procedure for conducting employee fraud investigations, and subsequently ignores that procedure, is heading for major problems.

4. **Reporting lines.** It is a good idea to set up formal reporting lines early, at the start of the investigation. The potential audience for a large employee fraud includes:

   - Chief executive officer.
   - Chief financial officer.
   - Chief internal auditor.
   - Chief personnel officer.
   - Chief fraud advisor.
   - Compliance officer.
   - External auditor.
   - Shareholders.
   - Director for the area affected.
   - Company attorney.
   - Investigators.

The more people who know about the fraud and the investigation, the more chance there is that unauthorized persons—even the fraudster—will find out that an investigation has begun.

**Status.**   A big decision at this stage is whether the investigation should be open or closed; that is, whether it should be made public, perhaps with suspension of the persons suspected of being involved, or kept entirely confidential at this stage. Some investigations have to be made public, such as when funds are missing and this is well known throughout the organization, or when a vendor complains that a huge payment to the company is missing. Investigative journalists may carry out an operation and tell everyone there is a fraud going on in a particular organization; again, the problem will become public knowledge. If the investigation is covert and has to be kept secret, then the tenor changes somewhat. The project will have to be reported on a need-to-know basis and time becomes quite an issue. The work will become public sooner or later, but the idea is to do as much as possible before it breaks. When surveillance is being considered, the time factor becomes even more crucial.

**Other matters.**   There may be special factors involved in the investigation. This will obviously vary with each case, but it may be that the suspects are related to a senior manager or that they are implicated as part of a criminal gang that is being investigated by the FBI. The investigation becomes more difficult when there is no suspect and any of dozens of people in a section may be involved. The police department may ask that no action be taken by the employer at this stage, because of various sensitivities. In some cases, management may have acted in a negligent manner and so violated the insurance coverage, or made the organization culpable. When a very senior executive is implicated, the investigation may have to be fast-tracked, with the CEO being intimately involved in setting direction and ensuring quick and effective action. When a group of tough managers conspires to defraud the company, using threats and menace to intimidate the staff, the work takes place on a heated battlefield, and there may be little time to convene too many panels and meetings. At the other extreme, the problem may be much simpler and related to general abuse that has become custom and practice in a section; this is more of a human resource management issue than a real fraud.

## 5. Support

Building on the defined reporting lines established earlier, the support infrastructure for the planned investigation has to be made clear. Extending the material from Chapter 4, several roles should be clearly defined, including those of:

- **CEO**. The chief officer will want to see the fraud dealt with efficiently and will approve a budget for the project and ensure that it is properly spent.
- **Director for the area where the fraud occurred**. We have argued that executive responsibility for managing the risk of fraud lies with management. One way to do this is to make the relevant director responsible for the way the fraud is handled. The director may well join the fraud panel and make executive decisions as a result of the work done and reports issued by the investigators. All this is on the understanding that the director is in no way implicated in the problem through direct involvement or indirect negligence.
- **Fraud panel**. Relevant key officers will sit on the panel, review the progress of the investigation, and make executive decisions based on recommendations from the investigating team. Personnel, legal representatives, the chief internal auditor, and a representative from the CEO's office may sit on the panel whenever it meets.
- **Chief fraud advisor (or compliance officer)**. This person will oversee the work of the investigators and present their reports to the fraud panel. The chief fraud advisor is also responsible for quality control over the work of the investigators and technicalities such as contacting the organization's insurance carrier.
- **Investigators**. The lead investigator will undertake the bulk of work and may employ a small team to assist with this task. He or she may need to call upon accounting, IT, and technical forensic experts from time to time. The investigators may well be from a firm of external consultants. The police department may also be asked to work with the investigators, or simply to provide advice and support, although they will take the case on when there is enough evidence to think about prosecution. When the fraud starts to fall outside of the organization and search warrants are required to deal with third-party bodies, the police will have a greater role. Most police services are underresourced, so when the organization can launch a professional investigation, expensive police time will not be needlessly tied up.
- **Audit committee**. The audit committee will want to know that the organization has responded well to the fact of fraud and is managing the problem according to set standards. The chief internal auditor may need to be kept up to date and may provide advice to the investigators regarding corporate systems and procedures. Also, the auditors tend to have access to all organizational information systems,

and so could be asked to help as appropriate. Some internal audit outfits actually carry out entire fraud investigations and have a pivotal role in all major fraud work.

## 6. Definition of Barriers

One aspect of an investigation is to work out what could go wrong. What are the barriers to an effective investigation in conjunction with the set objectives? For larger frauds, it may be a good idea to set up a secure room with a few tables, chairs, marker board, and flip charts, so that the investigation team can start to put the fraud into context and bounce ideas around. One flip chart may list the known facts, including people, sections, systems, and the way the crime was perpetrated. Another flip chart may contain a "to do" list of tasks that are outstanding and must be completed at some stage. A marker board may be used to brainstorm ideas for advancing the investigation. There are some frauds that are very hard to crack; the investigators know what is wrong but cannot pin down the actual methods used or the culprits involved.

> In one case, company checks kept going astray and ended up in false bank accounts that could not be traced until the account holder had disappeared, after withdrawing the funds. It took many sessions of brainstorming before the breach was spotted in the system for preparing checks and getting them to payees. A mobile surveillance exercise resulted from the brainstorm. It turned out that various couriers who transported mail between company offices were removing checks and then passing them over to a criminal gang.

The weeks of frustration during which the fraud could not be traced went by very slowly before the breakthrough. Things that could get in the way of an investigation are many and varied, but could include:

- Missing or irretrievable documents.
- The absence of any known suspects.
- Time limits before the investigation goes public.
- The nonavailability or intimidation of witnesses.
- The possible involvement of management in the fraud area.
- Computerized evidence that could be destroyed.
- Requests by the police to restrict the scope of the investigation.
- The need for privacy in interviews.

- Noncooperation of key witnesses.
- Apparent alibis of the suspects.
- The danger of claims of entrapment.
- Claims of duress from suspects.
- The possibility that the fraud resulted from innocent mistakes, or that management authorized the questionable activities.
- The unstable mental state of the suspect.

Potential barriers must be considered very carefully. One aspect of this stage of the investigation is to get over the barriers and, if possible, get rid of them entirely. Some barriers are legal, in that only certain things are allowed by law. For example, setting up a wiretap to record conversations with the suspect may violate that person's rights. In some states, phone conversations may be monitored, but only as long as it takes to ascertain whether they are private or work-related. Even prior notification to staff that calls will be monitored may not be enough to preserve this right to listen to calls in all circumstances.

## 7. Strategy

Possibly, the most crucial stage of the investigation is that of setting the strategy. The team of investigators may go back to the flip charts and brainstorm how best to deal with the fraud, but at a minimum, it will want to ensure that:

- The fraud itself is properly understood.
- The offense is clearly defined in terms of which local and federal laws have been violated.
- The functioning of the systems and controls breached by the fraud is understood.
- The amount lost is established.
- The area affected by the fraud is isolated.
- The people potentially implicated in the fraud are identified.
- The witnesses who can contribute to the investigation are defined.

The remainder of the strategy is about preserving and gathering the available evidence required to prove the fraud, in a way that makes the evidence admissible. For example, if the police take charge of a case, the rules on law enforcement apply, and the employer's investigators become agents of the police. As such, the investigators will need search warrants for carrying out tasks such as desk searches. The assigned investigators will have to be professionals, as they may be required to testify in court.

## 8. Full Investigation

After the investigation team has been assigned specific tasks, the full investigation may be started. The techniques described earlier, such as interviewing, forensic examination of documents, and so on, will be used in the investigation proper. The main point to note is the need to set a clear objective for each task and ensure that the right resource is assigned to the right job, and that the working papers are beyond reproach. Use a standard form for each task that includes sections for:

- Task objective.
- Assigned investigator.
- Method employed.
- Results.
- Conclusions.

Paperwork, documents, reports, and the results of any analysis can be attached to the front sheet and precisely cross-referenced. Interview records should be carefully prepared and filed along with any attachments relevant to the case. Particular care should be taken with any consent forms received to allow access to personal records and searches, to ensure that they have been provided voluntarily, with no duress or inducements. Most investigations are a mix of creative thinking about what to look for and very basic gathering and documentation procedures that are applied meticulously. In fact, for bigger cases a documents manager may be assigned, who will ensure that all paperwork meets acceptable standards, originals are protected, sources are made clear, the chain of evidence is preserved, and the evidence is accounted for, from inception to presentation. Security is a key issue for original documents; all work should be carried out on copies of the originals. Automated files, such as CDs, floppy disks, and confiscated hard disk drives, may have to be protected from defense claims of contamination. Because electronic media are so vulnerable, there must be firm methods for protecting the material. Physical evidence, say from a search of the suspect's desk or a video recording from surveillance work, has to be preserved intact. When fingerprint checks or other forensic examination of documents and objects may be required, the items should be handled and stored with this in mind. Making someone responsible for the evidence is one way of ensuring good standards in line with an evidence control system. The master file may contain a chronology of events that fits with the logical order of the investigation. A short example of a simple investigation follows.

In one organization, all photocopying was done by an in-house reprographics section, managed by a young man called Maurice. In an innocent conversation beside the coffee machine, someone mentioned that the repro team was really busy, as they were on a big job over the weekend. The marketing manager overheard this comment, inquired about the job, and was told that it was a color mail shot on a new product. The marketing manager reported this to internal audit because he had given the job to repro, but was told that it would have to go to an outside vendor as they were too busy to do it in-house. The marketing manager was quoted $7,500 and grudgingly paid it from his budget. Internal audit:

1. Assessed the allegation and found that it had some grounds.
2. Briefed the CEO and director of operations responsible for repro.
3. Prepared a strategy for the investigation and sought advice from the lawyers.
4. Isolated the "target area"—that is, all staff in repro, including the manager, Maurice.
5. Examined the invoice for the job and ran some checks on the company and its directors.
6. Chased the returned check from the company bankers and found out where it was banked.
7. Commissioned a forensic examination of the marketing mail shot job and ascertained that it was produced on the company's own copier.
8. Checked attendance and access to the copier over the last weekend and found out who had used the copy machine.
9. Confirmed that Maurice was a director of the company that had been paid for the copying job.
10. Interviewed several key staff to confirm that Maurice had been working the copier over the weekend, and obtained written statements to that effect.
11. Established that other staff in repro were not implicated at all.
12. Presented the evidence to Maurice and his representative, and sought explanations, which were not forthcoming.
13. Concluded the case with the partially unsatisfactory result that Maurice disappeared, his employment contract was terminated, and the matter was handed over to the local police department.

14. Presented a report on the case and recommended various controls to ensure that the lax treatment of photocopy facilities and placement of local contracts would be tightened up.

This case was fairly straightforward, although there was some discussion with the director of operations about the way contract work was handled. Also, the investigators had to take quick action in taking copies from the photocopier under controlled conditions to be compared with the mail shots. Another simple case was investigated along the following lines.

Income collection from car parking was contracted out to a small firm that made nightly collection of cash from parking meters located around a city center. Cash boxes were removed from each meter; replaced by empty boxes; and taken to the firm's office, counted, and banked. Reports of proceeds were sent to the public body listing the cash received per numbered parking meter per day. Information was received from a former employee of the contractor that the operatives had gotten keys to the cash boxes and that cash was being removed before the cash boxes were taken to the firm's office. As a result, investigators met with the parking manager and obtained a detailed account of the system for collecting and recording parking meter income. The manager felt that there was no theft going on because the daily income figures were pretty constant. What he did not know was that the scam had been going on for years and the figures were being understated by 25 percent, or just over $10,000 a week. The investigators carried out the following tasks:

1. Brainstormed the case and devised a suitable strategy, which was presented to the CEO and head of parking control.
2. The strategy involved counting the cash in a selection of parking meters after the parking bays became free of charge in the evening, and marking the cash with an ultraviolet pen. Armed with hot coffee and doughnuts, two investigators then sat in their car and waited for the cash boxes to be collected.
3. The operatives were observed removing the cash boxes from the meters and were then followed back to the firm's offices. Luckily, the parking contract allowed unannounced access to the firm's records, so the investigators entered the firm's offices, identified themselves, and observed the cash count and made their own records.
4. Having established a shortfall on all marked cash boxes, the local police, who had been notified about the exercise some time ago, were alerted. The police obtained search warrants, found marked cash in the possession of the contractor's staff, and made several arrests.

5. The contract was terminated, a sum for restitution was negotiated with the contractor's directors, and several employees were charged. One pleaded guilty, two were convicted and found guilty, and one was found not guilty because he had no marked cash on him and could not be traced to particular parking meters.

In this case, a sample of losses was identified and proof obtained that the suspects had removed the cash involved. Again, recommendations were made to ensure better controls over this type of contract.

## 9. Interim Reports

It is important to drive fraud investigations so that there is constant momentum in the right direction. Some investigations can be quite frustrating when many hours of work are required to shift through reams of paper—most totally irrelevant—with the possibility of one or two items being highly significant. Even automated interrogations can be boring, as they may flag hundreds of records that have to be manually extracted and scrutinized in detail. Many fraud investigations are time-bound, in that a loss is identified but the case gets older and older as the work establishes what happened. Again, it is important to retain an energetic pace in trying to crack the case. This is why interim reports are so important. They provide an update on the investigation and a chance to assess any new evidence. It also gives the organization an opportunity to review the quality of the investigation and decide whether the right resources are being used. Finally, fresh approval can be secured, to embark on major new tasks and spend more money as a result. All ongoing investigations should involve interim reporting on a regular basis when:

- The investigation is taking a while to complete and lasts more that one week.
- There has been a major change in direction of the investigation as a result of new leads.
- There is clear evidence from which to prepare charges against the suspect.
- A decision is needed on whether to continue the investigation.
- The fraud panel is meeting and needs an update on work in progress.
- The police or other external bodies need to know of the progress on a case.

If there is a chief fraud advisor (or compliance officer), it may be a good idea for him or her to get an update on outstanding fraud investigations every week or two. For more significant investigations, regular progress reports may be required, perhaps delivered as oral presentations rather than formal reports. The interim report will cover such items as:

- The fraud and how it came about.
- Work carried out to date.
- Cost of the investigation to date.
- Details of known losses.
- Any special problems and sensitivities.
- Progress of gathering evidence and whether there are any suspects.
- Any suspension of employees so far.
- Any charges that are being considered.
- Further work required and possible time frames involved.
- Any items submitted for management decision.
- Any recommendations for management action.

The report should be brief and made available on a need-to-know basis only. The fraud panel will probably want a presentation of the work and this should be used as an opportunity to ask searching questions of the investigators and the direction of the investigation. The chief fraud advisor will need to perform some quality assurance work to ensure that the investigation meets acceptable standards. The evidence gathered by the investigators so far should be reviewed and legal advice obtained on the status of the evidence.

### 10. Witness Statements

Interviewing was described as an important technique in investigations; in a typical inquiry, many dozens of people may be questioned to ascertain the facts. When this task has been completed, formal witness statements may be obtained; that is, a formal record of the events in the words of the witness that is duly completed, signed, and witnessed. The format of the record should be such that it can be presented in court for civil or criminal action and can also be used as part of an internal disciplinary case against the employee. If the fraud results in a criminal prosecution, the police may wish to reinterview witnesses and obtain their own statements. If the investigator's version is acceptable, then the statements can go straight to the prosecution team—something of a compliment. Any exhibit referred to in the statements should be attached and clearly cross-referenced to the statement.

## 11. Suspect Interview

This is a most difficult part of the investigation. It is undertaken when there is sufficient evidence of an alleged offense that has to be presented to the suspect, to provide an opportunity to address the evidence. A file of evidence will have been compiled, including documents, statements, analysis, surveillance records, and other material relevant to the inquiry. The suspect may be asked to recount his or her understanding of events, and this will be compared with the known facts. When the investigators are in possession of all key facts, they will probably remind the suspects of their rights and place the evidence before them while seeking an explanation of each incriminating item.

Documentation via a written note or tape is essential; some investigators make a video recording of the interview. If there is an admission of guilt, along with dates, times, names, method, and an indication of intent, the interview may have to be terminated. Any statements should be signed voluntarily and include a written note of the suspect's willingness to cooperate and any explanations for the offense offered by the suspect. It may be best to secure a separate statement for each separate offense. When there are sufficient grounds to bring charges against the suspect, again the interview can be terminated.

The interview process should involve no intimidation or duress; it should simply be an attempt to get to the truth. The suspect has the right to make a formal complaint about the interview and this complaint will have to be properly responded to. The suspect should be asked at the end whether he or she is satisfied with the opportunities given to provide explanations, and additional details can be included if required. The suspects should be given an opportunity to make a full confession, and if the replies are unsatisfactory they can be asked to rethink their answers. Scenarios that suggest guilt can be laid out before the suspects and they can be asked to comment. Questions may also be posed about others who may be implicated in the crime.

Some investigators hand over the paperwork to the police department and ask them to conduct the interview with the suspect, as it can be a very detailed affair. Other investigators carry out the interview but restrict matters to charges relating to the staff disciplinary code of conduct rather than the criminal case.

## 12. Final Report

The final report is a formal document that may be considered by many different parties. Legal representatives for both the prosecution and the defense, and even a jury, may view the report. External bodies, such as external audit firms, or the government if the company is in receipt of government funds, may also wish to consider the report. Insurance carriers and regulatory bodies may request access to the report of the investigation, and the courts may order access by various parties to the proceedings. The point is that the report should be firmly grounded; it should not only look good, but also contain a valid account of the scope, findings, and conclusions from the investigation.

**Why report?**  A good place to start when thinking about the report is to consider why we bother to prepare one in the first place. The report is about communicating important information to produce a desired response. Think about the audience and what they want from the report and the message that is being communicated. The report will have an open message and a hidden message. The open message will be about the findings of the investigation and the action that should be taken as a result of these findings. It will give details of the offense, the evidence, who is implicated, and what the consequences are. The hidden message will be that all reasonable steps have been taken with respect to the fraud and that the organization can defend itself against charges of negligence or culpability. The recipient will also perform a subjective analysis of whether the investigation was carried out with due professional care, and check that there are no real gaps in the research, the evidence produced, or the chain of logic that links the evidence to any suspects. This is why the report is so important. It represents a product that attacks the criminal and defends the organization that has been defrauded, and not the other way round. As such, the report will need to:

1. Satisfy the recipients that a thoroughly professional job has been performed by the investigators.
2. Demonstrate that all legal means have been applied to identifying and using the available evidence of the fraud.
3. Illustrate how the objectives of the investigation were achieved.
4. Show that the work was done objectively, so there can be no claim of victimization or tampering with evidence.

**5.** Demonstrate that all reasonable steps have been taken to protect the reputation of the organization.

These five points will be uppermost on the minds of the reader of the report and should therefore also feature prominently in the thinking of the report writer.

**Types of reports.** There are different types of reports to fit different circumstances. The investigator needs to ensure that the right kind of report is prepared for the right circumstances. Unlike standard reports, a fraud investigation has certain peculiarities that make it a little different. There may be periods of extreme frenzy followed by periods of calm, collected analysis where the findings are harmonized. A simple model of "6 As," shown in Figure 6.3, can be used to reflect the changing stages of an investigation and the various reports required. The type of report is linked to the stage that the investigation has reached.

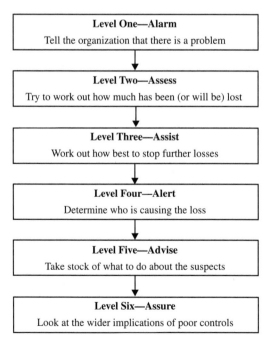

**Figure 6.3** Reporting at Stages of an Investigation

- **Level One—Alarm:**   Alarm bells are rung to tell the executives that something is wrong and there may be an employee fraud at hand. This is done via a brief memo that is presented to senior management or the board. An oral statement will highlight the suspicions and the fact that some quick research must be undertaken. A one-page memo may follow the short presentation of the allegations, as time is the essential ingredient here. Any contact with the press that is necessary should be coordinated by the press office.
- **Level Two—Assess:**   This stage seeks to drill down a little deeper and tends to happen after the case has been worked on for a few days. The report again is a short document that tries to identify the scale of the fraud and whether this is a big or less significant investigation. A schedule of known and anticipated losses will be the main feature of the written report.
- **Level Three—Assist:**   A careful consideration of ways to stop any more losses should be reported, although this will have to be done fairly quickly. The insurance carriers will not be impressed if an organization becomes aware of a problem and then allows it to accelerate and cause more losses than necessary. This report will talk about any quick controls that should be established and any action, such as suspending a suspect, that may be required to halt the fraud. Protection of the organization is the main thrust of this type of report.
- **Level Four—Alert:**   This is the longer, more comprehensive stage of the investigation, detailing anyone who is implicated in the offense. The report is longer because of the risk of defamation; the facts will have to be carefully checked and presented before it can be released at all. A formal interim report should link the findings to the detailed evidence with an index and chronological notations. This document may be considered by third parties and may form the basis for decisions regarding charges and police involvement, if this has not yet happened. A draft will go to legal counsel for due consideration before the report is released. Legal admissibility drives the style of this type of report.
- **Level Five—Advise:**   A report should eventually be issued that gives clear direction on the appropriateness of criminal prosecution and internal disciplinary action. This report will discuss the offenses committed, the charges that should result, and the determination of how the disciplinary code has been breached. It is hard to think of an

employee fraud that does not breach the code of conduct set by most organizations. The fraud panel and audit committee will probably want to see a copy of this report. Problem solving and closure should be key considerations for this report.

- **Level Six—Assure:** This type of report will be a less punchy document that looks at the longer-term implications of fraud risk that has not been properly managed. Aspects of control failure will be examined along with the need to install better controls. The report may stimulate a consultation process whereby buzz groups consider the proposals after formal presentations on any proposed changes to control structures. This report is about achieving assurances that effective controls are in place to guard against the risk of fraud.

The other types of reports that may be written by the chief fraud advisor are summary reports on recent allegations made, frauds investigated, and statistics on reports to police, prosecutors, and staff disciplinaries, perhaps on a quarterly and/or annual basis. It is highly embarrassing if an organization cannot give a figure on reported employees frauds for the year and point to action taken, along with a summary of the results of any investigations undertaken.

**Contents.** The final report of the investigation should contain all the information needed to understand the various stages of the investigation, and will cover matters that are of importance to the recipients. These will obviously vary, but the following areas may be covered:

- The objectives of the investigation.
- The scope of the work.
- Details of the team carrying out the investigation.
- The way the fraud was uncovered.
- Details of the fraud itself.
- Control weaknesses that meant the fraud was not prevented.
- The investigation strategy, reporting lines, and approval procedures involved.
- Personal data relating to the suspects (this may be held in a separate confidential appendix). Suspects may be referred to by a code name that should be read in conjunction with the classified personal data in a detachable appendix.

- Legal representatives.
- Any police involvement.
- Offenses committed and possible charges.
- Any recovery action that has been initiated.
- Detailed list of evidence and conclusions drawn from each item.
- Recommendations for supporting criminal prosecution, disciplinary action, and improving controls.
- Any other relevant information.

A great deal may end up in the official report of the investigation and terms such as *the suspect* and *alleged offense* should be used to retain objectivity. It is not the job of the report to assess the guilt or innocence of the suspect; that is the job of the courts. The job of the report is simply to document the preceding items clearly and objectively.

**Structure.**    The fraud report should follow a basic structure that makes for easy reading and understanding. It may include, for example:

1. **Cover.**    This should be marked *Confidential,* and for more sensitive investigations may be coded rather than given a title. It certainly should not display the name of the chief suspect.
2. **Executive summary.**    Introduction, brief account of the fraud, terms of reference for the investigation, suspects and proposed charges, and recommended actions required.
3. **Introduction.**    Objectives and scope of the investigation, how the fraud came to be noticed, who was assigned to undertake the work, and their approach.
4. **Detailed findings.**    Details of the fraud, the offenses resulting from the fraud, description of evidence relating to each offense (in chronological order), and any rebuttals of the evidence.
5. **Appendices.**    List and summaries of evidence, including witness statements, points by legal advisors, and any other relevant schedules.

It is generally best to get the report structure established before drafting the content. Once the structure makes sense, the detail should fit in quite easily.

**Attributes.**    We can now list some of the factors that make for a good report:

- The report must be based on a first-rate professional investigation. There is no real shortcut around this. If there are flaws in the actual investigation and evidence accumulated, there is a temptation to "report your way out of the problem"; the right response should be to go back and do the investigation properly.
- The report should focus on logic and sound reasoning. A quote from *Second Time Around,* by Marcia Willet (Headline Book Publishing 1997), may help clarify this point: "Arguing from the particular to the general was fraught with danger; an argument was worthless if it could not be taken to a logical conclusion."
- Think about the way the material is presented in the report. The findings should be clear, relevant to the points in issue, and objectively presented. Any opinion should derive from an interpretation of the evidence and not comment on subjective matters, such as the character of the suspect. Sentences should be short and to the point. The active voice should be used so that the report would say, "The compliance officer coordinated the investigation . . . " rather than "The investigation was coordinated by the compliance officer. . . ." There is certainly no room for ambiguity or vague comments, and anything not entirely factual should be discarded from the report.
- Check and double-check accuracy. Unfortunately, reports of fraud investigations have to be entirely accurate. Any error found in the report, however insignificant, may cast doubt over the entire investigation. The best way to ensure accuracy is to have the draft report reviewed in detail in conjunction with the file of evidence. All facts, dates, extracts, references, and exhibits should be verified to ensure reliability. A quality checking procedure should be in place, although any checks should not unduly hold up progress on the report. Not an easy task!
- Prepare the right type of report for the particular circumstances. This point was made earlier, as timeliness is a key issue in many investigations. A short briefing note prepared on the day may be more appropriate than a comprehensive progress report that takes days to complete.
- Arrange a formal presentation of the findings when the fraud is complex and difficult to convey in writing. Take advantage of charts, diagrams, and any visual aids that can assist a full understanding of the fraud, the investigation, and the overall context.

## 13. Action

Reports should be action-oriented. That is, they should lead to efficient action to deal with the problems that have been identified and encourage a response to any recommendations made by the investigating team. The problem is that a report alone does not necessarily lead to direct action; hence, this is a separate stage of the investigation. The reporting process should be fine-tuned so that the right people have access to the report and are able to make executive decisions. This is a fundamental point, in that investigators work on behalf of the employing organization and provide specialist advice based on the work carried out. It really is the organization, in the guise of the board and CEO, that needs to take responsibility for acting on the results of the investigation. Missing funds should be traced through lawyers who specialize in tracking and freezing relevant funds, with a view to recovery. Illegal funds may be transferred to family members by a fraudster or laundered into investments and schemes that fall outside the purview of the investigators, and may even be transferred abroad. Note that the Office of International Trade may provide assistance in tracing missing funds. The organization will also need to consider whether any case against the alleged fraudster is likely to be successful, and weigh the amounts involved and the costs of taking civil action for recovery. Likewise, the case for seeking a criminal prosecution will also have to be examined.

## 14. Review

The final stage of the investigation is often missed completely. This stage entails a reflective consideration of what went wrong and why. The review may cover a variety of areas, including, for example:

- How did the fraud happen and why was it allowed to continue for the period in question?
- What controls have failed and how do we correct the problem?
- What about the overall control environment and culture in place— should they be changed?
- How is our staff managing the risk of fraud?
- Could a similar fraud happen in another part of the organization?
- Did we do enough to recover lost funds?
- Are our procedures for carrying out fraud investigations adequate?
- How did we handle potential damage to our corporate reputation?
- What are the main lessons we can take away from this experience?

The list can be extended to cover other issues as well. If controls, detection system, the fraud policy, and the fraud response plan have been shown to be substandard, these weaknesses should be addressed. If the employer behaved in a way that compounded the problem, this failing needs to be addressed. And if the right messages are not reaching staff and customers and other stakeholders, the communications strategy has to be tightened up. Organizations that have a high level of employee fraud tend not to include the review stage (14) in their fraud investigation strategy and so do not really learn from their experiences.

## STAFF DISCIPLINE

The organization has a moral duty to uphold the law and support the judicial process through any investigation into wrongdoings. Society has developed a criminal justice system to ensure that the rights of the defendant are balanced against the government's need to promote justice and fair play. All criminals should be prosecuted and, so long as the evidence is sound, should be convicted and punished accordingly. This view rules all other considerations and is arguably the right position to aim for. Law enforcement and state prosecutors will want all fraudsters to go through the criminal justice system, so long as that is in the best interests of the people. However, another factor should be added to the justice model when the fraud is perpetrated by an employee. This factor is simply that an employer can rightly conclude that when an employee has committed a fraud against the organization, the mutual trust that binds the two parties has broken down and the continued presence of the employee at work becomes unacceptable. This is regardless of what happens with the criminal case against the employee. It is generally not a good idea to rely on the criminal justice system to deal with an employee when a breach of the organization's standards of conduct can be proved. It is much better to take action against the employee in respect of the breach as a matter of internal staff discipline. The key point is that disciplinary action is about standards at work and not the criminal aspects of the case. There are some issues to be addressed when considering disciplinary action, including the following:

1. Make clear the standards of conduct expected from all employees covered by contracts of employment or at-will arrangements.

2. Ensure that the staff understands these standards and that any serious breach (fraud by definition is always serious) is actionable by dismissal. The breach is about the employee's activities during the course of business. If people who execute fraud are simply asked to resign, they may well do the same thing elsewhere. It gets even worse when dishonest employees are given good references that enable them to leave and get a new job. This clean reference is a clear misrepresentation and makes the ex-employer vulnerable to civil action from the new employer.

3. Ensure that all managers understand the importance of not overruling the standards or condoning questionable behavior. One defense used by employee fraudsters is that their actions were condoned by management, and this stance can blur the line between right and wrong.

4. Carry out a fair and full investigation of the facts of the case. Use professional investigators to assess the entire situation, using the following criteria:

   - Make the investigation thorough and above board.
   - Make sure that no one is prejudiced or discriminated against in any way.
   - Investigators who have a conflict of interest, whether actual or apparent, should withdraw from the investigation.
   - Make sure the investigators are credible and can communicate their role properly.
   - Define reporting lines for the investigation.
   - Make the CEO responsible for ensuring the full and proper conduct of disciplinary investigations.
   - Treat the investigation like a project and implement good project management and risk assessment.
   - Monitor the investigation so that it meets the standards set by the disciplinary procedure.
   - Make sure the employee has access to suitable representation and all information relevant to preparing a defense to the case, including the ability to call his or her own witnesses.
   - Use a procedure whereby the investigators pass the case over to a senior manager who will present the case against the employee to the disciplinary panel.

**5.** Implement a formal disciplinary procedure involving an independent investigation and the presentation of charges by a senior manager. A disciplinary panel should be convened to hear the case against the employee, and the members should have the right skills and insights to understand their responsibilities to act in the best interests of the organization, while observing the rights of the employee. One format for hearing disciplinaries appears in Figure 6.4.

The CEO sits above the entire process and ensures that the disciplinary proceeding is fair and above board. Thus, it is not a good idea for the CEO to comment on the case or the guilt of the suspect. The disciplinary panel should consist of senior managers and an experienced person from human resources. A skilled manager should present the case on behalf of management; the employee's case may be presented by a representative of the employee. A file of evidence prepared by the presenter should be copied to the employee and the panel members beforehand. Witnesses should consist of the investigator, managers for the area in question, and any other person whose evidence is relevant to the hearing. Remember, the standard of proof is not as exacting as "beyond a reasonable doubt," as the disciplinary hearing is not a criminal action. The disciplinary hearing should contain an element of natural justice and may follow a variety of formats. One example is:

- Disciplinary panel convenes after examining the file of evidence.
- Presenters should go through the charges and how they will show the panel why the employee is guilty of the charges.

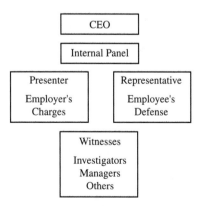

**Figure 6.4   Displinary Hearings**

- The employee's representative makes a statement about the case for the defense.
- The presenters work through the evidence and cross-reference this to the charges.
- The employee's representatives present their case and question, throw doubt on, challenge, or refute any evidence against the employee. The employer's witnesses may be cross-examined and witnesses for the employee may called and examined.
- The presenters sum up their cases and also discuss the past disciplinary record of the employee if this is relevant. They will then ask for a remedy (for example, dismissal).
- The employee's team sums up its case and asks that the charges be dismissed or that any mitigating circumstances be taken into consideration in making a decision on the remedy. Any special circumstances that put the employee in a good light or provide mitigation should be commented on.
- The panel adjourns and makes a decision that is communicated to all parties, either in writing or at a reconvened hearing. The decision may be to discard the charges, or apply various sanctions such as dismissal, demotion, reprimands, suspension, probation, or reduced salary.
- If there is no appeal from the employee, the CEO sanctions the decision of the appeals panel.
- The employee may ask that the case go to appeal, giving specific grounds for this request.
- The CEO considers any appeal and, on advice from personnel and legal, may then ask that an appeals panel be set up to hear the appeal. The appeals panel should not go through the entire case again, but should just consider the matters that form the basis of the appeal.
- The appeals panel confirms or overturns the decision of the original disciplinary panel and relays the decision to all parties involved.
- The CEO sanctions the decision of the appeals panel.

6. The organization should really act in good faith in dealing with all employees and this is part of employment legislation in some states. This means an employer would follow its disciplinary procedures and not, for example, discriminate unfairly against an employee.

The employee's rights will also be respected and great care taken to ensure that there is no invasion of the employee's privacy. When dealing with an employee, it should be clear that the remedy applied against the person for, say, breach of procedure is appropriate and fairly reflects the severity of the case. The internal disciplinary panel should be removed from any criminal prosecution, although this task has to be handled carefully. Breach of procedure normally results in a reprimand and is cumulative in that if it occurs again the remedy becomes increasingly more severe. Misappropriation may be treated as a breach of procedure rather than a criminal offense of theft and concealment. At the same time, the case must be shown to be serious, but in a way that does not suggest the employee is being charged with a crime. Only the courts can convict someone of a criminal offense, and the internal case must not be blurred with any ongoing prosecution. Any suspension that applies to an employee should be given a time limit and should not be executed in such as way as to imply guilt in any way at all.

7. Try to achieve a satisfactory solution for the organization. Dismissal of the fraudster will solve the main problem, and if the case gets to court the prosecution may be asked to go for a restitution order and recover missing funds in this way. There are many reasons why a case may not make it to court, or the charges get thrown out or not proven. The employee may be asked to pay back the missing funds, and this restitution may be used as a mitigating circumstance when the case comes to the sentencing stage. The employee may want to give back the money anyway and simply hand it over, although the company lawyers will have to advise on whether acceptance impairs any case against the employee. Some organizations go for a release package whereby the employee is asked to part company with the employer and signs a legal document of voluntary release that stops the employee from suing the organization, while admitting to no wrongdoing. This happens when there is no clear case against the employee, just a basic suspicion of wrongdoing. Still others engage in civil proceeding against the ex-employee and after pretrial motions and discovery, seek to recover the funds in court. The defendant may file a counterclaim and so ensure that a legal battle ensues. A case may even go to arbitration, where an impartial party decides the case based on the evidence that is submitted.

8. The preceding considerations should be placed in the staff handbook and included in orientation training. The employee's personnel file is highly confidential and should contain an official record of all disciplinary action.

> In one case a director of information systems spent a great deal of time being entertained by a major IT supplier who was trying to sell a new computer upgrade. Each leisure event was followed by an attempt by the director to get approval for the new computer. There was much talk about bribes being paid to the director, although it was impossible to prove that money had changed hands. An investigation was launched which considered the degree of hospitality given by the vendor to the director. This was found to be excessive and to have affected the integrity of commercial decisions being made by the director. Charges of gross misconduct were brought against the director and he was subsequently dismissed. There was no mention of bribery or criminal activity during the disciplinary action and the case against the employee was based entirely on the extent to which the corporate policy on standards of conduct were observed by this person. The case against the director was strengthened by the fact that he spent so much time being entertained that he failed to meet service targets for his section.

Successfully bringing criminal charges to court is a much more demanding process.

## CONCLUSION

The standards and procedures referred to in this chapter are pretty straightforward. Professional fraud investigators will have handbooks that go into much more detail and cover specialist areas and various forensic techniques. However, it is not our intention to go any deeper into the task of conducting the investigation. The aim is to provide material by the nonspecialist in a way that is readily understandable. The hope is that nonspecialists will take some responsibility for investigating fraud when it affects an area that they are responsible for, and not leave this task entirely to the experts. Managers need to ask questions, check on the investigation, and get involved wherever necessary. The material in this chapter therefore represents a minimum of knowledge that senior and operations managers should have as part of their basic managerial responsibilities. This point will be developed further in Chapter 7.

# CHAPTER 7

---

# Integrated Fraud Risk Management

*Diamond cuts diamond.*

## INTRODUCTION

Our final chapter builds on what has been discussed in the previous chapters as a way of bringing forward and integrating all the material on employee fraud. Using this material, we have developed an Integrated Fraud Risk Management Model (IFRMM), based around a number of concepts:

1. Fraud is like a virus. Fraud may lie dormant and then attack the host when it is most vulnerable; it is the lack of good defenses that makes an organization a potential target.
2. The degree of fraud prevention installed in an organization should be as sophisticated and dynamic as the efforts of the fraudster to get around measures to prevent fraud.
3. Fraud prevention must be all-encompassing to have any chance of success. That is, it must involve the efforts of the entire organization in recognizing the potential impact of abuse from employees and outsiders and seeking to manage this problem properly.

4. Controls cost money. The less that is done to manage the risk of fraud, the less time, effort, and resources will be consumed. But in turn fraud costs money, worry, and possibly embarrassment for the organization. This means that fraud control should be pushed up the corporate agenda to sit alongside major business issues. Whereas new risks, such as strategic takeovers, arise from changing business contexts, the risk of fraud remains fairly constant, changing only to take advantage of new weaknesses.

5. All organizations are morally bound to address dishonesty within the workforce and management. This necessarily involves some form of integrated mechanism, designed with this obligation in mind.

These factors should drive the organization's antifraud strategy. The Association of Certified Fraud Examiners feels that fraud cannot be eliminated—it can only be reduced. If not tackled early, small frauds tend to grow larger and more significant.

## PUTTING PREVENTION INTO PERSPECTIVE

Before we discuss integrated fraud management, we need to go through some of the basic steps that can be taken to keep fraud at bay. The problems an organization is trying to prevent may include:

- Organized crime.
- Corrupt managers.
- Employee scams.
- Misappropriation.
- Financial misstatement.
- False accounting (e.g., bonus schemes).
- Financial frauds.
- Computer hackers.
- Any other significant corporate abuse.

Key control objectives may be set to focus on fraud and can be applied to all organizational systems to supplement the basic system objectives. Systems are designed to perform a defined function, such as to pay employees, or collect income, or to maintain the information systems, and so on. The associated control objectives would incorporate complementary aims, such as the following:

- All people interacting with the system should be accountable for their actions.
- All decisions should be made with full integrity and no conflict of interests.
- All actions taken should be transparent and, as far as possible, open.
- All assets and resources should be accounted for and protected.
- All transactions should be complete and accurate.
- All relevant information should be reliable.

These control objectives should be kept in mind when designing and implementing organizational systems. People should understand the significance not only of being successful, but of being successful with integrity and accountability. Moreover, embedded within all systems should be the view that all reasonable steps are taken to address the risk of irregularity.

# FRAUD CONTROL

A big component in fraud prevention is the opportunity presented to the potential fraudster. Many controls are available to restrict or even remove any opportunity to commit fraud against an organization. Management conduct plays an important role in fraud prevention when control procedures are seen as important and poor operational practices, such as cluttered desks and lax discipline, are dealt with adequately. The people who commit fraud are those who somehow get around controls or are implicitly trusted. Relying on the trustworthiness of staff in high-risk areas, such as the accounts section, is a poor method of fraud control. Controls must be in place and must be observed; they cannot depend on the trustworthiness of everyone. At the same time, there must be some balance: If employees trust the employer, there is less reason for them to abuse the systems.

Most common frauds are quite simple, involving misappropriation, fictitious suppliers, diverted checks, false expense and payroll claims, cash skimming, and alteration of performance figures for bonuses. Simple controls that are firmly established, reinforced, and reviewed are available for each of these low-level scams. When there is collusion between an employee and a customer, it can get more difficult, because the record of underlying transactions may not be reliable. Smash-and-grab frauds are not concealed and are mainly permitted by poor security arrangements. An extreme example of smash-and-grab is the often-told story of the powerful business executive who boards a plane to Rio immediately after transferring $5 million to a Swiss bank account. A list of possible fraud prevention measures can be broken down into several main categories .

## Security

Many employee frauds involve unauthorized (and authorized) persons performing unauthorized activities. To ensure proper authorizations, security is the first line of defense. Many organizations have a security function but do not have a strategic security resource. That is, they employ people in uniforms, but those persons have a low-level checking role that relates to what they can see a few feet in front of them. This is far removed from a high-level resource that is able to assess threats against the organization from unauthorized persons or activities and then go on to develop strategies for addressing these changing risks. A great deal of fraudulent activity is assisted by excessive access facilities. For instance, the theft and conversion of company checks requires physical access to the checks and the ability to remove them. A vendor's address field may be altered so that the payments fall into the hands of the fraudster. If access is secured, this type of fraud is harder to perpetrate. Points in respect of security controls to help prevent fraud include the following.

**Develop a proactive security strategy.** There should be a corporate approach to security, with someone on the board holding ultimate responsibility for this important role. There should be protection for assets, people, information, resources, and corporate reputation, and threats should be anticipated and dealt with efficiently. This is what is meant by strategic security.

**Make security a corporate issue.** An experienced and senior official should be employed as the full-time head of security.

**Know where everything is.** This applies to assets, people, information, and resources, so that they may be protected. A database of resources should be maintained, indicating the location, responsible custodian, security markings, known problems, and people authorized to access or use the resource. The custodian should be required to maintain control over the condition and safety of the resource, with advice from the head of security if required.

**Undertake a risk assessment.** We need to identify those items, locations, assets, and people at risk and classify the risks, whether they are high, medium, or low. Within this assessment, the issue of ownership should be determined. So, for example, someone should be designated as responsible for the safety of IT equipment or cash income at a remote location. It may well be the site manager or someone based at the site with a defined security role.

**Install access restrictions.** Access controls and an early warning system can ensure that any breach of security is detected and acted on, in conjunction with any assessment of risk that has been undertaken. Intruder alarms, security guards, hi-tech sensors, robust physical access controls, and alert staff who challenge strangers are all measures that can be employed.

**Collect intelligence.** Find out about local crime, latest trends, and any available information on possible criminal activity. If certain buildings, systems, or people are being targeted in a particular area, this should prompt an alert. Some companies have levels of alert, with red being the highest level, and increase security to correspond with the current level.

**Protect inventories.** Effective stores management and control are important in organizations where goods are held and moved around among production, warehousing, and delivery. Statistics on wastage and turnover should be compiled to monitor the state of the systems, and investigations launched when there are any clear concerns. Most of the controls revolve around physical security and matching the records to the actual items on hand. Risks such as pilferage or shoplifting should be assessed and steps taken to ensure that these losses are prevented, or at least detected swiftly and reduced to a minimum.

**Protect the IT systems.** Both external hackers and employees can access a database and cause problems or access data to facilitate the commission of a crime. A full-blown IT security policy should be in place to cover access rights for employees and associates; change control rules when a program has been amended; and establish clear restrictions on data privileges, such as read, write, delete, change, and so on. Access controls should be in place, using devices such as passwords, fingerprints, smart cards, and retina scans, to ensure that only authorized persons have physical access to restricted areas. Audit trails can be used to track transactions to users, and these should be examined for inconsistencies (e.g., nighttime or unusual patterns) and stored for possible use during an investigation.

**Watch out for Internet fraud.**    Businesses encourage open access to corporate Web sites, and total connectivity is based around flexible access facilities. The security implications are profound. An expert fraudster can set up a dummy Web site that looks and feels just like a well-known company's site, and redirect users to this dummy site (via the domain name server). When someone logs onto the dummy site, his or her credit card details can be obtained, after which an error message is sent out that aborts the connection. The user will then log back onto the authentic company Web site. Armed with the credit card details, the fraudster could buy shares in a company that shares are already held in and so force up the price. The shares are then quickly sold at the high price and the fraudster disappears. The problem with the Internet is that it is impossible to rely on initial appearances; the real identity of a Web site owner is unknown, no matter how impressive the site looks. A hacker can defraud a company by accessing a company's network and changing the address details on the payments database. Firewalls may be used to protect the network and the corporate intranet from outside intrusion and security will need to scan for indicators of problems such as an unusual temporary loss of memory.

Downloads and uploads can be particularly dangerous, so corporate security may need to monitor employees' usage. One approach is to classify all external interactions as suspect until cleared by virus protection and authentication routines. Some of these tasks and considerations can be built into the role of the organization's network manager. There should be an official policy on private use of the Internet, so that it is clear that employees do not have an expectation of privacy when using company IT facilities. Training staff and keeping up to date with current developments are all important aspects of IT security. It may be a good idea to locate very sensitive data offline and keep it away from possible external access, although the data will not hit the main server and will have to be carefully backed up. This offline policy could be applied to both business systems and personal home computers.

Sending personal details over the Internet can result in identity theft if the information gets into the wrong hands. Encryption can also be very useful here. As a rule, Internet purchases that are paid for before the goods are delivered and examined are always open to abuse. Employees may have to be restricted to known sites that can be trusted. A company that prosecutes all instances of Internet fraud will gain a reputation for severity that may deter other fraudsters. Some fraudsters are able to take over an Internet connection by planting software that turns the site into a slave server; they go on to commit a fraud via a PC and then trash the system to hide any evidence. Contingency plans play a key role in recovery when computer systems are brought down by accident or on purpose.

Organizations are starting to redefine the role of the head of security to recognize the need for sophisticated IT interventions to tackle cyber crime. Much of the defence will be based around good intelligence and effective incident reporting mechanisms. Many police agencies are now coming to the same view and are equipping themselves to handle IT abuse. Some companies actually employ reformed hackers to test their security. Others not only look at current threats, but also examine future threats that might arise as businesses throw themselves into total connectivity, where the threat of attack is compounded by the difficulty of identifying the actual attacker.

**Secure company information.**    Most companies have an edge because of what they do, who they employ, and what they know. What they know can relate to commodities such as processes, prices, customers, deals that are about to break, and much more. An intentional breach of this confidentiality through deceit can be a criminal offense, and some kind of security should be installed to protect all such corporate information. Prices submitted in bids for a big contract may be worth a significant amount to another potential bidder. Make clear what is confidential, who has access to the information, and any restrictions on usage. Staff will need to sign up to a confidentiality clause on joining the organization and on leaving. The provisions may be applied to many groups of people, including temporary staff, associates, consultants, and anyone else who may be given access to the files. Again, risk assessment can be used to determine which information is at risk. Employees have a key role in protecting information, particularly with regard to paperwork, files, and automated files on floppy disks and PC/laptop hard disks. All files should be classified and have a security rating attached. The measures to protect the information would then fit with the assigned security rating. There should be tight procedures over escorting visitors, maintenance workers, and customers who may need to access offices, and the conference rooms may have to be "swept" electronically on a regular basis to ensure that there is no violation of security. Late-night or early-morning cleaners can present a particular problem if they go through the entire building and take away trash, because even this trash may contain confidential trade secrets.

Good security underpins good fraud prevention but one should always ask, "Who monitors the activities of the head of security?" If this question cannot be answered, the head of security may be the person most able to perpetrate fraud and abuse.

## Separation of Duties

A key weapon in the fight against employee fraud is separation of duties. The way work is allocated, to involve more than one person, is less of a control and more of a control concept that underlies the entire system of internal control. The idea is to ensure that no "at-risk" process can be carried out from start to finish by one person only. Any process that is susceptible to fraud, error, or breach of procedure should be considered with this in mind. When collusion is required to perpetrate a fraud against an organization, there is less risk that the fraud will materialize. By separating parts of a function, several people come into the picture, and each person constitutes a control over the activities of the others involved in the process. It is important to ensure that different aspects of a transaction are carried out by different people, in terms of:

- Authorization of the transaction.
- Processing the transaction.
- Receiving or providing the benefit.
- Making payment for the transaction or receiving income.
- Accounting for the transaction.
- Monitoring management information from the transaction.
- Reviewing the integrity of the transaction.

If, for example, we need to equip a sales team with laptop computers, we would expect that:

- The purchase is authorized by the budget holder.
- The order is processed by the purchasing section.
- The laptops are received by the stores (or IT) section and checked before they are sent to the sales team leader.
- The invoice for the laptops is approved by the budget holder.
- The invoice is matched with the receipt note and paid by the accounts section, which codes it to the budget in question.
- The budget holder checks the spending on laptops against the budget provision.
- The arrangements are reviewed by the auditors.

- The IT section may update the laptop inventory and carry out annual checks on the laptops.

The hope is that someone could not buy and misappropriate laptops because he or she is in sole charge of the system for acquiring the machines. The involvement of different people and sections makes it harder to carry out this type of fraud. The preceding system for acquiring laptops could be abused when:

- There is an emergency override system through which one person can get the goods in and approve the invoice for payment because it is urgent.
- Forged paperwork makes it look like the items were properly ordered and purchased when this is not actually the case. Twenty may have been ordered and paid for, but only ten find their way to the sales team.
- There is a breach of one part of the system; say, the delivery is left in boxes at reception and intercepted and stolen by someone who knows the delivery is expected.
- There is collusion between various parties to the transaction so that, for example, the company pays for 20 laptops but only 10 are delivered.
- A member of the purchasing section accepts a bribe to place the contract with a particular supplier.

Ideally a number of people should be involved in transactions to avoid one person being in sole charge of the deal, but there are still things that could go wrong if other controls such as security and supervision are not also in place. A lot can be achieved through separation of duties, but this control must be properly used if it is to help manage the risk of fraud. One influence that makes segregating duties less popular is the move toward greater empowerment. People are now given much more responsibility to initiate transactions, as processes cut out the involvement of different sections and locate responsibility with one key caseworker. Transactions that involve high fraud risk items such as finances, contracts, goods, and claims, have to be excluded from the total empowerment concept. It is essential that more that one person be involved in these types of systems to minimize the risk of fraud. Moreover, other controls should swing into action when there is an emergency ordering system. If a single manager is able to initiate, authorize, and pay various employee claims, there should be further checks in place to verify the relevant transactions.

## Financial and Operational Controls

There is no definitive model of controls against fraud that can be applied to organizations as a solution to the growing incidence and impact of employee fraud. In fact, endless lists of controls are in the main counter-productive, resulting in a checklist approach to controls that do not fit the context of what goes on in a particular workplace. Controls must come from management and staff, as they work through the risks that confront them and decide how best to manage those risks, including the threat of fraud. Nevertheless, a few points can be made as to some of the basic controls against fraud, and this is the stance taken here, as we briefly discuss some of the possible control mechanisms that may be considered by finance and operations management.

**Payments.**    Releasing payments to third parties is always an at-risk function. Experienced fraudsters may try to get into the system and get payments made to themselves. Experienced employees may do the same and then prepare a cover-up so that the suspect items will be lost among the thousands of payments that go through a big accounting system each week or month. Much can be done to guard against these threats and ensure that payments go to the right party, for the right amount. Most people in business are aware of the basic payment system, which involves matching the requisition, order, receipt (goods or services), and resultant invoice so that each document not only comes from a different source (segregation of duties), but also adds to the verification of the transaction before the funds are released. Some argue that a good payment system will have the following attributes:

- Restrictions on who can requisition an order. The person initiating the purchase must have a budget, and is responsible for managing that budget and monitoring anything spent against it. Some auditors have concerns about company ATM cards or company credit cards, as they give authority to spend to whomever has possession of them.
- Formal ordering system operated by professional procurement staff who have a procedure for making buying decisions and selecting vendors. A big control over payments is the association of a formal

order with each material payment invoice. Rules regarding gifts and hospitality should be in place to secure some degree of independence of the purchasing staff.

- Efficient coding system, so that payments do not get lost in general descriptions that cannot be analyzed in the accounts. All commitments should be accounted for in the budgeting system and periodic analyses of payments made. Fraudsters often try to hide illegal payments under generic spending codes such as "fees to consultants," or in a huge suspense account of unallocated payments.

- Restrictions on the number of people who can authorize invoices for payment. Make these people responsible for the integrity of payments approved. Rapid scans of a schedule of payments by the approving officer generally does not constitute effective control over "planted" invoices. Authorizing officers should be trained to apply healthy skepticism and ask searching questions whenever required.

- Restrictions on access to the ordering, stores, and payments system, so that a fraud cannot be hidden through altered automated records.

- Payment database scans for unusual items, using automated interrogation techniques. When checks or transfers are going to the home address or bank accounts of employees (or associates), the items should be considered further. Compliance teams may wish to visually scan paid invoices for inconsistencies such as post ofice box addresses, cell phone numbers, no order number, fictitious vendors, or invoice numbers that do not match up.

- Checks should go out immediately after being cut, and should not be returned to the person requesting the check. In fact, if they go into the mail straight from the location where they are printed out, there is less opportunity for anyone to tamper with them. Any associated correspondence can always be mailed by the section concerned, with the check detail noting "correspondence to follow." Special controls should be applied to voided checks and checks that have been returned to the organization. One popular fraud involves sending checks out to unknown addresses, with the knowledge that when they are returned they can be intercepted by someone who has access to returned mail.

There are, of course, other controls that may be in put in place. So long as payments are seen as a high-risk process, measures can be implemented to reduce fraud (and error) to a minimum.

**Income.**    Income is susceptible to skimming, where it disappears before it enters the books. If the income does not hit the records straight away there can be problems. A few basic points relating to the management of income follow:

- The most basic form of income systems is found in cashiers or retail outlets, where the physical movement of cash (and goods) is what has to be controlled. Closed-circuit televisions, security guards, observant supervisors, refunds authorized by managers, end-of-day reconciliations, audit trails to individual cashiers, sequential tapes, rules on under/overbanking, and controls over staff discounts are all important. Cash should be banked intact, as soon as possible and IUOs should be banned along with any interference with the actual day's take. Voids should be watched carefully, as they could indicate monies received but not put in the till. Customers can be involved in control routines as they view the register display and obtain and check their receipts. It is a good idea to listen to any complaints from customers and figure out if they indicate an irregularity. Random cash counts can be used as a deterrent for problem areas (say, a location with regular underbanking). Credit card payments by customers should be carefully vetted and staff trained in detection routines. Most of these controls revolve around good procedures, well-trained staff, and alert supervisors.
- The mail receipt system is at the front line of income fraud. If income comes from checks received through the mail, there should be sound controls over the mailroom activities and subsequent routing of mail through the offices, in particular to the accounts section. There should be at least two staff in the mailroom and an immediate recording of checks that is verified by the office supervisor. The audit trail starts here and should follow the items through the system to recording, accounting, and reporting. Any complaints from customers or associates about nonreceipt of payments they have made to the company should be quickly followed up. Checks should be tamper-proof and the bank account reconciled to company records on a daily basis.
- Establish a monitoring arrangement whereby income patterns are checked against expectations and other available information. Anything odd that appears from the analysis should be followed up as

potentially suspicious. The possibility of fraud should always be borne in mind when carrying out the monitoring procedure.

- Take particular care about the writeoff system. When an account that is due and payable is written off, an opening is created for the potential fraudster. Writeoff requests should be checked and double-checked, and it should be a disciplinary offense for staff to neglect to recover income that is recoverable. Once an account has been written off, look out for any payments that subsequently appear. An experienced fraudster will arrange an unnecessary writeoff, intercept the payment that comes from the customer, and divert the funds to a controlled bank account. Unfortunately, it is the accounts personnel that tend to do the most damage in terms of employee fraud, particularly in smaller organizations.

- Establish safeguards against money laundering. Point-of-sale staff should be properly trained and a full-blown compliance program should be in place for this threat. Analyze and understand the threat; take special care when the client is not known to the organization and there is a great reliance on regular cash transactions.

**Claims.** There is a whole industry of fraudsters and fraud investigators involved in the battle over claims and loans, be it welfare, food stamps, car and theft insurance, bank loans, mortgages, worker's compensation, medical claims, government grants, or one of a whole assortment of inherently risky commodities. These are specialist areas of external fraud, whereas we are mainly concerned with employee fraud and employee claims. Anything that can be claimed from the company is at risk, in that it could be forged, altered, duplicated, or illegally intercepted. Like payments, there should be tight controls over employee claims, although the amounts will tend not to be significant. This is the problem with fraud. Risk assessment looks for big items—but the smaller ones attract less control and are more vulnerable. Frauds, once carried out successfully, tend to grow as the perpetrator becomes more confident. Employee claims covering travel, expenses, overtime, allowances, reimbursed petty cash, and so on all need to be controlled so that they do not grow out of proportion. The best approach is random checks followed by the most severe action possible, including dismissal. There may be little justification for assigning a full-time staffer to check and double-check all claims. It is a good idea to reinforce the responsibility of the appropriate line manager for authenticating any claims before they are processed, and maybe to provide some training to this effect. When inflated employee claims are a regular occurrence, this falls under the description of custom and practice. In this situation, a form of amnesty may be used, whereby the organization asks its people to stop breaking the rules and publicizes the fact that all future breaches will result in disciplinary action. This approach may be preferable to firing dozens of staff members, but it does depend on the circumstances.

**Contracts.** There are risks inherent in the contracting arrangements in which most organizations engage. The types of problems found are limited only by the imagination of the prospective fraudsters, but at a minimum potentially involve:

- Kickbacks given to employees who can influence the way contracts are awarded by an organization.
- Collusion by the employee and the vendor to get fraudulent invoices passed by the vendor and paid by the organization.
- Expensive contracts granted for inferior goods, where the inflated profit is split between the vendor and a dishonest employee.
- Contracts awarded to vendors who have an undisclosed relationship with an employee who has influenced the awarding process. An extreme version is when an employee actually sets up a company that does business with his or her own employer.
- Frauds by the vendor, without help from an insider whereby fabricated accounts are submitted for payment or when invoices are not supported by work undertaken on the contract.

If these are the defined risks in contracting arrangements, then it is simply a case of establishing key controls to guard against the risks. So, taking each risk in turn, consider:

- **Kickbacks**:  Rules on gifts help here. Senior management should be on the lookout for signs of corruption, such as changes in lifestyle and close relationships with vendors. Noncompetitive contracts should be investigated once uncovered. Tight bidding procedures and approved lists are designed to ensure that there is open competition for bigger contracts; these should not only be in place, but also observed by the purchasing staff. Ongoing database interrogations can be run to isolate unusual patterns of tender bids, awards, and

payments. Some frauds involve kickbacks to secure inside information, and the vendor wins with a low bid only to beef up the value
with subsequent changes that lead to a high overall cost. Continuing
negotiations after bids are received can lead to pressure on influential purchasing staff to accept bribes. The organization should be
constantly on guard for all these situations.

- **Collusion and fraudulent invoices:** All payments made against a
contract should be carefully checked by people outside the contract
negotiations. The accounts submitted should match up with the contract, and work carried out by the vendor should be signed off by an
independent expert before the interim accounts are paid.

- **Inflated profit split:** This problem comes to a head when expensive consultants are employed and one senior employee has the
power both to negotiate the day rate and to employ the person in
question. When a job calls for special skills, there is normally justification to use a known person or vendor who has a history of deliver-
ing the goods. These close relationships can lead to unmitigated
fraud where the fee is divided and part is given to the dishonest
employee. This type of fraud is normally the result of inadequate segregation of duties, and depends on the number of different people
and sections involved in hiring consultants. Legal services staff normally acts as a key control when tailor-made contracts are being
negotiated, and should have a defined role.

- **Undisclosed relationship:** The corporate code of ethics should make
clear the need to avoid conflicts of interests and ensure that all relationships are properly disclosed if relevant. Any breach of the standard
should be met with severe action and all employees need to receive
advice—if not formal training—on how the code affects managers and
the workforce. Key staff who make buying decisions may be asked to
sign an annual declaration about disclosing relevant relationships.
Control in this environment should be aimed primarily at awareness,
detection, and the ability to take swift action in the event of a problem.

- **Fabricated accounts:** When a vendor has decided to defraud the
organization, this is a straightforward external crime. Deceit, false
accounting, and misrepresentation with the intention of securing an
illegal gain should be acted on quickly. A rigorous contract management system should be able to pick up any fabricated accounts
and query them. It may be good to include the ability to inspect a
vendor's books for transactions supporting accounts payable, as part

of any contractual agreement. Reporting all suspicious items, so that they can be reviewed by auditors or inspectors, is another control that may help reduce the level of fraud by vendors.

Contracts can go wrong and may end up in arbitration if negotiations do not go well. If fraud appears on the agenda, it can become very complicated, with claims and counterclaims that interfere with the business. Many controls can be installed over professional contract tendering and subsequent management, and close checks over all accounts before they are paid. In organizations that work with many big vendors, these controls should be designed and established to counter possible irregularity.

**Payroll.**    If a fraudster can set up a record on the organization's payroll, and activates this record so that salary checks (or bank transfers) are generated each month, the scam will accumulate much long-term income for the fraudster. This type of fraud has to be carefully concealed, because it will only make sense if it can continue for a while. False overtime claims also create extra income for the employee who can get them into the system without being detected. The point is that a payroll system is essentially a mechanism to generate payments, and is therefore a high-risk system. The payroll may be administered in-house or by an external service, although the ensuing payments hit the company's expenditure systems nonetheless. Most payroll software incorporates good controls over input, processing, and outputs so that access can be restricted, data that is input is accurate, and output containing personal data is kept confidential. In conjunction with this, there are other control provisions that can be established:

- Make sure payroll is administered by suitably trained personnel and is seen as a professional service.
- Link payroll to personnel/human resources, so that only personnel staff may set up new accounts (not general managers and people across the organization). Temporary staff and consultants may be paid through the normal payment system (not payroll) via invoices that are submitted and verified.
- Monitor patterns of payroll spending and look for inconsistencies, such as large increases in a section that has not been recruiting for a while.
- Make sure deductions make sense. When no tax code is attached to a payroll record, it may mean that items of personal data do not match up with national records.

- Look for inconsistencies, such as more than one payroll payment going into the same bank account.
- Get the compliance team to do sample checks on claims such as overtime or allowances, to verify that the claims are correct.
- Employ segregation of duties over account set-up, reconciliation, terminations, and distribution of payments.
- Make sure any change of detail is authorized by the appropriate officer. Human resources staff may need to confirm changes in address or rates of pay. Such details should be entered by a senior payroll clerk and verified.
- Make arrangements for payroll staff not to have access to their own payroll records.
- Ensure that terminated employees are removed from the payroll and do not continue to receive payments after their date of termination (other than back payments and any agreed severance packages).

Payroll is a pretty simple system, but it can still go wrong. Just because the amounts paid to one employee may not be material does not mean it should not be considered a useful tool for the potential fraudster. Payroll can be abused; some companies are the victims of organized crime gangs who use threats and menaces to get their "ghost employees" onto the payroll as a form of protection money.

## Financial Misstatements

High-level financial misstatement generally involves senior figures in the organization—in one sense, it is the organization itself that is committing the fraud. The perpetrators are hardly likely to install controls over their own illegal activities. It is normally quite the reverse, in that the senior executives and officers involved will tend to employ people who either don't understand what is going on, or simply don't care about the behavior of the executives. It is mainly the job of the board and external auditors to watch out for this problem and report it to the police or stock exchange commission. A great deal of information may come from an effective compliance routine. When an entire enterprise revolves around huge bonuses based on short-term income targets in a volatile and shrinking market, the chances are that the income figures will be fudged, ranging from being overambitious or massaged through to being completely fabricated. When share options are earned alongside these bonuses and the share price is sensitive to reported profitability, the fraud potential gets even worse.

## Budgets

Most employee fraud results in a financial loss to the employer and a similar gain to the dishonest employee. This equation can be quite straightforward and means that there will be a "hole in the accounts" to the extent of the fraud. The final accounts are put together each year, and there are many reasons why profits may be down or spending up, or why a particular figure has moved since last year. A more dynamic way of tracing authorized as compared to unauthorized spending is through an efficient budgeting system. The thinking is that the budget holder will be responsible for any spending against a particular code and will be accountable for anything that falls into the budget line. When the fraudster has been able to get inside the system and arrange a payment to himself or herself, the amount must be posted to an expenditure code of some sorts. The expenditure code will build up in a spend budget that should belong to someone in the organization. The dedicated fraudster will understand the corporate systems and carry out a scam that will not be obvious to the employer. When the budgeting system ensures that only authorized spending is processed and that all actual expenditure is reported and compared to budget, with variances being followed up rigorously, the system is much tighter. The opportunist fraudster who has already booked a flight to Rio may be unconcerned about the loss being found out, but this is an unusual situation. Most employee frauds are committed by people who think the fraud will get lost among the thousands of transactions that go through the company accounts each week. Good and dedicated budgetary control means that discrepancies will be spotted and dealt with. The converse is slack budgetary control, suspect payments readily slip through the system. In terms of fraud prevention, the budgeting system should take on board the following:

- Design the budgetary control system with a view to combating employee fraud as well as the traditional objectives of budgeting. Select a system that has good early warning alerts.
- Reinforce the concept of "authorized spends" so that all expenditure is allocated to a recognized code. This means the fraudster will have to get hold of a realistic code to commit a payment fraud.
- Establish the concept of budget holder. It should be possible to trace all spending back to a defined individual, and this person can be asked to verify any item that is at all suspicious.
- Train relevant staff in effective budget monitoring. Deficiencies and gaps can indicate that a fraud has happened, and the budget should

be monitored with a view to isolating strange trends and specific unauthorized overspends. Tight budgets monitored on an ongoing basis (not just at year end), as well as detecting problems after the event, can also act as a deterrent to the would-be fraudster.

- Make sure the suspense account is not overused for unallocated debits. The budgeting system has no real impact if many items can go through the payment system with no valid codes attached to them.
- Train the budget monitoring officer in fraud awareness and the need to track suspicious items carefully.

If these policies are followed, they will constitute an important tool in preventing payment frauds and ensuring that they are spotted if they occur. The success depends on a change in culture to a stance where transactions are not accepted at face value. Each transaction has to pass various tests where it is authorized, coded, reconciled, and monitored against expectations or some form of set standard.

## Human Resource Issues

Most of the controls discussed so far are based on not trusting people and being able to check up on them, or at least building this idea of double checking into our systems. Controls based around the human resource (HR) policies are different. They are based on employing trustworthy people in the first place and getting them to be loyal to the employer. Some of the HR control measures that can be employed to help in the fight against fraud are listed:

- Check references very carefully when recruiting new staff. This should be a positive process to verify qualifications, extract an independent reference from the most recent employer, carry out a medical test, test suitability via personality tests, do a check on criminal convictions, check credit rating, and anything else that gives an insight into whether the person appears honest and reliable. Note that legal advice should be sought on testing and checking; it may be necessary to secure voluntary consents from the applicant. Controls should be as devious as the fraudsters, and the job applicant can be asked to provide a whole array of information which is then subjected to extensive vetting. Anything that comes back as "misrepresentation" should mean the job is not offered. This policy entails some difficulty, as some argue that the majority of information provided on a typical résumé ranges from slightly overexaggerated to completely untrue. One more sinister issue relates to the growing incidence of personal identity theft: An organization may end up employing someone who is not actually who he or she purports to be. Imagine the damage that could be done by someone who forges an entire identity!

- Make clear the standard of conduct expected from staff and link this to the corporate values and the internal disciplinary procedure. Most of the points relating to codes of conduct were mentioned in Chapter 3.

- Provide orientation training for new staff that brings home the need to be alert to fraud, to control frauds, and to report possible violations. Bring out important aspects of staff conduct like the rules on accepting gifts and declaring conflicts of interest. Make it clear that the employer will prosecute all frauds and dismiss the culprit.

- Make clear the employee's role in the organization; levels of authorization; access facilities to IT systems; and staff responsibilities and duties to record transactions properly, check the work of other staff, and adhere to all organizational procedures.

- Add to the staff role responsibilities for assessing the risk of fraud and managing these risks in conjunction with the fraud reporting system.

- Make sure staff are properly motivated. A well-motivated workforce has less excuse for "getting back at the rotten bosses." Staff attitude surveys can be used to get into the minds of employees and discover the feelings people have about work and whether they are being treated fairly. Surveys can isolate factors such as whether staff feel valued and whether they trust top management and feel committed to organization goals. Motivation means all things to all people and we could spend much time discussing what makes the workforce tick. Some argue that this is about sensible targets and a fair and transparent performance appraisal scheme. Others feel motivation is more about good teamwork and people pulling together in the same direction. Motivated staff tend to have the right competencies for the job and are continuously developed along some kind of career line.

- Provide a counseling service for staff with problems such as alcoholism, and look out for financial pressures that are bearing down on employees. The company may provide financial assistance when this is appropriate and not seen to embarrass the employee or impair career development. Financial advice may be more appropriate but it does depend on the person coming forward and admitting to a financial problem.

Many of the listed measures help create a type of culture in the organization. Assessing this culture is important in measuring the fight against fraud. Do the people at the top override controls as and when they feel like it? Do work practices imply that bending the rules is the "macho" thing to do? Do people view work as a positive experience, or do they hold grudges and have numerous complaints against "the system"? Do they feel stuck in a corner with no rights and no way of expressing their worries? People tend to behave in a fair way when they feel they are being treated fairly. The type of culture in place is a vital aspect of the control environment.

## Compliance

We have said that controls cost money and that they must be linked clearly to perceived threats. Once good controls have been developed, they provide assurance that there is a reasonable likelihood that the chance of fraud is reduced to an acceptable level. What is acceptable will vary with the organization and how it responds to employee and external fraud. Whatever the adopted stance, there is still due reliance on the controls that have been designed and implemented. Some control frameworks provide a high-level concept of control, such as the control environment and audit committee oversight, but there are also more basic control procedures, such as authorization of invoices for payment. Control concepts are aspirations aimed at by the organization, whereas control procedures are basic arrangements that have to be adhered to. In other words, compliance is a fundamental part of the control cycle. When it comes to fraud and irregularity, compliance is a key issue. Controls that are ignored may mean that more fraud occurs; for example, when the ordering process for invoices and big payments is overridden based on the mere say-so of a senior manager. Compliance routines should be in place to ensure that procedures and standards are being properly observed. A small team may work through a sample of bigger payments to check that each is accompanied by an associated order, and if not, find out why. Payments that have slipped through the cracks may be picked up and investigated. There are two main models of compliance: We can either set up a separate independent team that covers the organization, or we may ask each manager to establish a compliance-type process that double-checks high-risk areas on behalf of the manager.

The concept can be broadened so that procedures are designed to ensure regularity and also quality services, and compliance checks become quality checks as well. Hence, quality teams and compliance teams may start to merge, as they both seek to identify problems with a view to enhancing adherence to quality procedures through appropriate recommendations. Compliance checks by teams that have both a degree of independence and professionalism provide a major contribution to the controls against fraud. Good teams will consider high-risk areas and assess the degree to which control procedures are being applied by staff. For this to work, the organization must ensure that:

- The compliance team is staffed by professional people.
- The team has some independence and reports to someone senior enough to make a difference.
- The compliance checks focus on high-risk areas where fraud is a potential issue.
- Compliance is seen to be about making procedures better rather than simply penalizing managers for identified problems.
- Compliance should include an awareness aspect, such that the team is prepared to demonstrate how fraud (and other corporate issues such as poor quality or slack service delivery) can be tackled through better procedures.
- The compliance team understands the nature of fraud and how it may be addressed.
- People can approach the compliance team regarding specific problems of breach of procedure.

Bearing in mind the preceding, one can see that compliance checks are an important aspect of control and that they can contribute to reducing fraud. Due diligence depends partly on an effective compliance program being firmly in place. Compliance checks may also report on peripheral matters, such as the quality of documentation, delegation of budgets, adherence to legislation, and whether the culture in place shows an awareness of applicable standards.

The actions of top management should also be within the ambit of compliance reviews, as there is little hope of success if senior managers flout the rules on a daily basis. When executives travel on business that looks suspiciously like pleasure, and abuse company resources with expensive cars and excessive IT equipment installed at home, this sends out the wrong message. We must, however, issue one word of warning at this stage: it concerns the potential impact of aggressive checking on staff and the fact that it may backfire and cause a degree of resentment amongst the workforce. An example follows:

> A post office worker was visited by auditors when he was ill and had to come downstairs to count the stamps. He felt so humiliated that he went on to commit a $1.4 million fraud against the post office before being found out.

## Monitoring

The basic control cycle may be simplified to appear as in Figure 7.1.

**Objectives.**   Controls are about achieving objectives, and this is where all control models should start.

**Standards.**   A budget, norm, expected position, plan, or standard must be set to represent a performance target. Control is implicit in setting standards and what is expected to be a benchmark against which to measure the resulting performance.

**Actuals.**   This is what is really happening. The outputs, performance, results, and deliveries represent the achievements in any given period. It is by comparing actuals with the standard that deficiencies are isolated.

**Review.**   The extent to which we are meeting set standards is determined through the review process. Review comes about through effective monitoring and it is here that the ability to monitor performance constitutes a key part of the control system.

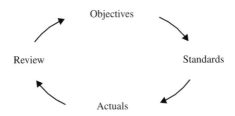

**Figure 7.1**   The Control Cycle

Monitoring, within the confines of this model, provides an opportunity to gauge the level of success and so make adjustments. It is a dynamic, ongoing process that feeds into the decision-making mechanism. In terms of fraud, monitoring is a control in that it seeks to assess whether outputs are consistent with set standards. The organization must assess whether staff are behaving appropriately, and whether there are any unexplainable gaps in outputs. Monitoring is also linked to supervision, as checks are made on the work of staff and supervisors observe that things are going according to plan. What has been called "management by wandering around" is key to keeping close to the front-line staff and knowing what they are involved in. Managers who understand that supervision is a two-way process, whereby they keep an eye on their staff and also keep a door open so that staff can talk to them, have access to a good control over the activities of employees. Monitoring extends this process by ensuring that managers are looking at returns, budgets, actual performance, statistics, and patterns of income, spending, and productivity. Although the drive is not directed primarily at fraud prevention, there is nonetheless scope to check for inconsistencies that cannot be readily explained. When explanations are not forthcoming, fraud can be considered as one possibility. The other side of the coin is that people know their activities are being monitored, and this may well act as a deterrent to would-be fraudsters. Managers can be trained to check returns, to examine figures and patterns, and to be aware of the possibility of employee fraud during these examinations. In this way, monitoring and supervision become powerful tools to prevent fraud and detect any related problems very quickly.

## Audit and Review

The final piece of the control jigsaw relates to the audit process. This works on two main levels. First, external audit acts as the principal control over illegal behavior of the board of directors and top company executives. Financial figures may be manipulated or loans secured and diverted to personal use. The lower levels of the organization will probably not be aware of these problems, outside of a basic belief that top management are distant and unapproachable. The main defense is the audit process, which will check that the financial accounts make sense and fit the reality of the organization's performance and results. Family-run companies should consider commissioning a full independent audit to report on the accounts. Remember that employees who commit fraud tend to be people who are trusted, including family members. Larger companies should commission a fraud risk assessment from the external auditors and ask whether they are able to isolate any particular problems. External audit can also take on special projects, such as the audit of share options issued to company directors.

The second audit function relates to internal audits, which review and assess whether controls provide proper mitigation of risks and whether the controls are working as intended. Again, the internal auditors may be asked to consider the possibility of fraud in those audits, as appropriate. Internal auditors may also review the extent to which employees understand the antifraud policies. It is not unknown for internal auditors to facilitate fraud awareness seminars as a way of driving home the message that everyone in the organization should be involved in the fight against employee fraud.

Auditors will not necessarily direct their attention at fraud risk management, but if asked, they will refocus the terms of reference for certain projects and act as an additional high-level control. Components of the entire audit process include the audit committee and any oversight committees that deal with relevant issues such as ethics and fraud investigations. These forums may be used to monitor the way the organization is handling the risk of fraud and to determine whether the right resources are in the right place to provide suitably proactive and reactive responses.

## Getting a System

We have covered some of the controls that help in the fight against fraud. The adopted controls should fit together to form a system of control that is interconnected, integrated, and coordinated. For example there may be good separation of duties over the payment system, ensuring that only supplies properly ordered (by the purchasing section) can be paid for by the company. But if there is lax security over the purchase orders themselves, so that orders can be fabricated and attached to invoices for payment, then the separation-of-duties control will not work. Authorization is a strong control, but if documentation standards are so poor that the paperwork accompanying a contract for approval is unreliable, an item may be authorized even though it is entirely incorrect. Good procedures that are prepared to direct staff in important routines (say, daily banking of customers' checks) will have less value when senior managers ignore the procedures for expediency and set a poor example. Controls should be viewed as an entire process that fits easily together. The need for integration forms the basis for the next section of the book.

# WHY INTEGRATION?

Before we delve into the concept of integrated employee fraud risk management, two short stories bring out many facets of the type of employee frauds that have to be tackled.

An airline's finance chief, who embezzled almost $2.8 million because he had not been given a performance bonus, was jailed for four years. DS, aged 31, took the money from the airline company in an act of "revenge and greed," the court heard. The $42,000-a-year financial controller believed he had saved the airline $8.4 million but did not receive the bonus he thought he deserved—so he took a cut of one-third of that amount by siphoning cash off through a fake business, the court was told. He was also angry when he was told he "would not go any further with the company" after he had a relationship with a junior member of staff which failed. The prosecutor said, "He set up [his company] to recompense for the money he believed he was entitled to, which was 30% of $8.4 million." DS rented a post office lockbox, then created and registered false invoices from the company for engineering work. He told a colleague to set up a monthly money transfer to the company and authorized payment of the invoices, which went into his account. Then he splurged the cash on high living, a magnificent home, cars, holidays, jewelry, and clothes, as well as buying land, shares, and pensions. The alarm was raised by a clerk who could not find invoices from [the finance chief's company]. When police officers arrived at DS's home he looked at his briefcase and told them, "It's all in there." He had banked 36 checks worth $2,514,000 and still had two others worth $224,000 in the briefcase. Although police praised his cooperation in a letter to the court, civil action is being taken to find money still not accounted for.

The defense said DS was a "very vulnerable young man with a fragile personality." Before the offense, he had been under terrific pressure, working 70 to 80 hours a week, including weekends. His life was also filled with self-contempt. He blamed himself for his father's death when he was just 18; he had also lost friends and regarded himself as a pariah. He had tried to kill himself on numerous occasions and had a "monumental" drinking problem. The judge told DS, "It is probable what you did was a mixture of revenge and greed at a time when you were under great pressure and stress and consuming a large quantity of alcohol. As a result of what you did you have lost everything."

Graham Lord, in his book *Sorry, We're Going to Have to Let You Go* (Warner 1999, p. 315), described a fraud committed by Skudder, a newly appointed CEO:

Mulliken (Chair of the board), frowned. He shook his head, "God, what a nightmare," he said.

Jim (the legal director) said, "He (Skudder) was siphoning off the pension fund. He was piggybacking his own cash on the back of the company's investments so that he could increase his own rate of interest and buy more shares in the company. He was giving himself thousands of unjustified share options. And he was planning to sell his shares just before the next audit so that he could make a killing before anyone realized the true situation and the value of the shares collapsed."

"Bloody hell, Jim. How long have you known about this?"

"A couple of months, maybe three."

"So why didn't you blow the whistle on him weeks ago?"

Jim Donaldson looked shifty. "I wasn't sure you'd believe me. Well, he was your appointment . . . "

"The bank's."

"Well, yes."

"The Millennium Bank head hunted him for us, as you know, but that's no reason to let Skudder wreak havoc on the company for so long. You should have come to me yourself, long before this."

"I thought I needed more evidence to convince you."

Mulliken fixed him with a beady stare. "Are you saying it's my fault?"

"Good God, of course not . . . "

"How much evidence did you need? The man is patently a crook. He's been robbing us blind for months."

Donaldson said nothing.

"You were accumulating evidence for so long that the company nearly went bust?"

"I was about to come to you any day."

"Too bloody late, Jim. You should have come to me long ago."

Donaldson bristled. "Well, why didn't anyone else do anything about it?"

Mulliken looked aggrieved. "I've got half a dozen companies to run, Donaldson, not just one. And do you know how many boards I'm on? Seven. I can't be expected to know precisely what's going on in every piddling little corner of one of them. That's what I pay people like you for. To keep your eyes open. To blow the whistle."

Donaldson took a deep breath. "Come on, Willie, you knew things weren't right. Peter Hallam told you for a start, months ago, nearly a year ago."

Mulliken frowned. "Hallam . . . "

"Yes. But you wouldn't listen."

There are also external frauds, such as hackers who try to break into the customer database and extract credit card details. Or the small-time criminal who sends bills to various local companies for thousand of calendars that were not actually ordered or delivered, hoping that some will simply pay without checking. What we need is a model of fraud risk management that takes care of most types of frauds and scams. One model that may suit many organizations, and which forms the remainder of this chapter, is illustrated in Figure 7.2.

This Integrated Fraud Risk Management Model (IFRMM), which draws on and summarizes all the material in this book, is used in two ways. First, we provide a brief description of each part of the model. In addition, we will use the model as a basic self-assessment tool, to give readers a list of key

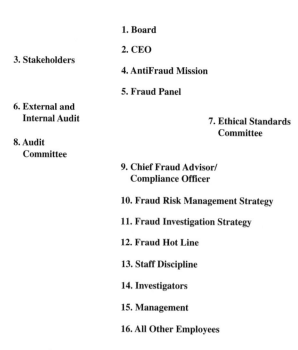

**Figure 7.2**   Integrated Fraud Risk Management Model

attributes for some of the stages of the model to be used to assess their own organization. In this way the IFRMM can be used as a crude benchmark against which different organizations may measure their achievements. Crude, because every organization is different in the extent to which fraud is a perceived threat, and the model can only provide a general guide.

## Describing the Model

**1. The board.** The board must assume ultimate responsibility for managing fraud and ensuring that there is a suitable mechanism (ours is the IFRMM) to discharge this responsibility. The directors must ensure that the selected method is properly implemented and need to oversee its actual effectiveness. To this end, the board should:

- Ensure that a good understanding of fraud is built into the competencies for directors.
- Undergo some type of fraud awareness training.
- Prepare an overall policy statement on fraud risk management.
- Make corporate fraud risk management an agenda item that is discussed at least twice a year.
- Build fraud risk management into the corporate objectives of the business.
- Inform shareholders of any significant frauds that affect the organization.
- Inform the external auditors of any significant financial frauds.
- Locate responsibility for effective fraud risk with the CEO and ensure that this officer has a good understanding of the subject.
- Ensure that suitable arrangements within the organization cover all aspects of the IFRMM.
- Receive regular plans and reports from a forum that has the role of the fraud panel (see the following section on the fraud panel).
- Receive assurance statements and annual declarations from senior management regarding the management of fraud risk.
- Allow the CEO, CFO, chief fraud advisor, legal director, external auditors, and internal auditors to bring to the board's attention any concerns regarding the way fraud is being managed in the organization.
- Prepare a formal statement on fraud risk management for the annual report to shareholders, based on the assurances received from the CEO, top management, the audit committee, and external and internal auditors.

**2. CEO.** This officer has executive responsibility for implementing the fraud policy and ensuring that everyone involved has a clear role and is able to meet the requirements of this role. More than anything, the CEO sets the trend with key messages to the workforce about fraud and whether it is an important organizational issue. The CEO sets what many call the "tone at the top,"; no matter how many formal policies are prepared, the fact is that actions speak louder than words. Finally, the CEO has a quasi-judicial role in ensuring a fair balance between protecting the organization and observing the rights of all employees. The CEO's input and tasks include:

- Personally possessing adequate knowledge of fraud and how it can be managed, and ensuring that any shortfall in this knowledge is addressed through input from experts in the field.
- Attending an update event at least annually through conferences, seminars, workshops or special presentation. The chief fraud advisor may provide some guidance.
- Approving a version of the IFRMM that suits the organization and is designed in a way that meets all business needs.
- Adopting a risk management model that is properly implemented and ensuring that all employees understand and live up to their responsibilities.
- Defining a suitable budget for dealing with fraud awareness and resourcing the risk management system.
- Ensuring that sufficient expertise is available and applied, mainly in the form of a chief fraud advisor (CFA).
- Delegating authority to the CFA to have unrestricted access to all records, files, systems, people, building, and information needed to achieve defined objectives of fraud detection and investigation.
- Assuming a judicial role in ensuring that employee fraud is dealt with fairly and that there is an appeals process to check that due process is properly provided.
- Overseeing a robust disciplinary procedure that ensures fairness to all employees.
- Ensuring that the issue of fraud risk management is built into the role and responsibilities of all executives, managers, and employees.
- Establishing and maintaining an ongoing program of staff awareness.
- Notifying the board, chief fraud advisor, external and internal auditors, and any other relevant parties when there are significant frauds that affect the business.

- Making sure that ethical standards are firmly in place and that expert advice is available and applied to help assist the development of good ethical standards.
- Integrating fraud risk management into business strategy, business goals, and decision making processes, in terms of the need to reduce potential frauds and their effect on the business.
- Developing good audit and accountability arrangements based on the key components of accountability, integrity, and openness.
- Reporting to the board on the extent to which controls are managing the risk of fraud, and ensuring that effective steps are taken to prevent, detect, and investigate actual and attempted frauds.

**3. Stakeholders.** The IFRMM is designed to protect the interests of those parties who have a stake in the success of the arrangements. This covers the shareholders, government, customers, vendors, the media, employees, associates, and so on. Stakeholder—in particular influential ones, such as institutional investors who hold large numbers of shares—have a role to play. They should inquire about the organization's response to the threat of fraud and whether the organization is properly protected from all threats to resources. The annual report and press releases are the main vehicles through which the organization communicates with outsiders, and these documents should be considered by people affected by the business. The main role of stakeholders is to ask searching questions whenever appropriate. Customers or vendors who have been approached by an employee to engage in questionable practices should make themselves familiar with the complaint procedure and make known their concerns. The organization should make clear to all stakeholders its position on fraud and any action taken in response to particular problems.

**4. Antifraud mission.** There should be a clear corporate statement of where the organization stands with respect to antifraud measures. It is not actually possible to have no opinion on this subject. Most of the mission will be embedded in the documented fraud policy which should be firmly in place. The following are criteria for assessing the adequacy of the fraud policy:

- The fraud policy should be endorsed by the board and address issues of prevention, detection, and investigation.
- It should make clear the role and responsibilities of all employees and associates in tackling fraud.

- The fraud policy should contain a clear message on fraud and link the message to the business goals of the organization. If the overall corporate mission contains the word *integrity* or something similar, this is a good way of recognizing the importance of morality in business.
- The policy should be developed with advice from an expert in the field of fraud management (possibly derived from the role of the chief fraud advisor).
- The fraud policy should be properly implemented and team workshops considered as one way of driving home the main messages.
- Clear positions should be assumed as to hot lines, prosecution, speedy investigations, recovery, dismissal, and the concept of zero tolerance.
- The policy should be reviewed at least annually and updated to ensure that it is well focused and responsive.
- The policy should be revised if there are any events indicating that it can be improved.
- The policy should have a focus on prevention and learning lessons, rather than just on investigation.
- The policy should be prepared with regard to the issues discussed in chapter 5 on this subject.

**5. Fraud panel.**   There should be a forum that has sole responsibility for overseeing all matters relating to fraud and regularity in the organization. Key players should sit on the panel and take an active role in deciding on the form and direction of fraud prevention, detection, and investigation. For large organizations, the panel (or equivalent forum) could meet each quarter; in medium-sized bodies, the panel should meet annually. Small enterprises may have an event every two or three years. The panel would also meet to deal with the outbreak of any specific fraud and thereafter to deal with progress on the fraud investigation. Criteria for assessing this type of forum have to be general, but could consist of the following features:

- Members selected because of their expertise in fraud-related issues. They would include legal, personnel, a representative from the CEO's office (e.g., the deputy CEO), and others as appropriate. The chief fraud advisor will attend the panel meetings as the main advisor. No officer should attend the fraud panel if he or she is implicated in a fraud directly or indirectly (for example, managerial negligence) or if there is a conflict of interest that may impair his or her judgment.

- The panel will report directly to the CEO and have executive responsibility for all matters pertaining to internal and external frauds. It is responsible for decisions on the resources for, shape, and direction of individual fraud initiatives (e.g., general detection routines) and ongoing fraud investigations.

- The fraud panel should have clear terms of reference and its role should be defined in the fraud policy.

- The panel will also deal with employee fraud that is investigated with a view to taking disciplinary action, when appropriate.

- The panel may be chaired by a representative from the CEO's office who is senior enough to ensure that decisions are properly implemented. The chair must have successfully completed a fraud awareness training program.

- The panel will ensure that the organization's fraud policy is being properly implemented and that all allegations are dealt with efficiently, in line with the fraud response plan.

- The panel should ensure that all investigations are professionally conducted by a suitable resource under the direction of the chief fraud advisor (CFA).

- The panel will also receive reports from the CFA and make decisions based on the recommendations in the CFA's reports.

- The fraud panel will advise the CEO on the way fraud risk management is being handled in the organization and ensure that sufficient resources are in place to discharge the obligation to manage fraud.

- The panel will commission and oversee any proactive measures to detect fraud based on advice from the CFA.

- The panel will ensure that any shortfalls in the adopted IFRMM are addressed and corrected.

- The panel will have a say in the appointment of the CFA and will monitor the performance and standards adopted by this officer.

**6. External/Internal audit.** The external auditors should be appointed by the shareholders (or their public-sector equivalent) so that they can bring to bear an independent consideration of the way the financial accounts have been prepared. External audits may report on the way fraud risk is managed, if so commissioned. Likewise, internal auditors need to bear in mind the possibility of fraud when carrying out audits, and recommend better controls against fraud when appropriate. The two main considerations when fitting the audit process into the fraud management task are, firstly, that the board may provide both sets of auditors with the results of the fraud risk assessment and ask them to take strategic risk into account when preparing their plan of audits for the year. Secondly, the board may ask the auditors to review the antifraud arrangements (say, every two or three years) and provide any advice possible on improvements or a better focus on problem areas. Some internal audit teams take a pivotal role regarding fraud issues, and the chief internal auditor may double as the chief fraud advisor, although this depends on the parameters set for the audit team and its adopted policies. It just happens that auditors, particularly internal auditors have the right type of skills to undertake fraud investigations; views vary on whether they *should* assume this special responsibility.

**7. Ethical standards committee.**   There may be a high-level committee of the board with independent members, which oversees the way corporate ethics is defined and promulgated, and that any breach is properly dealt with by the organization. The most effective antifraud strategies consider the behavior of employees as a factor in tackling corruption, abuse, and criminality. Employee behavior can be viewed in conjunction with standards set for from managers and staff and the employer, as a form of mutual understanding. An ethical standards committee represents a high-level resolve to place corporate ethics firmly on the agenda. The committee can deal with standard setting that falls outside the purview of the audit committee or the fraud panel, and can oversee the way these standards are being employed. At times, the audit committee concentrates on the audit and accountability process and is immersed in the audit, compliance, and review functions. The fraud panel is a practical decision-making body that solves urgent problems and arranges "sweeps" of high-risk parts of the organization. The gap left by these two functions relates to the softer issues of staff values, the rules of the game, and the way people behave, as cornerstone factors in the fight against deceit, which is what fraud prevention is all about. Establishing a forum to deal with these soft issues from board level and below is one way of recognizing the importance of moral direction, as an overall framework.

**8. Audit committee.**   There may be a committee of the board whose independent members oversee all matters concerning audit and accountability. This audit committee (AC) would ensure that the external and internal audit processes are discharged in a manner that maximizes the benefits of objective audit and review. The AC will want to see, as part of the accountability process, that the risk of fraud is understood and is being managed properly. When integrated fraud management is in place, the AC may sit back and take comfort in this fact. The AC swings into action when gaps and problems show all is not well. The strength of the AC is inherent in its composition of independent directors who have an oversight function; when the board and senior directors are at fault, the AC may point this out and also strengthen the external audit process to address this concern. The AC should review its terms of reference and make sure that oversight of fraud risk and compliance is part of its role, and that this is properly understood by all the members. For example, the AC may ask the fraud panel to make an annual report on its activities, as a way of reinforcing its input into strategic fraud management.

**9. Chief fraud advisor (or compliance officer).**    There should be a senior person who has responsibility for advising on all matters relating to fraud and regularity. The chief fraud advisor (CFA) will advise on measures to prevent fraud, commission steps to detect fraud, and direct all investigations into employee fraud. All reported allegations of fraud should be conveyed to the CFA. Some organizations employ a compliance officer or a head of security who could assume the responsibilities of the CFA. Whatever the titlet, the CFA has several key roles:

- Advise the fraud panel on the success (or otherwise) of the IFRMM.
- Ensure that all fraud efforts are properly coordinated and are consistently undertaken in line with set standards.
- Assume full-time responsibility for all fraud-related matters.
- Provide, at least annually, a report to the fraud panel on all relevant matters, such as reported fraud, investigations, and detection exercises.
- Compile a database of frauds and seek to make projections about future threats and ways to anticipate and reduce them.
- Be responsible for a team of in-house fraud investigators, when such a team is in place. Think very carefully about employing a full-time team; a worst-case scenario is where the organization employs a whole bunch of full-time investigators who sit around waiting for a fraud to materialize. Eventually a stage will be reached where this team encourages poor controls, so that the resulting frauds will keep

them in work. There is no incentive to promote a proactive control environment when everyone embarks on securing safeguards against the risk of fraud.

- Employ and oversee extra resources as and when required.
- Prepare and amend the fraud policy and fraud response plan for review by the fraud panel and adoption by the board. The policy and plan should be prepared, based on best practice, after consulting with management, who hold prime responsibility for managing fraud.
- Define standards for investigating employee fraud and ensure that these standards are applied or that any external team meets an equally valid set of professional standards.
- Advise managers on steps they may take to prevent fraud. Other experts such as the head of security and the IT security manager, may help in this task.
- Ensure that employees have a good awareness of the threat of fraud and that they are equipped to discharge their responsibilities to manage this risk. Awareness workshops, presented by the CFA or through a trainer employed by the CFA, are one way of ensuring this happens.
- Review orientation programs to ensure that new starters have a good appreciation of the corporate fraud policy.
- Advise Personnel on checking references and information provided by persons applying for employment with the organization.
- Provide advice on ways that teams and managers can undertake fraud risk assessment; as required, facilitate or arrange facilitation for fraud risk assessment workshops.
- Provide an annual report on the state of fraud risk assessment and make recommendations to the fraud panel as appropriate.
- Carry out fraud detection surveys, in conjunction with management, when it is deemed appropriate and ensure that the results of these surveys are followed up. These projects will be agreed on with the fraud panel.
- Receive all allegations of fraud and irregularity from employees and external parties and ensure that these are dealt with according to the fraud response plan.
- Keep up to date with best practice on fraud management and ensure that specific alerts affecting the business are built into the business by management.
- Be the first point of contact on all matters relating to fraud.

- Liaise with law enforcement on criminal investigations.
- Liaise with professional investigators on employee investigations or allegations of fraud by external parties.
- Liaise with the company attorney and personnel department in detection routines and actual investigations.
- Liaise with the press office on communications with the media, as and when required.
- Liaise with the head of security and IT security manager, as and when required.
- Advise the CEO on the way the organization is managing the risk of fraud, and present papers on this subject to the main board, audit committee, and any ethical standards committee. The CFA may also arrange awareness workshops for these groups.

**10. Fraud risk management strategy.** There should be an ongoing process of identifying, assessing, and then managing the risk of fraud. This point has been referred to many times already. The idea is to implement a cycle of activities along the lines shown in figure 7.3.

Each stage is briefly explained.

1. **Business aims.** Start by working through business aims and ensuring that staff can see where fraud prevention fits in with their overall objectives. If the organization ignores fraud issues and simply writes off any unexplainable losses, there is little point in carrying out risk assessment. Unfortunately, this type of organization is in a questionable position, because the directors are failing in their duty to safeguard the resources of the organization. The reason that fraud is at times sidelined by managers is that no one tries to link antifraud measures with the real business of the day. So risk

**Figure 7.3** Risk Management Cycle

assessment must start with what the business is seeking to achieve and move on from there.

2. **Risk identification.**   The next stage is to work through the types of frauds that could arise in the relevant area of responsibility. The concept of risk ownership is crucial, because managers are responsible for managing risk, but only in the areas that they are responsible for. Risk identification can be carried out by work teams brainstorming their fraud risks. Reference to the material in chapter 2 may help with this task. The idea is to capture all possible attacks and abuses that could be targeted against the organization. It depends on team workers understanding that some of their colleagues, customers, vendors, or associates may be dishonest; sensitivity training may be included to open people up to this rather uncomfortable possibility.

3. **Risk assessment.**   This simply means working through the risks as identified and giving each one a score to reflect its relative importance. The next step is to agree which ones are material, in that the fraud could have a big impact if it comes about and is likely to happen because there are not many controls in place to prevent it. The end result is a top-ten list of significant fraud risks that have to be tackled.

4. **Risk management.**   The next stage is problem solving, where the team will work through the measures that can be taken to mitigate the key risks as identified and judged to have an important impact on business success. All the material described at the start of this chapter covering fraud prevention should be considered as part of the process of managing the risks involved. Staff and managers could work through each part of fraud prevention and decide what is required to provide the proposed solutions. The problem with most risk workshops is the failure to concentrate on control solutions after the risk assessment has been completed. So much time and effort is focused on the risk identification and assessment stages that a typical workshop leaves only a short time at the end to think about controls that may be designed and implemented. A better approach would be to stop the workshop after the assessment stage and then resume with a presentation and debate on what control is about and how control mechanisms and compliance routines can be applied to form a robust system of internal control. Only after having done this should you consider the types of controls that may be established. The results of the risk workshop may be captured in a risk register that details the assessment, the risks that were isolated,

and the resulting action plans. These risk registers can be reported upward to the board, and can form the basis for assurances on internal controls and the formal report on controls in the published annual report.

5. **Review.** This is about revisiting the risk management workshop and keeping the findings and action plans up to date, particularly against a changing environment and new threats such as cyber fraud. The workshops are not an annual event; rather, they should be part of an ongoing process for dealing with risk. Much of this process is about getting the right culture in place that fits with the fraud policy and takes the responsibilities seriously. Fraud risk may be added to the wider business risk assessment thinking that forms the basis of existing workshops, rather than having a separate series of team events for fraud only.

The preceding risk model can be used to measure success in managing fraud risk then the above risk, with the key question being: "Have we got something in place that more or less addresses all the stages of the risk management cycle?"

**11. Fraud investigation strategy.** A formal strategy and accompanying standards for conducting investigations into fraud and irregularity should be in place. Alternatively, there should be access to professional parties who work to a set of formal standards. Most of the relevant material is found in chapter 6, on investigations, and this should form a minimum baseline of knowledge that is brought to the investigation, including standards of evidence. Advice should be sought from the local police department and legal advice taken when sensitive techniques such as surveillance and phone taps are being considered. The terms of reference for and scope of the investigation should be drawn up by the CFA and discussed at the fraud panel. It is good practice to include on the fraud panel the director for the area affected by the fraud, so that management's responsibility for dealing with fraud is reinforced. The investigation team should work with the CFA and should provide advice at each stage of the investigation. The fraud panel will make all executive decisions. For employee frauds, the organization can be broken down into several main categories:

- Main suspects.
- Possible suspects.
- Management in the area where the fraud occurred.

- Culpable managers.
- Potential witnesses.
- All other employees.

Standards should cover the way each group of employees is treated. The organization needs a bottom line on investigations that encourage it to take a tough stand where this is needed. Fraud cannot be swept under the carpet,; if there is a strong allegation, there should be an equally strong response, to investigate thoroughly and clear the air.

**12. Fraud hot line.**   There should be an agreed procedure for conveying concerns about the integrity and activities of staff and external parties who create a threat to the welfare of the organization or are otherwise engaged in unlawful acts. The organization should actively encourage reporting of illegal activities. Again, the material on whistleblowing in earlier chapters should be used as a baseline to compare the current arrangements. Exit interviews for all staff may be used to elicit information from people who may have no reason not to act in good faith.

**13. Staff discipline.**   The internal disciplinary process should cover breach of procedure as a result of fraudulent activities by employees. The response should be robust and determined in finding out the truth and taking appropriate action. The procedure in place should ensure that "crooked" employees are quickly dismissed and that innocent people are properly protected. Once the procedure is established, it should be followed in detail and constitute a reasonable way of dealing with employment issues. The internal disciplinary procedure should, ideally, define clear roles that suit the organization; one approach may be to design a structure along the following lines:

- **Disciplinary standards.**   There should be a clear set of standards that cover what constitutes a disciplinary offense, and also frauds by staff members.
- **Disciplinary panel.**   The organization should be able to convene a panel of senior managers who will represent the organization in hearing charges against the employee and the defense to these charges. They then make recommendations about the future of the person in question. The panel should have access to legal advice and may include a representative from personnel and at least one senior manager.

- **Judicial balance.** Disciplinary proceedings should be fair and balanced. The CEO should oversee the process and should not take sides or make inconsistent remarks about the case or person involved. The CEO will endorse recommendations made by the disciplinary panel. Legal advice should be available to the CEO.
- **Presenting officer.** A senior manager should be in charge of taking the finished case from the investigators and presenting it to the internal disciplinary panel. This may be a senior line manager from the area affected by the fraud.
- **Employee and representative.** The employee being charged should be allowed to provide an explanation to the investigators after presentation of the evidence against the employee. This explanation should be given due consideration before a decision is made to go ahead with disciplinary charges. Moreover, the employee should be permitted to present a case for the defense to the disciplinary panel and challenge all evidence against the employee, or have a representative (arranged by the union) present this defense. To prepare the defense, the employee should be given access to all material relevant to the case, including potential witnesses for the defense, even if the employee has been suspended for the duration of the investigation.
- **Investigators and final report.** The alleged disciplinary offense should have been fully investigated by professional investigators.
- **Line manager.** The employee's line manager may be asked to act as a witness in the case, and should answer all questions fully and honestly.
- **Witnesses.** Other persons may be asked to give evidence at the hearing on behalf of the employer or the employee and be cross-examined accordingly.
- **Charges and remedies.** Formal charges should be brought against the employee if the results of the investigation so indicate, and these should be what is considered by the panel. All evidence should relate to the charges against the employee. The panel will consider the evidence as presented and recommend a suitable remedy, such as not proven, dismissal, demotion, formal sanctions, and so on. The CEO will consider the recommendations and endorse them if appropriate.
- **Appeals.** The employee should have access to an appeals process if the disciplinary panel decides against the employee. The CEO should consider the grounds for appeal and, if justified, convene an

appeals panel of senior managers to hear the appeal and decide whether there are grounds to change the decision of the original disciplinary panel.

- **Proceedings.** The disciplinary hearing should follow a set procedure that provides a judicial response to the problem; that is, a response that is fair to both the employer and the employee.

**14. Investigators.** There should be resources available to carry out professional investigations into fraud and irregularity. The resource may be in-house or consist of a contract with a source that provides this service. Each investigation should be headed by a lead investigating officer, who will report to the CFA. The investigating team should possess the requisite competencies to carry out the work.

**15. Senior management.** The responsibility for managing the risk of fraud should be clearly defined as resting with management. This is so even when a chief fraud advisor and in-house team of fraud investigators are employed by the organization. These teams provide investigative services and give advice based on the investigation, but executive decisions should be made only by senior management. Managers discharge this responsibility by installing controls that guard against this risk and its effect on staff and the business. The performance appraisal scheme should reflect the new responsibilities for managing the risk of fraud. We could refer to the various controls mentioned earlier in this chapter and argue that the manager's responsibilities center around designing and implementing suitable controls over fraud. To provide a better focus on areas of responsibility we set out various ways in which managers may discharge their obligations. All managers should:

- Take executive responsibility for managing the risk of fraud, including investigations.
- Familiarize themselves with the fraud policy and fraud response plan.
- Make sure all staff likewise understand the policy and its implications for the work role, and implement fraud awareness events as appropriate.
- Ensure that information provided by staff is verified, and establish an ongoing program of checking information to evaluate the honesty of employees, on advice from legal staff.

- Register all assets and resources and ensure that they are accounted for at all times.
- Establish clear procedures for staff to follow, look for breaches of procedure, and deal with serious breaches under the disciplinary policy.
- Understand the various indicators of fraud and respond when they suggest that fraud might be being perpetrated by employees.
- Undertake fraud risk assessment, as described earlier.
- Provide a formal assurance on controls as part of the overall corporate governance reporting requirements.
- Make sure staff know that they should report any suspicions and concerns to management and the CFA.
- Seek advice from the CFA and chief internal auditor on dealing with fraud issues.
- Seek to promote a culture where fraud is seen as a real business issue and people at work are alert to the problem.
- Make the corporate standards on fraud, regularity, and conduct known to associates, vendors, and customers. Emphasize that the same standards are expected from third parties.
- Be suspicious of unfamiliar or unusual people and situations. Personnel managers have special responsibility for checking out job applicants before they are given a contract of employment.

**16. Employees.** All line managers, supervisors, team leaders, staff, workers, consultants, associates, partners, vendors, and anyone else employed by or associated with the company should have a good awareness of the risk of fraud and the need to respond positively with controls that prevent, detect, and address perceived problems resulting from actual and attempted frauds. Employees need to understand the fraud policy, be aware of fraud indicators, report any suspicions, improve controls, and cooperate with any investigation. Work teams should respond positively to all information about fraud and current threats, and engage in a continual search to minimize these threats.

## CONCLUSION—THE RED STOP LIGHT

There are many reasons why people don't worry about fraud at work. It is someone else's burden. Most people are concerned about fraud against them in their private lives, and take many steps to manage the risk to credit cards, personal details, their home, valuables, car, and family: they have set procedures for locking doors, concealing cell phones and laptops, and taking care when dealing with strangers on the phone, the doorstep, and over the Internet. Generally, we are all on guard for con artists and out-and-out criminals. If we could transfer this thinking to the workplace, there would be much less employee fraud, and even if the occasional fraud popped up it would be spotted quickly. We protect what's important to us, but not what is outside our jurisdiction or what our managers are not bothered about. The stop light model tries to get everyone to red; that is, acting as safeguards against fraud. This can happen only when people feel they should have a role in protecting the organization rather than simply doing a day job. More than anything, it is about changing workplace culture. The employer needs to figure out how far people are from the red stop light and how much they need to change to get there, if this is an issue. The integrated fraud risk management model is one way of carrying out this assessment and the points made earlier on each aspect of the model can be used as a checklist for findwork out where the organization stands, set development targets, and then measure any progress.

We close with three further points and one final model:

1. **Healthy skepticism.**   Take nothing for granted. Janet Cooke fabricated an entire news story that was sold to more than 300 newspapers and won the 1981 Pulitzer Prize. The lesson learned was that a failure to double-check the facts and a lack of basic controls meant that no one felt they should ask any tough questions. If employees adopted a healthy skepticism at work, these tough questions would be asked whenever necessary.

2. **Risk workshops.**   Insist that fraud issues be on the agenda for risk assessment workshops. Ordinarily, the topic of employee fraud is avoided by workshop members. The solution is to get the facilitator to step outside of the mere facilitation mode for a few moments, ask to be excused by the group members, and note "employee fraud" as a potential risk, even if there has not been past experience with this problem. Remember, facilitation is mainly about encouraging, but it should also be challenging.

3. **Attitudes.**   The Red Stop Lights approach to fraud is mainly about changing attitudes. Period. Everything else is based on how these attitudes may be changed and how these changes can be made to stick.

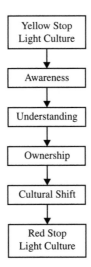

**Figure 7.4** Getting to the Red Light

Finally, we come to a working model for getting to the red light, as shown in figure 7.4. Start at yellow, where people at work are not bothered about fraud in their organization. Secure some kind of awareness. This may be done by pointing out what fraud is, and that it can and does happen in business and government. The next stage is to get people to understand the implications of corporate fraud; that when it happens, it affects on the business. Ownership brings home employees' responsibilities for managing the risk of fraud and the fact that this task is not reserved to managers and their staff. If the risk of fraud is embedded in business plans, and if everyone gets involved in the fight against fraud, the would-be fraudster is presented with a clear and bright red stop light.

# APPENDIX A

# Forensic Statement Analysis

Communication is strategic. Everything we say or write has both a meaning and a purpose, and involves a deliberate choice of words as a means to an end.

Each of us has a unique style of communication, which is developed from childhood and continuously fine-tuned to achieve the best results. Most of this is done subconsciously, influenced by our cultural background, work environment, and the stresses of everyday life. But everything we do and say is ultimately designed to perform one of two functions, communicate information, or cause someone to believe in the truth of something.

Consequently, we have to look at written statements on different levels and ask certain questions. What is the writer's intention? Is it to covey information, or is it to convince us of something? If it is to convince, then what is the person really saying?

Conveying information is straightforward. If we believe in what we say, our statements are absolute. Trying to convince someone of something we know not to be the truth, or have no real commitment to, creates a stress that we subconsciously try to distance ourselves from. This is reflected in our choice of words.

Each word we use is a matter of choice. The selection is done largely subconsciously, and is an extremely complex mental process, because we have an enormous number of words in our vocabulary to choose from. However, when we manipulate information to convince someone of something, such as when we lie, the mental processes involved become even more complicated. This creates emotional stresses that are reflected in what we write. Spot the indicators of stress, and you can uncover deception.

*Forensic statement analysis* is the systematic study of the basic elements of written statements in order to determine truthfulness or deception. Its origins lie in the 1950s with the development of sociolinguistics, which was designed to study the interaction between language and social life. By the mid-1980s, "Discourse Analysis" had evolved, facilitated by the development of audio and video recorders, which enabled the study of language and behavioral interaction in detail.

The analysis of written statements to identify the motives of the author and the veracity of statements was a natural next step. By the early 1990s, the analysis of verbal transcripts and other written statements was being developed to identify deception, as part of criminal investigations.

Forensic statement analysis is based on the premise that, under low arousal (nonstressful, nondeceitful) conditions, statements are characterized by the use of repetitive words with consistent attributes, with an almost rhythmic pattern to sentences. The construction of narratives is balanced, with equal importance given to all the component parts: prologue, principal issue, and epilogue. Statements are absolute and reflect the emotional commitment of their authors.

Deception creates emotional stresses that subconsciously stimulate the "fight or flight" reaction. Words appear, disappear, and change, reflecting the author's needs to shift attention away from himself, or distance himself from the things that cause him stress. Sentence patterns fluctuate, depending on whether information is being withheld or embellished. Statements are qualified, reflecting the authors' lack of commitment to what is being said.

An analysis of semantics (from Greek *semantikos,* meaning "significant") suggests specifically where in statements deception is occurring. *Semantic indicators* are words that indicate the presence of deception. They function by highlighting the relationship between the author and other people, objects, actions, and emotions referred to in the statement. An example of distancing from an event can be seen in the following excerpt:

> On July 18th, 1969, at approximately 11:15 P.M. in Chappaquiddick, Martha's Vineyard, Massachusetts, I was driving my car on Main Street on my way to get the ferry back to Edgartown. I was unfamiliar with the road and turned right onto Dike Road, instead of bearing hard left on Main Street. After proceeding for approximately one-half mile on Dike Road I descended a hill and came upon a narrow bridge. The car went off the

side of the bridge. There was one passenger with me, one Miss _____, a former secretary of my brother . . . . The car turned over and sank into the water and landed with the roof resting on the bottom.

The author refers to himself as "I" in every sentence, except in the three sentences that refer to the actual accident. The only evidence that the author was present in the car is the phrase "There was one person with me," but here he is presented in a passive role, and not in control of the situation.

Another semantic indicator is the phrase "my car," which reveals a close personal association between the author and his vehicle. This changes when the accident occurs to "the car," another indicator that the author is distancing himself from the situation.

The reduction in length from the first two sentences to the short "The car went off the side of the bridge" is also significant. Taken together, the cluster of indicators suggests that deception is present in this excerpt.

Certain types of statements suggesting subconscious conflict show a lack of commitment to what is being said:

One cannot entirely condemn such behavior. I am inclined to accept the offer. Perhaps we can work something out.

The change in pronouns, from "One" in the first sentence to "I" in the second and "we" in the third, reveals that the situation is causing the author stress, and he is attempting to shift focus away from himself. The excerpt is also littered with words that qualify the action verbs, such as "entirely condemn," "inclined to accept," and "Perhaps we can work something," all indicating a reluctance to commit.

There are also statements from which the author wishes us to believe she carried out certain actions:

As a matter of fact, I decided to call the auditor to confirm the figures. I then started to prepare the accounts.

Phrases such as "I decided to call" and "I then started to prepare" do not say that the call was made, or that the accounts were completed, although the author wishes us to think so.

In the right hands, forensic statement analysis can be a powerful weapon. It can be applied to a multitude of documents in any market segment, wherever there is a reliance on written documents. As a reactive tool, it provides a quick and cost-effective way of scanning a wide range of documents for indicators of deception. It clearly identifies deception and fraudulent activity in both narrative and nonnarrative documents, and indicates the degree of commitment that the authors have to what they are saying.

As a proactive tool, forensic statement analysis makes companies less susceptible to fraudulent activity, as a result of increased awareness. It puts out the right message to employees, customers, and stakeholders, and helps create a zero-tolerance antifraud culture in organizations of any size.

Isabel Picornell
Director QED Limited
November 2001

# APPENDIX B

# An Introduction to Data Mining as a Fraud Risk Management Tool

## INTRODUCTION

The concept of data mining is not new.

Virtually every commercial organization in the world now stores, collates and analyzes information about its business, client's vendors, employees, and competitors. Information is stored electronically in such different areas as accounting systems, telephone management, access control, manufacturing, airline registration, banking, and so forth. Many key elements of information are also stored in manual systems and paper records, and information about corporate activities and transactions is captured in a myriad of different ways and at various levels of detail and sophistication. Managers and key executives who are required to make crucial decisions are suffering; at one level, from information overload and data saturation, and on

*Richard Kusnierz, founder and CEO of Investigative Data Mining Limited, and international consultant Jane Bell are the authors of this Appendix. Further author information and contact details can be found at the end of this Appendix.

another level, from an inability to "join" salient facts from different information sources and systems so that an informed decision may be made.

In this respect, data mining is a methodology that allows appropriate information assets to be sifted and compared, resulting in the presentation of relevant facts and the identification of hitherto unknown relationships and trends. It brings order out of chaos; it cuts through information overload and can be used to confirm or deny perceptions of how an organization is run.

The objective of this paper is to briefly explain how data mining can effectively be used to seek out the indicators of malpractice (possible fraud) and to identify exposures in corporate control mechanisms. While it is an extremely effective tool, there is no "magic silver bullet" which will unfailingly identify fraud and control weaknesses in an organization. However, by adopting some of the concepts in this paper, managers will be able to enhance their control mechanisms and actively identify the symptoms of fraud before catastrophe strikes.

# AN OVERVIEW OF DATA MINING:
## FROM INFORMATION TO KNOWLEDGE

Management has the prime responsibility of ensuring that risk, in all of its forms, is managed and either reduced, eliminated, or transferred. But how does a manager go about assessing the current level of risk in an organization? Reliance on internal audit or external consultancies may be misplaced. Much of the underlying information produced by such groups is based on subjective and personal comments or observation. Determining if such risks or exposures are real and not imaginary requires the ability to quantify risk against a base line of valid data. In many cases, the information is spread across the organization and is in both paper and electronic form.

Figure B.1 provides an overview of the data mining process. There are a number of steps that should be followed if management wishes to use data mining to review controls and identify fraud:

1. *Fully understand the systems and processes.* With many organizations having an ever-increasing base of PC literate users, more and more end user computing takes place. The ability for departments to download data into local PCs and create entire systems using Access or other similar databases means that quite often there is no overall

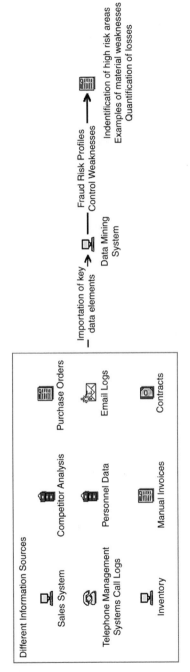

**Figure B.1**

understanding of how data is being used and where satellite systems exist. Before embarking on a data mining review, it is important to understand what data/information is available and how it is stored. A brainstorming session with key managers and users for the function under review will enable the process and data sources to be mapped out.

2. *Consider your worst nightmares: Creating a fraud profile.* As part of the same brainstorming session, the next step would be to consider different fraud scenarios. Managers and users are asked to "think like a criminal" and to work out ways to divert funds, issue bogus payments, reroute electronic payment messages, steal stock, over order parts, scrap current stock, set up bogus vendors or employees on the system, and so forth. In effect, how could the controls be broken and how would the company suffer a loss. Once such ideas (fraud theories) have been discussed, identify all the indicators that should point to such an event having taken place. For example, if an organization has a rigorous policy of going out to tender for contracts where the estimated contract value is in excess of $250,000, how would you test for collusion in the tendering process? An indicator might be one company consistently winning contracts when competing against the same three competitors. Of the 20 contracts issued, company A wins 100% and companies, B, C, and D always lose. By describing such indicators, management can create a number of fraud profiles.

3. *Test the fraud theory using fraud profiles: Investigative data mining.* Step 1 has identified what information is available, how it is stored, and a number of fraud theories. Step 2 identifies fraud profiles that would indicate that frauds may be actively in progress or that controls have broken down to such an extent that the company faces an unacceptable fraud exposure. Step 3 is to use data mining techniques to test the fraud theories by applying the profiles against the available base data.

For example:

- **Fraud Theory:** Managers with financial authority could authorize payments for nonexistent computer consultancy services to a family member

- **Fraud Profile:** Details about the computer consultancy, such as address, zip code, bank details, or contact telephone number match employee details held in the personnel file
- **Data Mining:** Obtain a copy of the vendor master file and the personnel file and conduct tests to match the zip codes and other key fields between the two files. Once a successful match has been identified, expand the search within the vendor master file to identify what other companies are based at the same address as the computer consultancy. The reason for expanding the search is that criminals are generally greedy, and once one scam is seen to work well, they will try to maximize their profits by repeating the process in other areas.

This process need not be restricted to only extracting data from existing computer systems. In many organizations, valuable data is still held in manual records and, therefore, might be excluded from conventional data mining. In many cases, it is easier to manipulate paper systems than it is to alter computer records and, therefore, such systems may be at greater risk. Just because the information is stored in manual, handwritten, ledgers does not mean that it cannot be analyzed by computer. The following case study is based on a real data mining review that is currently ongoing. The names and detail have been changed to protect the guilty.

## PROCUREMENT FRAUD

### Background, Fraud Theory, and Profile

The VP of Corporate Security for a large domestic organisztion was concerned that the tendering process for building maintenance and small construction works was being manipulated.

The annual budget for such expenditure was $2.7 billion in the financial year ending December 1999, $3.5 billion in 2000, and $4.3 in 2001. The organisation had regional offices, distribution centers, manufacturing plants, and an assortment of research laboratories in most states, and the total number of locations exceeded 3,500. Generally, small ad hoc work with a monetary value of less than $5,000 could be awarded to a single supplier; between $5,000 and $10,000 required three quotations (but that was not mandatory); and anything over $10,000 required a formally issued invitation to tender and a review panel comprising of purchasing professionals, technical specialists, and user management. Records of tender review panels were recorded manually in formal minutes of the process. Internal Audit had reviewed the process and reported that, due to the independent nature of the review process, the number of different people involved and the documented purchasing policy, the potential exposure was low and the process well controlled.

Since the records were held manually, data mining was not initially considered an option. However, having discussed the concerns of the VP of Corporate Security, the following profiles were identified:

- Companies that were repeatedly invited to tender but were not interested in responding, that is, they did not respond.
- Companies that were repeatedly invited to tender but whose contract price was consistently higher than any of the other bidders and therefore always lost the bid.
- Companies that won 100% of the bids that they were invited on (during the course of the review, we had to refine the profile to exclude single bids and focus on cases where the company had been invited to tender for more than five contracts).
- Companies that were successful in one geographical region (state) but unsuccessful in another state.

Based on these profiles and given the potential size of the losses, it was decided to perform a pilot data mining review based on an area where there were two regions (hence, different tender panels). Since the prime sources of information were the formal minutes of the tender review panel meetings and there was no format or structure to these minutes, a methodology was devised to capture the relevant information. An Access database was developed to manually capture information so that "Win/Lose" analysis could be performed based on the agreed profiles. Once analyzed, the results were diagramatically represented in the link analysis chart shown in Figures B.2 and B.3.

In this diagram, two different regions of the same company have their own tender procedures and use a number of different contractors. Three companies, 2, 4, and 7, are used by both two regions. The green and red links represent cases where the companies either failed to tender ("FTT") or lost the bid on price. A number of companies stand out. Companies 7,

This link chart shows diagrammatically how a "Win/Lose" analysis of a company's tendering proccess may be represented.

In this diagram there are two tendering regions.

Three companies 7,2 and 4 have been used by both regions.

The patterns in the  Region 1 are unusual and represent potential tender manipulation.

Companies 7,16 and 12 appear to be used to manipulate the process in favour of companies 14 and 15.

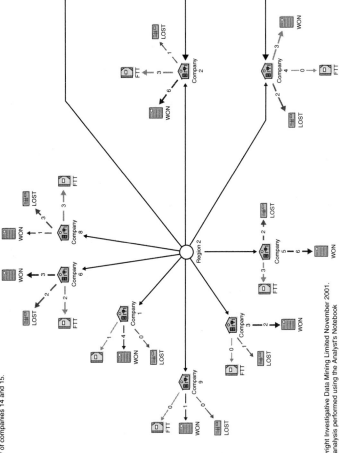

**Figure B.2**   Overview of Data Mining

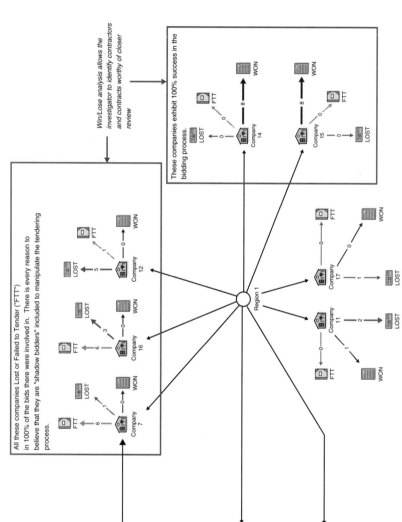

Win/Lose analysis allows the investigator to identify contractors and contracts worthy of closer review

All these companies Lost or Failed to Tender ("FTT") in 100% of the bids there were involved in. There is every reason to believe that they are "shadow bidders" included to manipulate the tendering process.

These companies exhibit 100% success in the bidding process.

**Figure B.3**   Example of Win/Lose Analysis

12, and 16 (all used by Region 1) have lost or failed to tender all the bids in which they have been involved. Furthermore, two companies (14 and 15) have won all of the bids they entered and appear to have been much more successful than any other company shown. This compares with Region 2, where all of the companies invited have won at least one bid.

A second, equally useful profile is to review the tender books by contract and to display the associated companies that bid for those contracts. Using the same type of link analysis techniques, it is possible to identify groups of companies that are consistently bidding against each other and, thereby, identify possible cartels or tender rigging groups.

## CONCLUSION

In the above example, the information used from the pilot data mining review was passed to a firm of forensic Quantity Surveyors who were instructed to review the bids, evaluate the work, and report on the quality and value for money. So far, the work undertaken by companies 14 and 15 has proved suspect. In one case, even though the work was signed off as having been completed and had been invoiced and paid, the Quantity Surveyors could find no evidence that the work had been started or that there were plans for the contract to be completed. The investigation continues. Data mining is a powerful tool and can be used with scalpel-like precision to identify fraud and control weaknesses. However, when used by the inexperienced analyst, it becomes a shotgun and generates numerous false positives. The secret of successful data mining is in ensuring that the fraud profiles are correctly defined and appreciating that even if the information is not contained in an electronic format, it is possible to create databases against which tests may be successfully performed.

---

**Richard Kusnierz** is the founder and CEO of Investigative Data Mining Limited ("IDM"), a specialist consultancy dealing with all aspects of data mining and automated fraud detection. Richard is an internationally recognized expert, frequently speaking at international security and auditing conferences. He has over 14 years of security experience that include over eight years developing innovative data mining solutions. He is a member of the

U.K. Fraud Advisory Panel, the Guild of Security Professionals, the Institute of Professional Investigators, the American Society for Industrial Security (ASIS), and an associate member of the Association of Certified Fraud Examiners. He has contributed to the U.K. version of the AFCE Fraud Manual by writing the first-ever section dealing specifically with "Data Mining" as well as enhancing and developing the sections on computer and internet crime. He can be reached by phone at   011 44 20 8997 1933, e-mail at *Kusnierz@idmfraud.co.uk,* or visit his website at IDMFRAUD.co.uk.

**Jane Bell**  has eight years experience in commercial fraud investigation, detection, and prevention. She is a graduate of Liverpool University, with a Bachelor of Science Degree in Mathematical Sciences with Management, and a member of the Association of Certified Fraud Examiners. In 1999, she become the Director of Fraud Analysis for ArmorGroup, a worldwide security organization. With ArmorGroup, she continued to expand and extend the use of data mining and automated techniques in the fight against fraud and spoke regularly at seminars and conferences on the subject. Jane now works as an independent consultant based in the New York metropolitan area, assisting firms in the United States and United Kingdom. She can be reached by phone at (203) 434 6780.

# INDEX